A HISTORY OF THE IGBO PEOPLE

By the same author

History of Religion

POLITICAL THINKING AND SOCIAL EXPERIENCE: SOME CHRISTIAN INTERPRETATIONS OF THE ROMAN EMPIRE

VICTORIAN QUAKERS

African History

THE IBO PEOPLE AND THE EUROPEANS: THE GENESIS OF A RELATIONSHIP – TO 1906

A HISTORY OF THE IGBO PEOPLE

ELIZABETH ISICHEI
M.A., D.Phil.

Senior Lecturer in History
University of Nigeria, Nsukka

ST. MARTIN'S PRESS NEW YORK

For information, write:
St. Martin's Press, Inc., 175 Fifth Avenue,
New York, N.Y. 10010
Printed in Great Britain
Library of Congress Catalog Card Number: 75–14713
First published in the United States of America in 1976

CHRISTO VERO REGI

Eze kasi eze nine bu Jesu Christi

Contents

List of Plates

The above are reproduced by permission of the following: *Nigeria Magazine* (1*a*, 2*b* and *c*, photographed by Donald D. Hartle; 5*a*, 6*b*); National Museum, Lagos (1*b* and *c*, 2*a*, photographed by Arthur Brooks); Philip Amaefuele (4); *African Arts/Arts d'Afrique* (5*b*, photographed by Herbert M. Cole; 8).

Plate 3 is taken from James Barbot, *An Abstract of a Voyage to New Calabar River . . . in 1699*, in Churchill's *Voyages*, v (London, 1746); Plate 6*a* from *The Interesting Narrative of the Life of Olaudah Equiano* . . . 4th ed. (Dublin, 1791); Plate 7 from 'A Centenary Tribute to the Founder of the Holy Rosary Sisters', anon. (Dublin, 1971).

List of Maps

Map 1 is based on Barry Floyd, *Eastern Nigeria, A Geographical Review* (1969); Map 2, in part, on Michael Onwuejeogwu's articles in *Odinani*, I, 1 (1972); Map 6 on D. Forde and G. I. Jones, *Ibo and Ibibio-speaking Peoples of South East Nigeria* (International African Institute, 1950); Map 8 on CO/520/18. Map 12 was redrawn from the official map produced at the time by Sylvanus Chukwu Nwairo.

Preface

This is a book which has been some eleven years in contemplation and over seven years in preparation, though I realise that in saying so I invite comparison with the mountain which has laboured to produce a mouse. It is a book which at one time I feared it would be impossible to write.

I laid the foundations of my work in Igbo studies by research in a widely scattered range of archives and libraries. The nature of my source material meant that the bulk of my data reflected relationships with Europe – though before the twentieth century, this was certainly not the major theme of Igbo history. In this area, however, the material was so extensive that I was forced to divide it into two books. The first, *The Ibo People and the Europeans: The Genesis of a Relationship – to 1906*, has already been published; the second is still in preparation (a process which the pressure of heavy and frequently changing university teaching duties has prolonged much more than I originally envisaged). The nature of my theme and its sources meant that my first study concentrated heavily on the Niger area.

In 1972, I came to live and work in eastern Igboland. I rapidly accumulated, from a wide variety of sources, a great deal of new material pertaining especially to the east. I began, moreover, to see new dimensions of meaning in the material I had already collected. It came to seem increasingly that a history of the Igbo people was a real possibility. When I was at this point two things encouraged me to abandon, for the time being, the detailed monograph I was working on, and write this book.

The first was the question, asked in the correspondence columns of the *Renaissance* (the local newspaper), 'Where do the Igbos come from?' I felt immediately that I had a duty to answer it. This book is my answer – an answer no doubt both tardier and longer than the correspondent originally envisaged. At this stage Christopher Harrison, Macmillan's West Africa representative, invited me to tackle a standard history of the Igbo. I am most grateful to him for providing the final challenge and impetus.

This study has been greatly enriched by two categories of source material, both the work of Igbos. The first consists of locally published local histories. Some of these are now extremely hard to find. I am grateful to those of my students who managed to track down, in their home areas, some extremely rare examples of the genre, which I had been unable to locate in any library in Nigeria. (I arranged for these to be xeroxed, and copies deposited in the University of Nigeria, Nsukka, library.)

The second consists of the special projects submitted by our students in the Department of History and Archaeology, Nsukka, in partial fulfilment of the requirements for the B.A. degree. The second part of these projects consists of their field notes, *in extenso*. In the two years this scheme has been in existence,it has borne fruit in field materials of great richness and interest. I have learnt something from every project I have read, and I have cited them as widely as possible in this study, in the hopes that in a work of synthesis of this kind, at least, they may reach the wider audience which I feel they deserve. Three of these I have found of especial value. The extremely interesting fieldwork done by Mr Joseph Ejiofor in Agu-inyi shows the historical interest which may lurk in an area with apparently 'no history'. Two students working under my own supervision – Mr Oji Kalu Oji of Ohafia, and Mr James Afoke, an Ezza – have by their enthusiasm, energy, and intimate local knowledge transformed our knowledge of their respective important peoples.

I very much hope that all our student historians will persevere with the writing and research in which they have made such splendid beginnings, although in the nature of things only a tiny minority will become professional academics. The key difficulty lies, not in the lack of ability or zeal, but in the lack of obvious outlets for publication. Yet the successful publication of a study of Uzuakoli which is essentially a secondary-school project would suggest that local histories of this kind would be a more viable publishing proposition than might be supposed. Certainly, they would enrich our knowledge of the Nigerian past, and be of consuming interest to the communities with which they deal.

The indebtedness which I accumulated in writing this book is so extensive that it can scarcely be described without writing another book. I laid the foundations of my work in Igbo studies in three years as a post-doctoral Research Fellow at Nuffield College, Oxford, a period of my life I shall always recall with gratitude and pleasure. Here, in Enugu and Nsukka, I have received almost infinite help and encouragement from colleagues and friends. I have created a great deal of work for the staffs of the National Archives, Enugu, the Nigeriana research collection at Enugu Public Library, and the University Library, Nsukka – the last named an institution the singular helpfulness of whose staff does much to compensate for its present lack of books. Joseph Anafulu, the Africana librarian there while I was writing this book, was quite remarkably helpful and well informed. Arthur Brooks, head of the university's Medical well informed. I am grateful to Arthur Brooks of the university's medical illustration unit, for his help with the illustrations.

For reasons on which I need not expatiate, no library in East Central State has an adequate Africana collection. Where the resources of available libraries, and my own library, failed, I borrowed from my friends – especially in the History Department, Nsukka, and at Bigard Memorial Seminary, Enugu. My thanks to them all. Professor Donald Hartle not only lent me a great deal of archaeological material, but also kindly read an earlier version of the first chapter. Professor Adiele Afigbo lent me much material, and has given me the most unstinted and generous encouragement in a field of study which he has done so much to transform.

A debt of a different kind: I could not have written this book without the help of the young people who have, for varying lengths of time, formed part of my household, and by their cheerful and willing assistance with domestic chores freed so much of my time and energy for academic work. I thank them all, and especially Sunday Kalu of Ebem, Ohafia, and Virginia Nwakuna of Orsu, near Ihiala.

Again, I must thank my four beloved children, Uche, Emeka, Nkem and Chinye, for their forbearance, for much of this book was written in time which was rightfully theirs.

By far my greatest debt is to my beloved husband, Dr Uche Peter Isichei, and the fact that I have said so repeatedly, in the prefaces to earlier books, shall not discourage me from reaffirming it. The full story of all I owe to his loving encouragement and wise counsel will only become known in eternity. I embark upon no project, large or small, without his advice and approval. Had his attitude been different, I would long ago have ceased to write books.

The University of Nigeria, Nsukka and Enugu E.I.
February 1974

A Note on Orthography

One of the difficulties which at present beset Igbo studies is the existence of two alternative spellings, 'Ibo' and 'Igbo' – a difficulty which the inconsistency of my own usage has done nothing to help. When I began writing studies of Igbo history and religion in the late 1960s, 'Ibo' was in almost universal use, both among the Igbo themselves and internationally. Although a handful of linguists and anthropologists used the technically more correct 'Igbo', I opted for 'Ibo', on the grounds that academic usage should differ as little as possible from that of everyday life. (In one of my articles, however, a journal editor insisted on 'Igbo'.) Having once opted for 'Ibo', I naturally retained it on grounds of consistency.

It is now, in 1974, clear to me that things have changed. The overwhelming majority of the Igbo now prefer the form 'Igbo', which they regard as indigenous, in contradistinction to the inaccurate 'Ibo' of colonial days. The only criticism of my earlier writings which has ever been made to me by Igbo readers concerned the spelling of their name. Among my fellow scholars, some use 'Igbo', some 'Ibo', and some, like myself, have changed horses in midstream. On the grounds that people should always be referred to by the name with which they prefer to describe themselves, I have accordingly switched to 'Igbo', with apologies for my inconsistency.

In the transcription of Igbo words and phrases in the text, I have followed the following principle. Where following a written source, I have copied the orthography of my source exactly. Where copying a spoken source, I have sought the advice of an educated local informant. Since the purpose of a writer is to communicate, I have concentrated on intelligibility, rather than pedantic accuracy. Thus I have opted for the familiar 'Ezza' rather than the more correct 'Ezaa'. In any case, I am not a linguist, and had I worried too much about the problems of transcribing a multitude of different dialects would have found myself in the position of the centipede, who spent all his time considering how to run!

'People will not look forward to posterity who never look backward to their ancestors.'

'To be attracted to the sub-division, to love the little platoon we belong to in society, is the first principle, the germ as it were, of public affections.' (*Edmund Burke, in 1790*)

I The First Phase

1 The Dawn of Igbo History

'We did not come from anywhere and anyone who tells you we came from anywhere is a liar. Write it down.'

An elder of Mbaise, in 1972[1]

ORIGINS AND SETTLEMENT

No historical question arouses more interest among present-day Igbos than the enquiry, 'Where did the Igbos come from?' It is sometimes discussed in the press, and often put to the author, in conversation. It is as if the question of origins contained, somewhere, a key to the elusive problem of Igbo identity. In a sense, this whole book is an attempt to answer the question.

The interest in origins stems essentially from a mistaken stereotype of the history of other Nigerian peoples, resting on an ageing historiography which is now increasingly under attack,[2] for historians are increasingly sceptical about traditions of lengthy migrations in the history of other groups.

The first human inhabitants of Igboland must have come from areas further north – possibly from the Niger confluence. But men have been living in Igboland for at least five thousand years, since the dawn of human history. One of the most notable facts of Igbo history is its length and continuity. Igbo began to diverge from other related languages, such as Edo and Yoruba, perhaps four thousand years ago;[3] 4500 years ago people in Nsukka were making pottery which was similar in style to that still made in the area today.[4] The words of the elder of Mbaise, quoted as epigraph to this chapter, embody an essential historical truth.

The first cradles of human habitation in the Igbo area were probably the Cross River and the Anambra Valley-Nsukka escarpment. In each of these areas, later Stone Age sites have been excavated. A rock shelter at Afikpo was first inhabited about five thousand years ago, by people who made rough red pottery and a variety of stone tools – hoes, knives, pounders and so on. Excavations at the University of Nsukka uncovered the pottery, 4500 years old, mentioned above, and Ibagwa, a town in the Nsukka area, has a rock shelter which yielded both ancient pottery and tools of stone.[5]

This picture of an early nucleus of settlement in northern Igboland is confirmed by Igbo traditions. The traditions of the Umueri clan – which includes the ancient state of Nri – state that both they and the Igala are descended from a still more ancient community in the Anambra valley. 'We are all descended from Eri, but Igala went one way, Aguku another, Amanuke another, Nteje another and Igbariam another. This separating of the Igala from us happened so long ago that now we do not hear Igala, nor can they hear our language.'[6]

As time went on, these proto-Igbo populations dispersed more widely in the forests of Igboland. They came to concentrate especially in what much later became Owerri, Okigwi, Orlu and Awka divisions. Most scholars follow G. I. Jones in regarding this as an Igbo heartland, basing their views on linguistic and cultural evidence.[7] It is also strikingly confirmed by demography, for a glance at the modern population map opposite shows that it is also the area of densest population. As one moves further from the heartland, the population density falls, in a series of steadily diminishing rings.

The traditions of Nri, in the northern part of the high-density belt, preserve a memory of the original migration to the south. 'At the time of Ndri's arrival in this part of the world, there were no other towns in the immediate vicinity, nothing but open country, and so the settlement was called Aguku, meaning, the great field.'[8]

This theory of the Igbo heartland, however, suggests a number of problems. In particular, why did the population concentrate on sandy uplands of limited fertility, with frequent water shortages, rather than on the well-watered alluvial soils of the river valleys? There are a number of possible answers to this question. Floyd points out that the uplands offered a number of positive advantages to agriculturalists with limited technical resources: the land was more easily cleared, and the well-drained soil favoured yam cultivation, the staple crop.[9] Why did they avoid the more fertile river valleys? Tsetse fly is one stock answer, but trypanosomiasis (sleeping sickness) seems almost unknown among the present-day inhabitants of

Igboland's river valleys, and I can see no convincing reason why it should have been more common in the past. There are, of

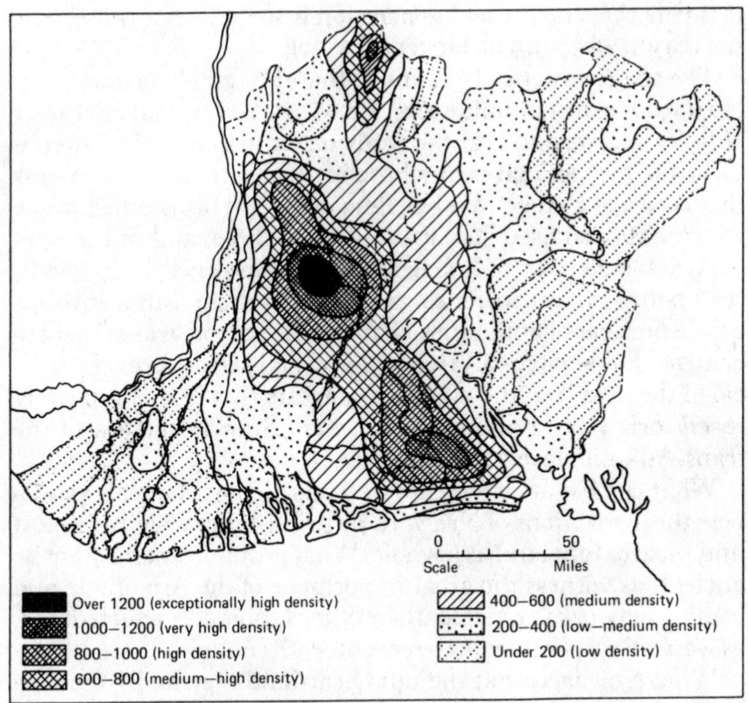

Map 1 Density of population in south-eastern Nigeria, 1963 (estimated number of persons per square mile)

course, other water-linked diseases, such as malaria, borne by mosquitoes, and schistosomiasis (bilharzia) which are both very common in Igboland. The tendency of the rivers to overflow their banks in the rainy season may have been a factor. Defence certainly was, because riverain settlements were very susceptible to canoe-borne attack. Onitsha was placed on an inland site for this reason, and Illah moved to an inland site, to avoid piracy.[10] There was a remarkable demonstration of this factor in the 1890s, after the extension of British rule to the Cross River, when a major shift of population occurred, with whole villages moving to a riverain site.[11] Whatever the reason, Igbo communities regarded settlement near water with definite apprehension. 'The ancestors believed that these streams were meant to quench the thirst but not to serve them as 'homes'. The streams and rivers are the homes of gods and other spirits. It is true that the present generation is too wise . . . but that is the reason why man no longer lives long.'[12]

The suggestion has been made that the Igbo heartland, isolated from external influences, shows us the original character of Igbo culture, and that the study of, for instance, the Owerri-Orlu-Okigwi area gives us a baseline with which we can assess the nature of change in other Igbo areas.[13] This is a technique which has been used very fruitfully elsewhere, and in the Igbo context it is suggestive (the heartland, for instance, lacks witchcraft beliefs, secret societies, and title societies). But it involves us in a number of difficulties. The heartland, too, was subject to change. Thus the institution of *osu* (ritual slavery) is very typical of the area, but the evidence suggests that it is of relatively recent origin, and adopted its present form in the era of the trans-Atlantic slave trade.[14]

What is most ancient is not necessarily most typical, as witness the institutions of Nri, with its priest-king, which are most untypical of Igboland as a whole. What is important may not be ancient, as witness the great importance of the Aro oracle and trading network in nineteenth-century Igboland – which dated, as we shall see, only from the seventeenth century.

What is clear, is that the Igbo heartland repeatedly built up levels of population pressure which the ecological environment was unable to sustain, and which from time to time gave rise to migrations to other parts of Igboland.

> One can assume an early dispersion from this centre to the Nsukka-Udi highlands in the east and an early drift southward towards the coast . . . One can more positively distinguish a later and more massive dispersal . . . which was mainly south-eastwards . . . into what is now the Eastern Isuama area. From this subsidiary dispersion area there was one movement south-south-east into the Aba Division to form the Ngwa group of tribes, and another movement east into the Umuahia area and thence to the Ohaffia-Arochuku ridge, with an offshoot that struck north . . . to develop into the North-Eastern Ibo.[15]

The antiquity of these migrations is reflected in the high population densities obtaining throughout Igboland, and the remarkable extent to which the original vegetation has been modified by the human presence. Igboland is in the rain-forest belt, but it is difficult to find any rain forest; the whole countryside is covered with farms, or secondary vegetation where farms lie fallow. Nor is this a recent phenomenon – a British forestry official described it over sixty years ago, and so did a number of nineteenth-century observers, though with less technical expertise.[16]

AGRICULTURE

The invention of agriculture is the most fundamental of human discoveries. It marked the watershed between the hazardous wandering life of the hunter and collector of wild edible plants, and a settled, more comfortable life, which in its turn made the development of further skills possible.

In the Igbo context, the fundamental discovery was that of yam cultivation.

This is how it is described in traditions recorded in Nri over sixty years ago.

> Cuku gave them [Ezenri and Ezadama] each a piece of yam; yams were at that time unknown to man, for human beings walked in the bush like animals. After eating his portion, Ezadama went to ask for more. Cuku gave him another piece and instructed Ezadama to tell Ezenri to send his eldest son and daughter. The Ezenri sent them and Cuku told them to bring a big pot, which he sent back again. The Ezenri was to plant this pot wherever he chose and no one was to look into the pot for twelve days; when they looked in and saw yams growing they went to Cuku and told him, and Cuku said, 'Plant them, put sticks, and lift up the runners.'[17]

One version of tradition among the north-eastern Igbo states that the founder of the Izzi searched in the bush for food for his starving parents and sisters. He found a number of specified wild yams, some of which have since been domesticated.[18]

The work of historical botanists places these traditions in a more precise factual context. Until fairly recently, scholars tended to think that the knowledge of agriculture spread to

West Africa by diffusion from Asia, and that the varieties of yam commonly found in West Africa were Asian in origin. More intensive research has shown that most West African yams are varieties of *Dioscorea rotundata* and *Dioscorea cayenensis*, both of which are indigenous. *D. cayenensis* still grows wild in West African forests, while *D. rotundata* is a cultigen. Other species of yam, such as *D. dumetorum*, widely grown in Igboland, are still in process of ennoblement. It seems almost certain that yam cultivation was independently invented in the quite small area which forms the 'yam belt' of West Africa.[19]

When did this take place? The variety of cultivars in existence has been taken by botanists as reflecting at least three millenia of development. The five thousand year-old pottery referred to above may provide a *terminus post quem*, for the invention of pottery precedes the invention of agriculture throughout the world.

All that one can say with certainty is that between five thousand and three thousand years ago, the peoples of the 'yam belt' learnt how to cultivate yams. By constant cultivation and experiment, they improved the local varieties, increasing their yield and, in certain instances, reducing their toxic content. The discovery formed the economic basis of Igbo civilisation; it was of supreme importance and was given ritual and symbolic expression in many areas of Igbo life.

The later introduction of further food crops may be conveniently dealt with here. The food crops which are indigenous to the area are surprisingly few, among them yams, okro, egusi, oil palms, some varieties of rice, and kola nuts (these last are, of course, less a food than a stimulant). Coco-yams, bananas and plantains came from Asia. It used to be thought that they spread across the African continent by diffusion. More recently, scholars have found difficulty with this thesis, and suggested that they may have been introduced to Nigeria by early Portuguese voyagers. Tomatoes, cassava, maize and chili peppers are native to America and were brought by the Portuguese from the late fifteenth century onwards. Cassava was well established in the Delta by the late seventeenth century – still keeping its Portuguese name[20] – but it often reached Igbo communities much later. Thus it was introduced in Onitsha in the mid-nineteenth century, where it created a minor economic revolution.[21] Other foods, among them guavas, cashew nuts and coconuts, were introduced in the late nineteenth century by the Royal Niger Company, and diffused in Igboland, often by missionaries. Sometimes this is reflected in their names – the coconut is *aku-oyibo* ('oyibo' means European) – or in the fact that they have, like the guava, no Igbo name at all.

Igbo audiences tend to be sceptical about the foreign origins of so many of Igboland's staple foods. But it is clearly established by botanical studies; thus, maize has all its 'relations' in America, and none in Africa. It is equally difficult for an Englishman to envisage an England lacking tea, tobacco and potatoes, or for an Italian to accept that there was no spaghetti in Italy, till his ancestors learnt the art of its preparation from the Chinese!

IRON WORKING

Another extremely important, though much later, development was the discovery of iron working, which excavations at Afikpo show had reached Igboland by the beginning of the Christian era.[22] Iron ores are found very extensively in Africa, but the process of extracting the ore is so complicated that it was once thought improbable that it should have been invented more than once. It is well known that the Nok complex of northern Nigeria is an ancient centre of iron working. It used to be thought that the knowledge of this craft reached Nok from North Africa, possibly from Meroe, a famous iron-working city on the Nile. But the date of Nigerian iron working at Nok is now known to be earlier than Meroe – 500 B.C. or even earlier[23] – and this may well indicate an independent invention. It doubtless reached Igboland by diffusion from Nok.

The discovery transformed the quality of life; it is not difficult to imagine the difficulty of cutting firewood, tilling the ground and slicing food with implements of wood, stone and bone. (Clearing the bush was probably easier – the Igbo doubtless used fire for the purpose, as they still do.) It laid the foundation for a highly skilled and sophisticated tradition of metallurgy, which had reached great heights of artistry and technical mastery by the ninth century.

Again, the traditions of Nri describe it in poetic and symbolic terms, making explicit reference to the ancient iron-working centre of Awka.

NINTH-CENTURY IGBOLAND: NRI AND IGBO-UKWU

Nri is unique in Igboland. The first ethnographic description of Igboland, based on fieldwork in the 1890s, stresses the 'reverence and precedence' which was paid to Nri by other Igbo communities, a precedence which was crystallised in a proverb: 'The street of the Nri family is the street of the gods, through which all who die in other parts of Iboland pass to the land of Spirits.'[24] Another early ethnographic description called the Eze Nri 'the spiritual potentate over a large extent of the Ibo country.'[25] Nri ritual specialists travel through much of east and west Igboland, purifying communities from abominations.

In modern times, the Eze Nri has been a sacred, quasi-divine ruler, whose cult has many parallels with that of the Atta of Igala, doubtless reflecting their common origin. He lives in seclusion, surrounded by restrictions, and performs rituals which safeguard the prosperity of his people. At his accession he goes through a symbolic death to humanity and rebirth as divinity. He is buried in a shallow grave, and then exhumed, and painted with white clay, a symbol of innocence and immortality. Symbolically, he makes a palm tree flower and fruit. When he dies, he is buried seated in a wood-lined chamber.[26]

Long ago – Mr Onwuejeogwu, an anthropologist who did detailed fieldwork at Nri and evolved his own chronological system, dates it between 909 and 1049 – a section of Nri migrated to Oreri and founded a rival ritual centre there, with its own, smaller, sphere of influence. The traditions state that the founder of Oreri took with him a roped bronze vase.[27]

Archaeology is a field where many important discoveries have been made by accident. We know a great deal about the richness and antiquity of Nri culture thanks to a farmer of Igbo-Ukwu, a small town twenty-five miles south-west of Awka. In 1938 he was digging in his compound when he discovered a number of remarkable bronze works of art. It was not until 1959 that the area was excavated by an archaeologist, and not until 1970 that the results were published in full. (The long delay before excavation reflects the relative indifference of colonial governments to African culture and history.)

Professor Shaw, who conducted the excavations, worked on

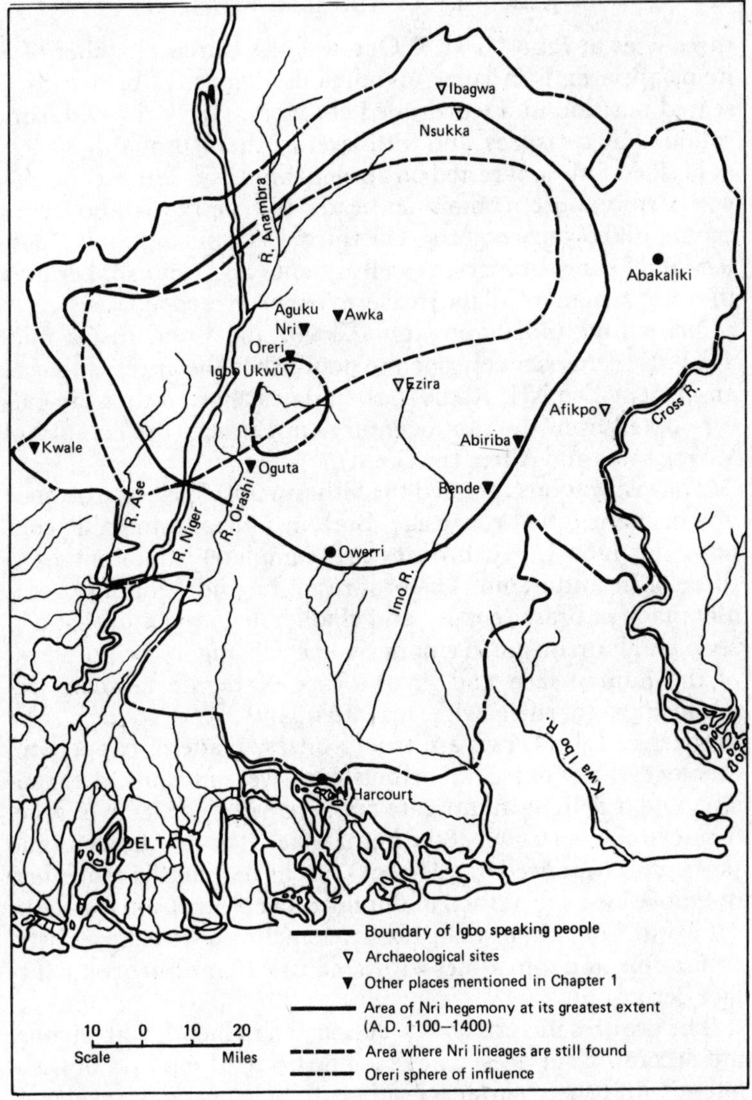

Map 2 Nri spheres of influence, and archaeological sites

three sites at Igbo-Ukwu.[28] One was the burial chamber of a man, apparently a ruler or religious dignitary, buried in a seated position in a wood-lined chamber, richly dressed, surrounded by treasures, and with several others, probably slaves, at his feet. One foot rested on an elephant tusk. The second site was a storehouse, containing beads, bronze bowls and many ceremonial bronze objects. The third was a pit containing pottery and further bronzes, as well as bones and rubbish. Perhaps the most famous of all the treasures is a bronze roped vase . . .

Nri is nine miles from Igbo-Ukwu, and Oreri just a mile away. It seems scarcely open to doubt that the grave is that of an ancient Eze Nri. Radio-carbon dates showed that the culture dated from the ninth century (in Europe, the century of Viking raids and Alfred the Great).

The excavations revealed the hitherto unsuspected existence of a brilliant Igbo bronze age. Both in style and metallic content, the Igbo-Ukwu bronzes are completely different from those of Ife and Benin. The bronzes of Ife and Benin are actually made of brass (copper and zinc). They are naturalistic in style and humanistic in emphasis, specialising in the portrayal of the human face and, in the case of Benin, of social relationships (a ruler with his attendants, and so on). The bronzes of Igbo-Ukwu are true bronzes, made of copper, tin and lead. They reflect an astonishing level of technical virtuosity, and a delight in intricate craftsmanship for its own sake. There is one portrayal of the human face (the first known Igbo portrait, reproduced in this book) but in general the craftsmen of Igbo-Ukwu specialised in duplicating objects from the natural world, sometimes realistically, sometimes with surrealistic stylisation, and sometimes with a realistic shape but ornate surface decoration.

The bronzes include shells, duplicated in metal, with elaborate decorated surfaces. They include bronze bells and bowls – again with ornate surfaces – a bronze belt, made of seventeen different ornamental plates, and elaborate scabbards and sword hilts. There are stylised rams' heads, elephants' heads and leopards' heads. The snake is a recurrent motif, sometimes depicted swallowing eggs or frogs. The delight in technical accomplishment is shown in the recurrent insect motifs. If one studies closely the shell photographed in this book (Plate 1c) one notes the bronze flies. There are five bronze crickets on an elephant pendant. A bowl is decorated with rows of bronze beetles and praying mantises.

All were made by the very difficult technique known as the lost wax method. They are made of bronze, rather than pure copper, because the alloy is more suitable for casting; this reflects the artist's knowledge of metallurgy. Interestingly enough, objects such as copper wire jewellery, (bracelets and anklets) and calabash handles, which were made by beating and drawing, are of pure copper, which is more suitable for this purpose.

Not all the finds were of copper and bronze. Professor Shaw discovered iron sword-blades and razors, together with the slag from which they were made. There were items of pottery, demonstrating, in a different medium, the technical assurance and inventiveness of the bronzes, in their 'marvellous wealth and variety of form and decoration.'

Three elephants' tusks were found, which, like the elephant pendants, reflect the importance of ivory in the economy. There were fragments of cloth, made of different fibres, and woven in quite different ways. A textile institute which studied them commented that the nature of the techniques used 'suggests that the craftsmen possessed a high degree of textile skill, as does also the quality of the material.'

Were these ancient craftsmen the ancestors of the modern Igbo of Nri? One would *a priori* assume so, and the research of Mr Onwuejeogwu has revealed a degree of continuity between the Igbo-Ukwu discoveries and the modern culture of the area which would seem to put the matter beyond cavil.[29] The *ichi* facial scars on the human face recall the facial scarification characteristic of titled men from Nri in recent times. The geometrical designs on the elaborate pottery are strikingly similar to designs still carved on wooden doors at Awka. The roped vase suggests the roped pottery which is still made in the area. The animal skull and elephant and leopard motifs remind one of the continuing vitality of these symbols of headship, power and authority. The snakes may well reflect the reverence which is still paid locally to the sacred python, *eke*. And there are further parallels. Some may be beside the mark, but together they add up to an astonishing degree of cultural continuity, over a period of more than a thousand years.

Among the treasures was a vast collection of beads – over 165,000 of them – many stemming originally from India, and some, perhaps, from Venice. They provide dramatic evidence of how closely the Igbo were linked with the rest of the world by international trade. It was once thought that the Igbo, and the other forest peoples of West Africa, spent centuries in great isolation, cut off by their allegedly impenetrable environment. But just as the forest did not hinder settlement, in the first place, it clearly did not prevent the Igbo from becoming part of a vast complex of international trade. The copper used in the bronzes was undoubtedly imported from far afield, for there is no copper in modern Nigeria. It came either from distant mines in the Sahara, or from Europe, via the trans-Sahara trade routes.

The treasures reflect, of course, the prosperity of the community which produced them. We can only guess at what was exported in return. Slaves may have been exported, but there is no evidence either way. Traces of kola nuts were found in the excavations. But then as now, problems of preservation made long-distance trade difficult, and it seems unlikely that in the ninth century they were exported over great distances. The elephant tusks suggest a more likely export. A great deal of ivory was to be purchased by European traders in centuries to come in the Delta, and early this century British officials met parties of Hausa elephant hunters in Igboland. Its former importance is reflected in the name of the Alaenyi (land of elephants) clan.

One of the bronzes, a sword hilt in the form of a horse and its rider, suggests fascinating questions about the relationship of Igbo-Ukwu to regions further north. In modern times, horses have been used in Igboland only for ritual purposes. But the forest kingdom of Benin had a cavalry for centuries, despite the obstacles of its environment, and horses disappeared from it only in the nineteenth century.[30] It is not impossible that something similar happened in Igboland, and that the great importance attached to the horse in the rituals of the northern Igbo preserves a memory of it. Alternatively, and perhaps more probably, the horseman may reflect contacts with areas further north – an Igbo who had travelled to Idda, or beyond, a craftsman from Idda, or an encounter with mounted Igala invaders.

IGBO-UKWU AND IGBOLAND

An important question remains: how typical was this tradition of craftsmanship of Igboland as a whole? Was it something unique and evanescent, or was it part of a wider and long-continued tradition? All the evidence points towards the latter possibility.

A site was excavated in Bende. Oral traditions and radio-carbon dates showed that it had been continuously inhabited since the ninth century. There were no spectacular finds, but it revealed pottery and iron objects, including an iron spear-head and metal bells.[31]

At Ezira fifteen miles east of Igbo-Ukwu, strikingly similar art works were uncovered, again by accident, when a farmer was digging clay to repair his house. The site was excavated by Professor Hartle, and proved, again, to be the burial of a prominent person, yielding a number of iron and bronze treasures, with the same ornate surface decoration – iron gongs, an iron sword, bronze anklets, bracelets, bells and ceremonial staves. They were stolen from the museum at the University of Nigeria, Nsukka, during the civil war, and survive only in photographs (reproduced in Plates 2*b* and *c*) and in Professor Hartle's descriptions: 'The bronze decorations are of particular beauty, consisting mainly of exquisite fine line designs that look like filagree or lace . . .' Radio-carbon dates show that they were made about six hundred years later, towards the end of the fifteenth century.[32]

A French visitor to the Delta at the end of the seventeenth century acquired several elaborate swords of Igbo manufacture[33] (shown in Plate 3). Baikie, in the mid-nineteenth century, visiting the Delta and the Niger, saw 'swords, spears and metallic ornaments' which were 'very neatly finished' and made in Igboland.[34] He thought them the work of the Aro, but it is generally agreed that they were probably the work of Abiriba smiths. The first European visitor to Bende, in the 1890s, gave an interesting description of bells, pipes, jewellery and brass-mounted staves made in Abiriba, 'whose inhabitants consist of nothing but blacksmiths, who do all the work in brass and iron for a very great distance around.[35] The researches of Miss Ekejiuba, in the 1960s, revealed the existence of ritual brass objects, used by the Aro, and apparently made by Abiriba smiths, which have many striking similarities, both in style and content, with the bronzes of Igbo-Ukwu and Ezira. They include bells with decorated surfaces, swords, a bracelet decorated with tortoise motifs and large manillas, used for ritual purposes and decorated with snakes, lizards and leopards. The ritual objects, known collectively as *Otusi*, include brass replicas of a leopard and a crocodile, 'with five other ivory and wood carvings of skulls of dogs, leopard and human head.'[35]

The tradition of brass working, as well as iron working, seems to have existed in the riverain and western areas of Igboland as well, which are not usually associated with these skills. In the 1930s, a British official discovered 'various brass objects now ancient with decay' in Kwale,[37] though we would need more information to know their age and origins. The University Museum at Nsukka contains finely worked ritual bronze objects, obtained at Oguta in recent times.

II The Middle Years of Igbo History

> 'It is like gazing at the bottom of a deep gorge from the top of a high mountain. The objects seen are veritable, but their true nature is blurred by distance.'
>
> *An Ezza elder, on our knowledge of an episode in Ezza history*[1]

The centuries that lie between the ninth century and the nineteenth are the most difficult period for the historian of Igboland to write about. For the ninth century, we have the vivid detail of archaeological discoveries. For the nineteenth, we have an ever-swelling stream of evidence, both oral and documentary. But the thousand years which lie between are full of question marks and obscurities. One historian has compared them with a dark tunnel, separating two areas of light.

Our knowledge of the middle years of Igbo history rests partly on the evidence of European visitors to the Delta. These never visited the interior, so what they say about it is not very reliable. The other source is to be found in the oral traditions of the Igbo people themselves. These again pose many questions. There is the problem of chronology, and hence of the relationship between different traditions. There is the problem of their relationship to external events, especially the impact of the trans-Atlantic slave trade.

Because much of the date is ambiguous, this is an area of history where scholars can and do differ sharply. Not all historians would accept, for instance, the present writer's interpretation of the impact of the slave trade. The chapter that follows deals essentially with probabilities.

2 Igbo Society in the Middle Years

A QUESTION OF IDENTITY

This book is a history of the Igbo people. It immediately suggests the question, to what extent were 'the Igbo people' a real entity in precolonial times?

There was, of course, no sense of pan-Igbo identity. The Igbo villager's view of external reality was a sharp dichotomy, 'them and us', with the sense of attachment to 'us' growing weaker as the unit grew larger – the family, the lineage, the village, the village group. Invariably, he felt a strong local patriotism. The people of Owerri felt superior, as warriors, to the neighbouring Isu, who were traders.[2] The smiths of Agulu-Umana looked down on the neighbouring 'Oheke' who did not share their skills.[3] The people of Arochukwu called themselves the children of God.

Igbo names for other Igbo groups are often based on geography.[4] Enugu and Agbaja refer to upland dwellers, hence the commonness of the names. Anaocha refers to the dried up 'white' land between the Niger and the Imo River. Enu-ani is the high land in the Asaba hinterland, west of the Niger.

One important conceptual category which seems to have developed in the era of the slave trade was the distinction between Igbo and Olu,[5] inland and riverain. In the words of Professor Henderson, 'olu meant riverain or riverain derived, slave-dealing, kingdom-associated peoples; igbo meant upland, slave-providing, kingship lacking populations.'[6] The Olu, with their well-watered farms and protein rich diet, despised the Igbo, for their food and water shortages, and their role as slave suppliers. To the interior Igbo, the Olu states, with their traditions of origin from elsewhere, were not really Igbo at all. As Professor Green put it in the 1930s, 'An educated Mbieri man . . . said that the people of his district would not till recently have called the people of Onitsha Ibo.'[7] This concept of Igbo identity is also mirrored in proverbs, such as *Igbo enwegh eze*, the Igbo have no king (in contradistinction to the riverain kingdoms), or a saying, found in the Owerri area (but not among the northern or riverain Igbo) *N'anIgbo nine n'eli ji ahube'em ihe deka nkea*[8] (I have never seen such a thing in the land of the yam-eating Igbo).

A sense of pan-Igbo identity came only when its people left Igboland – an experience first imposed by the slave trade – or when colonial conquest and rule violently extended the categories through which the Igbo perceived their world.

William Balfour Baikie was a British naval doctor and explorer, who visited the Niger and the Delta in the 1850s, and made enquiries about the Igbo whenever he could. He described their conceptualisation of themselves in words which are still true today. 'In Igbo each person hails . . . from the particular district where he was born, but when away from home all are Igbos.'[9]

A QUESTION OF CHANGE AND CONTINUITY

The question of whether the Igbo saw themselves as a people in pre-colonial times is, of course, quite distinct from the question as to whether they could be existentially described as such. But the process of describing the distinctive characteristics of Igbo society – what made them a people – involves us in two difficulties. The first is that of generalisation. The many local differences in Igbo culture make it difficult to describe them accurately in a book of this length. Each statement should be qualified, and one is in danger of describing the average of all Igbo societies which does not correspond with any actual Igbo society. This is a difficulty which is implicit, however, in all historical writing.

The second difficulty is more serious. It is necessary to describe the society, in order to understand the nature of the changes it was to undergo. But nothing is more repugnant to a historian than to describe a society in, as it were, a temporal vacuum. Societies undergo constant change; the historian, inevitably, focuses on changes, rather than on continuities. One's description of Igboland should be rooted in a particular moment in time, because the society was constantly changing. A description of Igboland 'once upon a time', in the *mgbe ndichie*, is bound to do violence to a constantly mutable reality.

The description that follows seeks to portray the main lineaments of Igbo society, as it developed in the middle years of

Igbo history. It is based on written descriptions of that society from the nineteenth and early twentieth centuries, on observations of contemporary traditional Igbo society made by anthropologists, and on a unique first-hand account of eighteenth-century Igboland. It is subject to all the qualifications I have mentioned, but it is necessary if we are to understand the nature of later change.

TRADITIONAL IGBO SOCIETY: GOVERNMENT

In Igboland, the insignia of a titled man varies – the thread or ivory anklets, the eagle feather, the red cap, the horse plume or fan carried in the hand – but a titled man is immediately recognisable, always and everywhere. In the same way, the details of Igbo traditional government varied from place to place, but its characteristic nature is always the same.

The basic unit of Igbo life was the village group.* The village was a small face-to-face society. Historians have sometimes written as if large political units are 'more advanced' than small political units, and as if the change from small to large units was a form of progress. This may be so in the modern world, when a large state, for instance, commands more resources for development, and more say, hence more independence, in international affairs. In traditional Igboland enlargement of scale offered no obvious advantages, and the small scale of her political institutions made true democracy possible.

Democracy, as it exists today in the Western world, is full of limitations. Governments take decisions that many citizens disapprove of, even among those that elected them. Minorities, even large ones, have little hope of having their political ideals put into practice. The average citizen has effectively no power to alter the network of regulations that govern his life. One of the things that struck the first Western visitors to Igboland, was the extent to which democracy was truly practised. An early visitor to a Niger Igbo town said that he felt he was in a free land, among a free people.[10] Another visitor, a Frenchman, said that true liberty existed in Igboland, though its name was not inscribed on any monument.[11]

Igbo political institutions were designed to combine popular participation with weighting for experience and ability. One

* West of the Niger, the town. In north-eastern Igboland, family groups lived in dispersed individual compounds.

finds, in different parts of Igboland, different political institutions, in varying combinations. Perhaps the most universal institution was the role of the family head. He was the oldest man of the oldest surviving generation, in the family, or in the quarter. He would settle family disputes, and commanded respect and reverence, because he controlled the channel of communication with ancestors.

An eighteenth-century Igbo wrote, recalling his childhood,[12] that government was conducted 'by the chiefs or elders of the place'. The composition of these elders varied. In Asaba, men aged 58–68 formed a governing age grade, the Oturaza. In Owerri, the council of elders, *ndi oha*, comprises the oldest members of certain specific families.

Igbo government has sometimes been called a gerontocracy, but not all elderly men had an equal say. A successful man, who was prosperous, with numerous descendants, would, as it were, register and legitimise his success by taking a title. (This was not universal in Igboland.) Usually, there was a hierarchy of ascending titles, to be taken in order, with an ascending scale of payments. But it was not a simple matter of the purchase of political power with wealth (a sight familiar to the student of English or American history). The title system served as a substitute for social security; the man who acquired a title paid to do so, and shared in the payments of later entrants. A title was a guarantee of character, as well as of success. The entrant went through protracted and arduous rituals, and his later life was surrounded by religious restrictions, which became more onerous as he rose in the title structure. They were scrupulously kept. The present writer recalls visiting a titled man in hospital, who was desperately ill, but who refused to eat, because hospital conditions made it impossible for him to conform with the ritual obligations surrounding meals . . .

Another political institution which was widespread, but not universal, was the age grade. Each age grade had defined obligations in community service. Each was jealous of its good name, so controlled and disciplined its unsatisfactory members.

Secret societies were a valuable instrument of social control. Their members would appear, masked, often at night, in the role of supernatural beings, and denounce and attack offenders.

Like the age grade, it was an intitution which cut across the vertical loyalty to the individual family and lineage. The anonymity of the members, and their supernatural aura, made the society a potent sanction against crime. As an Nsukka informant put it, 'They frighten people, and many people behave themselves just because they are frightened of what *omabe* will do to them.[13] In some areas, they were dominated by younger men, who were thus given a role in political life denied them by most other Igbo institutions for government.[14] In others, they formed guilds of wealthy men, similar to title societies elsewhere. A good example of this was the Okonko society found among several southern Igbo groups such as the Ngwa. This was responsible for maintaining the roads, and had the right to collect customs, in return. Its brightly decorated toll-booths are vividly described by early European visitors.[15]

A few Igbo states, such as Aboh and Onitsha, which had a tradition of origin from elsewhere, were ruled by kings. These kings were regarded as sacred, and lived in ritual seclusion. But they were not absolute, and took decisions in conjunction with titled men, and representatives of other groups. Their decisions could be challenged, and their persons deposed. Every morning, a drummer warns the Obi of Aboh that one of his predecessors was deposed and killed: 'Obonwe!* Obonwe! Kwulu wuzo. Obonwe! Obonwe! Watch your step!'[16]

The kind of decisions made most often in traditional Igbo societies were either what we would now call judicial – land or debt disputes, cases of theft, murder and so on – or decisions affecting relations with other groups. In a judicial case, the lineage head would attempt to settle the matter within the family. If he failed, the matter would go to the elders, who would hear the case in public. A decision which affected the whole town, such as a decision to make war, would normally be put to the people (i.e. to an assembly of free adult males).

Two further points should be noted. One is the essential fluidity of Igbo institutions. A noted orator could influence debate. A warrior of proven courage and judgement would have a leading role in warfare. In times of crisis, some communities tried the rule of one man, and gave it up when the crisis was past. Thus Aguleri, 'in times of war, the bravest and most influential

* Obonwe is the Obi's praise name.

men became dictators and controlled the town. Such was the case when Agave of Enugu* became the dictator.'[17] Agave founded a dynasty which endured for a time. Then kingship was given up, until in the second half of the nineteenth century another crisis (European encroachment on the Niger, and the military aggression of the Royal Niger Company) threw up another natural leader, Onyekomeli Idigo† who founded a royal dynasty which has endured to this day.

If the facts of a case were not clear, the Igbo had recourse to an oracle or to divination. The diviner had multiple functions in Igbo society; he explained the supernatural face of events, and he made misfortune intelligible, and so acceptable. He prescribed the sacrifices which would control the activity of supernatural beings. In some cases, disputing parties would have recourse to one of Igboland's regional network of oracles, such as the Agbala of Awka, or Ibini Ukpabe, at Arochukwu. These oracles depended on 'sons abroad' to bring clients, and to ascertain the truth of the matter. The oracles rested on a deliberate deception, yet were less exploitative than they seem, for their reputation and influence depended on their reputation for just judgements. Their main practical disadvantage – which they shared with most modern judicial systems – was that they were very expensive, which tended to put them beyond the reach of a poor applicant.

An anthropologist in the 1930s wrote that Igbo societies are governed by gods and ancestors. To the Igbo, the secular and the sacred, the natural and the supernatural, are a continuum. Supernatural forces continually impinge on life, and must be propitiated by appropriate prayers and sacrifices.

THE IGBO WORLD VIEW

The Igbo were nothing if not profoundly religious, and all accounts of their life reflect the fact. One of the earliest of these, a description, by a German missionary, of Aboh in 1841, is a good example.

The Igbos are in their way, a religious people. The word

* One of the component villages of Aguleri.

† Later baptised as Joseph, and often referred to by his title, Ogbuanyinya Idigo.

> 'Tshuku' – God – is continually heard. Tshuku is supposed to do every thing . . . – Their notions of some of the attributes of the Supreme Being are, in many respects, correct, and their manner of expressing them striking. 'God made every thing: He made both White and Black', is continually on their lips. Some of their parables are descriptive of the perfections of God.[18]

The missionary naturally concentrated on an aspect of Igbo religion which corresponded closely with his own: the idea of God, eternal, the Creator of all things.

God created the visible universe, *uwa.*[19] Many aspects of that universe exist on two levels – the natural level, and as spiritual forces, *alusi.* These include the sun, *anyanwu*, the sky, *igwe*,* the earth, *ani*, *ana*, or *ala*, in different parts of Igboland. To Niger Igbos, the Niger is the king of *alusi. Alusi* are found among temporal, as well as natural phenomena, in the four days of the Igbo week. Unlike *Chukwu*, who is always benevolent, the *alusi* are forces for blessing or destruction, depending on circumstances. They punish social offenders, and those who unwittingly infringe their privileges. Hence the key role of the diviner, who interprets their wishes, and the priest, who placates them with sacrifice (there are different types of priest: the hereditary lineage priests, such as the *ony'ishi*, and priests who are chosen by particular gods for their service, after passing through a series of ascetic and mystical experiences).

The *chi*, a personalised providence, comes from *Chukwu*, and reverts to him at a man's death. Each man has his own *chi*, who may be well or ill disposed. Each village has its sacred places and particular divinities, which inhabit a sacred forest, or rock, or cave, or stream.

The living, the dead, and the unborn form part of a continuum. The ancestors – those who live well-spent lives die in socially approved ways, and are given correct burial rites – live in one of those worlds of the dead† which mirror the world of the living. The living honour them with sacrifices. The ancestors watch over the living, and are periodically reincarnated

* *Chukwu* is closely linked with *igwe* and *anyanwu*. They are variously seen as his 'home', his 'messengers' or as metaphors of his attributes.

† In Onitsha, the number of the worlds of the dead is put variously at four, seven, and eight.

among them – hence the name *ndichie*, the returners. The unhappy spirits who die bad deaths, and lack correct burial rites, cannot return to the world of the living, or enter that of the dead. They wander homeless and dispossessed, expressing their grief by causing harm among the living.

The Igbo regarded their religion with great seriousness. Their sacrifices were real, and not token sacrifices; the sacrifice of a goat, for instance, represented a major loss of wealth in a poor society. Religious tabus, especially those surrounding priests and titled men, involved a great deal of what we would call asceticism. Whole communities deprived themselves of palatable and nutritious foods in religion's name – among them, the sacred fish of the Imo River. Perhaps few modern Christians would be prepared to undergo as much asceticism. Like the Jews of the Old Testament, they expected, in return for their prayers and sacrifices, blessings such as health, longevity and prosperity – and especially children, the greatest of blessings.*

Their religion led the Igbo into some oppression and injustice. Single births were regarded as typically human, multiple births as typical of the animal world. So twins were regarded as less than human, and put to death (as were animals produced at single births). The desire to offer the most precious possible sacrifice led to human sacrifice – for what is as precious as a human life? The belief that the worlds of the dead mirror the world we know encouraged the sacrifice of slaves at funerals, to provide a retinue for the dead man in the life to come. The intention was good – to aid and honour, for instance, a beloved father. The result was an institution of great cruelty (to which we shall return).

Certain Igbo beliefs attempt to provide an explanation of imperfectly understood natural phenomena. An interesting example is the concept of the *Ogbanje*. This is a wicked spirit which takes the form of a beautiful child. He is constantly reborn in a family, and constantly dies, tormenting the unfortunate parents. This may be an explanation of sickle-cell

* This is reflected in many personal names, such as Ifeyinwa, what is like a child, Nwakaego, a child is better than wealth and Nwabueze, the child is king. An unconventional realistic variant (chosen by a mother) is Nwadiolu, a child is work!

anaemia, which is very common in Igboland: the children of distinctive physical appearance, dying in infancy or childhood, born to apparently healthy parents who are carriers of the sickle-cell trait.

THE LAND

Olaudah Equiano, who was born in about 1745 and left Igboland at the age of eleven, recalled the agriculture of his area in these terms:

> Our land is uncommonly rich and fruitful, and produces all kinds of vegetables in great abundance. We have plenty of Indian corn [maize] and vast quantities of cotton and tobacco. Our pineapples grow without culture; they are about the size of the largest sugar-loaf, and finely flavoured. We have also spices of different kinds, particularly pepper, and a variety of delicious fruits which I have never seen in Europe . . . All our industry is exerted to improve these blessings of nature.[20]

This account may be romanticised. Everything about one's childhood is surrounded by a golden glow, and larger than life. In fact, the quantity and quality of land owned by Igbo communities varied greatly. Some indeed had so much land that they worked it with the help of migrant labour. But these were the exception. In the Igbo heartland – Orlu, Owerri, Okigwi – men struggled to wrest a living from inadequate and infertile plots. Thus the Nguru clan, in what is now Mbaise, worked leached eroding lands from which no industry or skill could wrest good harvests. Many of its people were forced to work as migrant labourers for the Etche clan, or eked out a living by various crafts, such as mat and rope making, or by trade.[21]

The fertility of the land made no difference to the reverence with which it was regarded. *Ana*, the divine Earth, has a key role in Igbo religion, reflecting the values of an agricultural community. Many offences were regarded as abominable, not so much in themselves, but because they offended her. In some expositions of Igbo religion, its core is the polarity between *Chukwu* and *Ana*, between the transcendant and the visible. In the words of an elder from Ihembosi,

It is *Chukwu* and *Ana*
That we invoke
Every people in their town
Call upon *Chukwu* and *Ana* . . .

When the *Akpu* tree matures
It falls,
And rots on the Ground,
No one can see it again.
When the *Iroko* tree matures,
It falls on the Ground.
When man matures
He falls on the Ground.[22]

The cultivation of yams was as central as the Earth. The Yam Spirit, *Ifejioku*,* is one of the major *alusi*. Part of every year is called the season of hunger. This does not mean a season of lack of food (though sometimes it is) but a season of yam hunger. Far from despising manual labour, the Igbo esteemed the successful farmer. Some parts of Igboland awarded him a title, such as *eze ji*, Yam King. Cassava was and is grown on land too poor for yam cultivation, but was regarded as very inferior, a poor man's food.

Few Igbo communities, even of craftsmen and specialists, were divorced from agriculture. The itinerant smiths of Awka were divided into two sections, which took it in turns to travel abroad, and to stay at home to work on the land.[23] The Aro were an exception, tending to concentrate on trade to the exclusion of farm work. Arochukwu itself bought food from neighbouring Ututo and Ihe.[24] The same thing tended to be true of the Aro settlements. Thus in Arondizuogu, boys were trained as traders from an early age, in commodities of ascending value (they started with lizards!) and farm work was left for the unsuccessful.[25] But this was very untypical of Igboland as a whole.

Traditions collected by Mr Ejiofor in Aguinyi cast light on changing patterns of agricultural productivity. His informants state that in pre-colonial times, the output of individual farmers was much lower. 'Even when I was a small boy, the barn of a rich man in those days did not contain up to one-quarter of the yams which the barn of a poor widow contains today. But

* The name varies in different parts of Igboland.

people were satisfied in those days, don't make mistakes about that.' Another informant stated that in the past, farms were much more carefully and frequently weeded, and domestic animals better fed – 'hence they were very much fatter than the goats we have now.'[26]

TRADE AND CRAFTSMANSHIP

The development of trade and of specialised craftsmanship was closely linked. A village where everyone was a blacksmith had to export its products, or send its sons abroad to practise their craft. Various forms of craftsmanship were widely diffused in Igboland, but were most developed among the Igbo of the heartland. Possibly, there was a correlation between a dense population and land shortage, and the development of other forms of economic activity.

The craft of iron working, was, as we have seen, of great antiquity in Igboland, probably going back to the beginning of the Christian era. We have noted the iron swords and razors found at Igbo-Ukwu, and dating from the ninth century, and from Ezira, dating from the fifteenth.

The most famous Igbo centres of iron working were Awka, Abiriba, and Nkwerre. Awka is close to Igbo-Ukwu and Nri, and is explicitly mentioned in Nri traditions about the introduction of iron working. The Awka smiths used raw iron smelted by the Agbaja of Udi division. As we have seen, the two sections of the blacksmiths' guild took it in turns to travel abroad – each blacksmith family had its own particular travel route, except for four families, which remained in Awka. Not all Awka men were smiths. There was a guild of ritual specialists (*dibia*) and a guild of wood carvers. Awka's travelling sons brought back clients to her oracle, and the information necessary for a just judgement.

Nkwerre, in southern Igboland, was another famous town of blacksmiths and traders; its smiths' skill in gun manufacture gave the town the name *Nkwerre Opia Egbe*. They were long-distance traders; in the words of a local historian, 'Every Nkwerre man or woman is a trader by birth . . . In days gone by the chief articles of trade were slaves, fowls, tobacco, cloths and all that blacksmiths of those days could manufacture.'[27]

Abiriba was another wealthy community of smiths and long-distance traders, working raw iron from the mines of the Okigwi-Arochukwu ridge.

These were the most famous centres, but there were many others. Historians have tended in the past to take too much of a bird's eye view of Igbo economic life, and to neglect the smaller centres which nevertheless were dominant in the local trading network. Thus although Udi was more famous for its smelters, it also had a community of smiths, at Agulu-Umana.[28] The metal goods used in the Ohuhu clan were made by the local blacksmiths of Umukabi Okpuala, using imported iron from the delta.[29] Both smelting and iron working were widely diffused in the Nsukka area,[30] and a missionary account from the beginning of this century gives an interesting picture of an Igbo smith at work, west of the Niger.

> I paid a visit to a blacksmith's shop. It was most interesting. With exceedingly primitive tools, and very meagre materials, these native smiths turn out some very neat work. While I was waiting he made a needle out of a piece of old knife. The eye and point all complete without being filed or ground. He was wearing a pair of armlets made from old knives. They were chased and polished . . .[31]

In all these places, the knowledge of iron working was the jealously guarded secret of certain lineages, surrounded by strict taboos.

Textile manufacture was another ancient and widely disseminated craft in Igboland. We have noted the high-quality textiles from Igbo-Ukwu. Equiano's account of mid-eighteenth century Igboland states 'When our women are not employed with the men in tillage, their usual occupation is spinning and weaving cotton, which they afterwards dye and make into garments.'[32] In the 1850s a British explorer found elaborately woven patterned cloth on the Benue and near its confluence with the Niger, which had been exported from Igboland,[33] possibly from the Nsukka area, where textile manufacture was highly developed. Traditions collected by Professor Afigbo reflect the fact that there was a time in the remote past when Nsukka textiles were made from bark fibre. Subsequently, cotton weaving was introduced 'very long ago when women were idle.'[34]

A missionary description of textile manufacture in a small Igbo town west of the Niger, at the beginning of this century, shows both the vitality of the tradition, and the way in which it was finally destroyed by European imports. 'Every woman here weaves cloth from the cotton which grows on the trees in abundance, and they do it beautifully, working patterns in, but foreign cloth is much coveted, and their own cloth despised.'[35] The southern Igbo town of Akwete made textiles so superb that imported cloth could not rival them, until finally, foreign producers copied them. 'Akwete cloth' bought today in a Nigerian market is liable to carry a small neat label, 'Made in Hong Kong'. . .

Not all trade exchanges, of course, involved craftsmanship. The various parts of Igboland, and her neighbours, were well suited to an exchange of natural products. We have already seen, in the Igbo-Ukwu context, the import of copper and beads from the north. A much more important exchange, and one which was well established by the beginning of the sixteenth century, was that between the Ijo states of the Delta, and the communities of southern Igboland. Their contrasting environments made them ideally suited for trade with each other. The swamps and waterways of the Delta were unsuited for farming, but excellent for fishing and salt manufacture. Southern Igboland lacked salt (some Igbo communities have made substitutes from vegetable ash until quite recent times) and its diet tended to be deficient in protein, relying too heavily on starches and vegetable 'soup'. The transport problem was solved by the technical skill of the Delta peoples. A Portuguese visitor, writing at the beginning of the sixteenth century, describes salt manufacture at Bonny, and the great canoes, carrying eighty men each, which carried goods through the Delta waterways to the interior.[36] This account does not mention fish (of which there is much later evidence) and describes the Delta as an importer of protein foods (cows and sheep) as well as of yams and slaves. Compare an Andoni oral tradition, 'at this time we were not fisher folk, but salt makers.'[37]

The other source of Igboland's salt was the salt lake at Uburu, in the north-east, where the salt was processed by an exclusive guild of women producers. Because of its salt, and its strategic location for trade with the north, Uburu developed into one of Igboland's great periodic fairs, under the aegis of the Aro, and attracting merchants from a great distance. Among other things, horses were sold there, for religious rituals.

The imported goods found at Igbo-Ukwu suggest the likelihood that they were imported via the Niger. By the nineteenth century, as we shall see, trade on the lower Niger was highly developed, and regulated by an elaborate system of inter-state conventions. We have no way of knowing when this trade first developed. It may well be that some of the great canoes the Portuguese saw travelling up the Bonny River were bound for destinations on the Niger. The present writer's view is that trade on the Niger probably began well before Igbo-Ukwu times, but that it expanded vastly in the seventeenth and eighteenth centuries.

Two aspects of Igboland's economic life which reflect the vitality of her economic life are the market, and her abundant and varied currencies. The Igbo market is an institution which marries the dimensions of space and time. Its name combines a place and a day – such as Eke-Agbaja or Afo-Umuduru – and Igboland was covered with a network of markets, carefully arranged in space and time, to avoid overlap. Since the four days of the Igbo week were insufficient to accommodate them, they were fitted into an eightday cycle, *izu ukwu*, the big week. Some markets were purely local, but the larger ones combined local exchanges with the import of goods from further afield by professional or semi-professional merchants, who faced the greater risks, and reaped the greater profits, of long-distance exchange of commodities. This is a theme to which we shall return. An interesting tradition recorded in the Nri area relates how the four-day week and the market structure were introduced by four strangers, who came trading in fish.[38]

Her amazing network of markets reflected the density of Igboland's population. It reflected too a society well above the level of subsistence, with time and material surpluses for a leisurely process of market exchange.

Igboland's currencies, similarly, reflect the vitality of her economic life. They included cowrie shells from the Indian ocean, horse-shoe shaped manillas of copper and brass, popular in southern Igboland, and brass rods, used on the Cross River. We do not know when each of these currencies came into use, though they may have been of considerable antiquity, for cowries were used in Benin before the Europeans came there,[39] and the Igbo-Ukwu excavations revealed objects very like manillas (see Plate 1b). There were also interesting types of iron currency. A seventeenth-century visitor to the Delta described the sting-ray shaped currency, the size of the palm of the hand, made by the southern Igbo of 'Moko'.[40] In the late nineteenth century, early European visitors discovered that in the area between Awka and Enugu, instead of cowries, a currency was used, which was made of iron, like the coins of 'Moko', and was similar in shape, 'resembling a miniature arrow-head'. The size, however, was much smaller, about half an inch in length.[41]

THE CONTEXT AND QUALITY OF LIFE

Equiano's memories of mid-eighteenth century Igboland reflect many other facets of Igbo life. He describes the thatched houses, and how they are built. 'The whole neighbourhood afford their unanimous assistance in building them and in return receive and expect no other recompense but a feast.'[42] Early European visitors have left us many descriptions of Igbo houses and communities. A British soldier invading Ezzaland wrote, 'The Ezza towns are models of cleanliness and good building and their farms are kept the same way.'[42] Some seventy miles further west, a missionary described late-nineteenth-century Awka, and the home of a titled man:

> As we passed through the town we were struck with its clean, well-kept houses and roads. The people certainly take a great pride in having their homes nice . . . As [our host] was a chief of very high standing his house was an elaborate one. The walls were beautifully smooth, and painted over with all sorts of queer designs. The door, boxes, and other wooden articles were quaintly carved.[44]

(The words 'queer' and 'quaint', of course, reflect the ethnocentricity of the observer . . .) At Bende, the first European observer described the house walls made of clay 'so beautifully polished with a rich chocolate maroon that we mistook them for old wood.'[45]

Across thirty-four years of exile, Equiano remembered Igbo cooking – the stews, flavoured with pepper and spices, and locally made salt, the plantains, yams, coco-yams, beans and corn. He describes the extreme cleanliness of the people and their love of scented pomades, and the invariable practice of washing before meals. He recalls the palm wine – 'when just drawn it is of a most delicious sweetness'. He describes the great richness of Igbo culture, and its musical instruments – 'We are almost a nation of dancers, musicians, and poets'.

He accurately noted, too, that Igboland was a society which lacked extremes of wealth and poverty. 'We are all habituated to labour from our earliest years. Everyone contributes something to the common stock, and as we are unacquainted with idleness we have no beggars.'[46] Practically no one, except the very young and very old, was exempt from manual work, and the skilful and productive farmer or craftsman was highly esteemed. The society did not encourage the accumulation of wealth. The technological limits of the society meant that the luxuries wealth could buy were limited. The most popular forms of accumulation, the well-stocked yam barns, were perishable. Wealth could not be invested except in long-distance trade, a risky and specialised profession. It could be hoarded – many Igbo homes had an inner strongroom – but the typical Igbo preferred to exchange his wealth for his community's esteem. He would purchase a title, the symbol of this esteem, and the outlay involved redistributed much of his wealth in the society again. The more fortunate helped their poorer relations, and were repaid by their gratitude, or by their help, if they fell on evil days. When they died, much of their property was redistributed by their heirs in celebrating a glorious funeral – and the more prosperous the man, the more splendid the funeral. These traditions have survived into modern times, creating many problems as social conditions change – a theme to which we shall return.

Igbo society was not of course perfectly egalitarian; no society is. The more prosperous accumulated wives and slaves. As in any society, it helped to have a prosperous father. Some were more gifted, more energetic than others. Some were impoverished through ill-health, an unlucky harvest, or a war. Igboland had its slaves, *ohu*, and its pawns – though again, Equiano's comments are instructive. 'How different was their condition from that of the slaves in the West Indies! With us they do no more work than other members of the community, even the master; their food, clothing and lodging were nearly the same as theirs. . .'[47]

HANDWRITING

It is generally held that the peoples of sub-Saharan Africa did not invent handwriting, and that, although they compensated for the lack by developing verbal memory to a high point, and by elaborate mnemonic devices, it proved, nevertheless, a serious obstacle to the preservation and progressive accumulation of knowledge. The best-known exception is to be found among the Vai people of Liberia, one of whom developed a script in the nineteenth century, in response to outside stimuli. The south-eastern Igbo and their neighbours, however, developed in pre-colonial times a widely used system of writing, which apparently owes nothing to external stimuli.

The best account of *nsibidi* is to be found in an article published by a missionary in 1909,[48] when, he noted, the art was already being eroded by European influence. He based his account on two informants from Abiriba, and a woman whose mother had held a school to teach *nsibidi*, and who preserved a copy of the signs made on cloth by her grandmother, many years previously. 'Nsibidi', he states, '. . . originated among the great Ibo tribe', but the precise area he mentions, north of Uwet and east of the Cross River, would suggest, rather, a non-Igbo area very close to the Igbo borderland.* Certainly, it was used among the Ibibio, and seems to have been most developed in those Igbo communities of the south-east which have strong Ibibio connections. It was the preserve of a secret society, and used especially by travelling smiths, though the knowledge of some signs was more widely diffused. He recorded ninety-eight signs, and stated, 'The use of *nsibidi* is that of ordinary writing. I have in my possession a copy of the record of a court case from a town on the Enion [Enyong] Creek taken down in it, and every detail, except the evidence, is most graphically described.'[49]

Nsibidi took the form of formalised pictograms, like Chinese. Had not the experience of colonial rule deflected the Igbo and their neighbours from their own patterns of development, it seems likely that, as in other societies, a knowledge of literacy

* The people who invented it are, he says, called 'Uguakima' or Ebe; the Efik know them as 'Uyanga'. Professor E. J. Alagoa identifies them as two small Cross River groups, Ugwakuma/Biase and Uyanga.

SOME NSIBIDI SIGNS

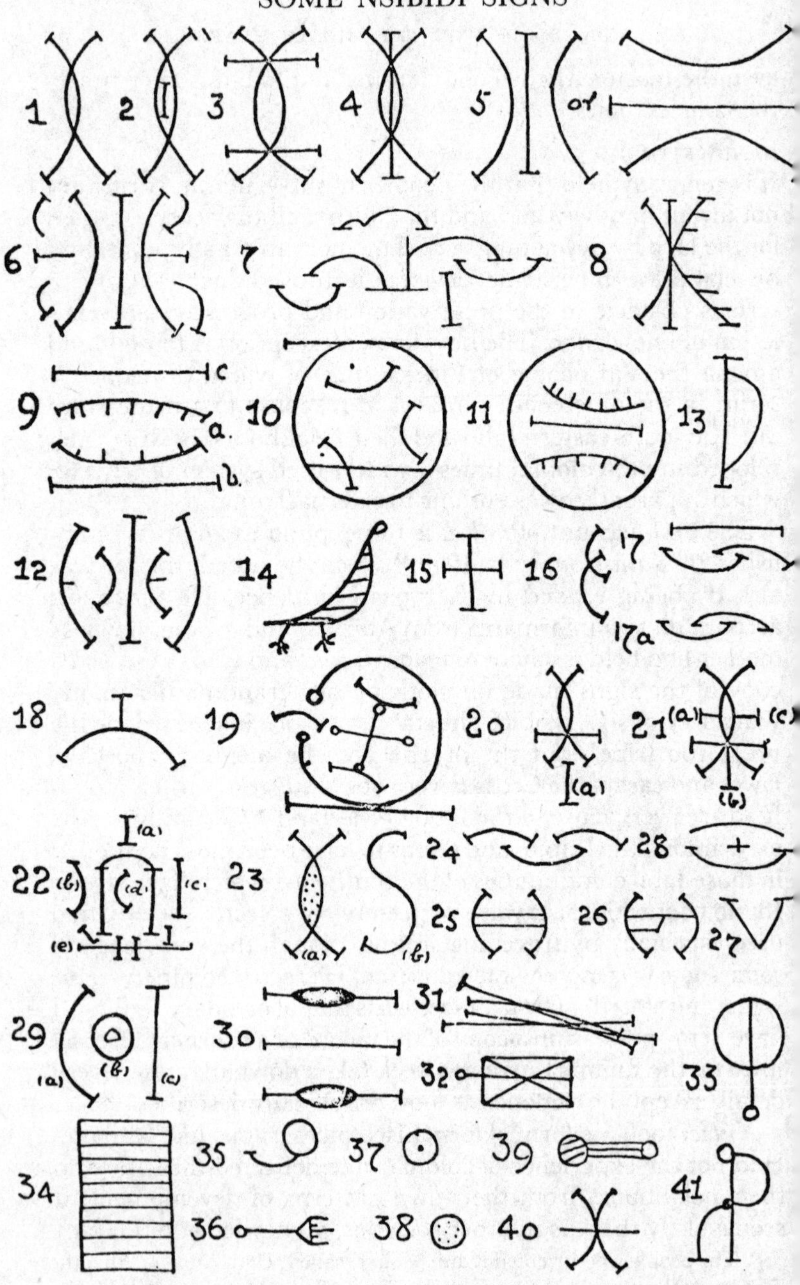

Source: Rev. J. K. Macgregor, 'Some Notes on Nsibidi', *Journal of the Royal Anthropological Institute*, XXXIX (1909) 215.

KEY

1, 2 Married love (2, with pillow)
3 Married love with pillows for head and feet – a sign of wealth
4 Married love with pillow
5 Quarrel between husband and wife, indicated by the pillow being between them
6 Violent quarrel between husband and wife
7 One who causes a disturbance between husband and wife
8 A woman with six children and her husband; a pillow is between them
9 Two wives with their children (*a*), of one man (*b*), with the roof-tree of the house in which they live (*c*)
10 A house (*a*) in which are three women and a man. The dots have no meaning
11 Two women with many children in the house with their husband
12 Two women on each side of a house. One on each side has a child
13 A woman with child (general sign)
14 The same; if a man writes this sign on the ground, it means that his own wife is with child
15 Palaver, the general term, by no means confined to marriage palavers
16 A woman who does not want her husband any more
17 A woman who wishes to put away her husband
17a Embracing? (unconfirmed interpretation)
18 A harlot
19 Two women who live in the same house have palaver every time they meet. A third woman is entering by the door
20 A man (*a*) who comes to a woman who has a husband and asks her to live with him
21 (*a*), (*b*), and (*c*) are three men who sought the same married woman, and quarrelled because of her
22 (*a*) is a man who committed adultery with a woman (*b*), who now lives apart from her husband (*c*). The guilty man has to pay compensation to the woman's family and her husband. (*d*) is the money paid, (*e*) are the parties to whom the money was paid
23 A man and a woman were 'friends'. The man wished to leave her, but she would not agree. One day he wrote this sign all over her house, and took his departure. (*a*) means that he curses her, saying that she has 'craw-craw'. (*b*) means that he has gone to another town
24 Love without agreement
25 Heart with true love
26 Heart without true love
27 Inconstant heart
28 Two persons agree in love
29 (*a*) is a woman who goes to bathe in the river at a ford (*b*), while her husband (*c*) watches to see that no one shoots her
30 Juju hung over a door or on the road to a house to keep danger – especially evil spirits – from the house. Sacrifices of fowls and goats are offered to it
31 Firewood
32, 33 Looking glasses (Also used for a man with a looking glass)
34 A native mat, used as a bed
35 A gourd for a drinking cup
36 Native comb
37 Toilet soap
38 Basin and water
39 Calabash with 400 *chittims* inside it. A *chittim* is a copper wire worth one-twentieth of a rod. Such calabashes have hinges of three strings
40 Slaves
41 Fire

would have become ever more diffused in society as a whole, and that, like Chinese, the script would have acquired more characters, becoming a richer and more flexible vehicle of literary expression. Its form meant that, like Chinese, it could be used by speakers of different dialects or even languages.

Incredibly enough, the same small area of Nigeria developed another entirely different script as well. Itu is an Ibibio community, close both to Arochuku and the Igbo border, and to the postulated homeland of the *nsibidi* script. It is the home of a Christian sect, Oberi Okaime, which has its own language, script and numerical system.[50] It claims that they were imparted by the Holy Spirit in 1931. The script bears no relation to *nsibidi*. It is alphabetic, and seems rather, like the Vai script, to be a response to European stimuli. The only scholar to have studied it finds many parallels with the Linear B script of Ancient Crete, but to postulate a link between the two seems almost as improbable as the direct intervention of the Paraclete! But for a small community with little formal education to invent an alphabet, a language, and a numerical system, and to use them consistently, is an enterprise of such staggering intellectual difficulty that one is tempted to look for a longer historical provenance. At the moment it is a mystery, which demands further research. Here is the first stanza of a hymn,* which, lite-

* From K. Hau, 'Oberi Okaime Script, Text and Counting System', *Bulletin de l'Ifan*, XXIII, sér. B, facing p. 304.

rally translated, begins, 'The Beloved Father sent message to the children in bondage . . .'

THE TRADITIONS

Much of our knowledge of the Igbo past comes from the oral traditions preserved in Igbo communities. It is clear, however, that not all these traditions are equally credible. Basically, traditions of origin fall into two categories. In the first category, a village group traces its descent to an ancestor, living in the era of the forefathers, *mgbe ndichie*. He may have come 'from the ground', or 'from the sky', or from a specific village six miles away. It is tempting to discard traditions such as 'from the sky' as obviously false, and regard the rest as true. But apparently impossible traditions may be a poetical way of stating a historical truth, and some statements which may seem impossible may be literally true. Thus the traditions of the Ndoki clan, in southern Igboland, refer to a time when the Imo River did not flow as it does now. Impossible? Geographers tell us that the Imo River is a classic instance of river capture, and changed its course in quite recent times.[51]

Many of these traditions, however, are not a narrative of events, but an explanation and validation of social relationships. What makes a group of scattered villages a unit, a 'town'? Their descent from a common ancestor – each component village being descended from a son. Why does a certain village claim seniority? Because it is descended from the eldest son. It is clear that the traditions of origin of many Igbo groups are of this type.

There is a second category of traditions, however, which clearly represent historical events. The history of the foundation of Onitsha is of this type, corroborated by the traditions both of Benin and of a whole chain of towns in western Igboland. At the present time, many historians tend to go too far in explaining traditions as charters of social relationships. According to this view, Onitsha, for instance, was not literally founded 'from Benin'. Its people admired Benin, and copied her political institutions, and developed a historical rationale of their action. I disagree with this view. I think that whatever the difficulties involved in the idea of 'an alien elite of political wizards',[52] the difficulties which arise if we suggest that a score of independent communities independently invented corroborating traditions are infinitely greater.

Only a minority of Igbo groups, however, have traditions of origin of this definite and provable type. The majority begin with the legend of an ancestor, and his children. Sometimes one can discern what seems to be a kind of amateur historical etymology, an attempt to explain a name whose origins are forgotten. The Ndoki legend of a child born during a dispute with Bonny, and named '*Anyi no do kwa ne ke*' (For what are we contending?), may be an example of this.[53] Another is to be found in the three rival etymologies of the name of the Ohuhu clan. One states that their Ngwa neighbours derisively called them Umu-Ohuhu, roasters, referring to their way of preparing their food. The second states that the Ngwa, admiring an Ohuhu trading venture, called them *ndi na-ahu uzo*, people with exceptional foresight. The third states that when travelling through Ngwaland, an Ohuhu group avoided a trap, and exclaimed triumphantly, '*Anyi wu ndi ohu uzo*' (We are a foresighted people).[54]

Typically, these traditions move from the legend of origin to events of relatively recent times, especially the major wars – major to those concerned – in which the village was involved. Few Igbo communities have traditions with anything like the time depth or amplitude, of, for instance, a state like Igala or Benin.

There are several reasons why this is so. The first is the small size of the Igbo village community, which made it difficult for it to maintain many specialists of any kind, especially in professions as non-utilitarian as history. In larger states, there was a niche for the professional remembrancer, with his highly developed verbal memory and special mnemonic devices. In larger states, moreover, the preservation of history appeared more necessary – a dimension of a state's identity, and of a dynasty's legitimacy.

At a more fundamental level, it has been suggested that Igbo ideas of time are not conducive to the preservation of different and unique and successive events.[55] The idea of recurrence is fundamental in Igbo thought. It reflects a community closely linked with the land and nature (the capitals of states like Benin form a much more distinctively urban setting), its attitudes moulded by the shorter cycle of the lunar month, the longer cycle of the seasons and the farmer's year. We have noted previously the idea of reincarnation. The ancestors, the *ndichie*, are 'the returners', and by returning they incarnate the past among the living.

> Time past and time future
> What might have been and what has been
> Point to one end, which is always present.

3 The Crisis of the Middle Years: The Trans-Atlantic Slave Trade

The first European visitors came to south-eastern Nigeria in 1472, or perhaps slightly later. They were Portuguese, and they came to Nigeria during their attempt to discover a sea route to India. One of these early visitors, the author of a navigator's guide written in about 1505–8, gives us what is probably the first written description of Igboland: 'a land of negroes, called Opuu, where there is much pepper, ivory, and some slaves.'[1] These first European visitors bought ivory, pepper, and locally made textiles, which they sold elsewhere in West Africa. They bought few slaves, because Portugal had little use for slaves. But unfortunately for Igboland, and Africa, soon after the Portuguese reached south-eastern Nigeria, Columbus discovered some islands off the coast of America. Many other Europeans followed him, and went on to explore central and southern America.

In the New World, the Europeans discovered vast potential wealth, both in mineral resources and land. Both sources of wealth needed ample labour for their exploitation. The native Indians could not supply it – they died in vast numbers of diseases the Europeans introduced. So they turned to West Africa. In 1518, the first load of African prisoners was taken directly from West Africa to the West Indies, ushering in over three centuries of the infamous triangular trade.

The triangular trade contributed vastly to the wealth of Europe. Her ships, with their suffering living cargoes, made profits which were invested in Europe's development. Since the Africans were bought with European products, such as textiles, the trade was to give a considerable boost to her industrialisation. But for the African societies it touched, the trade was a disaster. In Igboland, it spread across the fabric of life like a stain.

THE VICTIMS

We do not know exactly how many victims there were. We

know that the number of Igbos exported as slaves was relatively low in the sixteenth century. (Many of them were sent, not to the West Indies, but to plantations in Gabon and San Thomé.) In the seventeenth century the number increased. A French slaver who visited the Delta twice between 1678 and 1682 wrote of 'that vast number of slaves which the *Calabar Blacks* sell to all *European* nations.'[2] Bonny, Elim Kalabari, and Calabar became well-known centres of slave exports. Not all the slaves were Igbos, but many were.

In the eighteenth century, the slave trade rose to its climax in Igboland – a trade then dominated by the British. A number of independent observers claimed that 14,000 slaves a year were sold at Bonny. Captain Adams, who made ten voyages to the area between 1786 and 1800, put the number higher. He stated that over 20,000 slaves were sold annually at Bonny, 16,000 of them Igbo. Over a period of twenty years, he claimed that 320,000 Igbos had been sold into slavery at Bonny, and 50,000 at Calabar and Elim Kalabari.[3]

In the first half of the nineteenth century, the trans-Atlantic slave trade declined. In 1807 Britain passed legislation forbidding her nationals to engage in the slave trade. It did not involve other nations, nor did it abolish the institution of slavery in British dominions. As time went on, Britain made anti-slavery agreements with other nations, and established a squadron on the coast of West Africa to intercept slavers. By the 1830s, the Delta states were ceasing to export slaves. The trade lingered longest in Nembe-Brass, where the last slaver called in the 1850s.[4]

We have many descriptions of the sale of slaves in the Delta. Here is one of them, from an English slaver in the late eighteenth century.

> The Slaves taken on board at Bonny were procured of the Black Traders, who go up to Fairs in the Country to purchase and bring them down to the Coast. They pass through several Hands, and come from a great Distance. They bring them in a miserable Condition from the Fairs, half-starved and exposed to the Wet, in Boats, with hardly any Covering . . . Mr Falconbridge believes that none of the Slaves they had on board were Inhabitants of the Coast. A Woman, big

> with Child, told him, that she was caught as she was returning from a Neighbour's House, and passed through many Hands before she came to them. And an old Man and his Son told him, that they were kidnapped as they were planting Yams.[5]

The victims of the slave trade were taken to the New World in a dreadful voyage. Many of the captives tried to starve themselves to death. The slavers would break their tightly clenched teeth, and force their jaws apart with a sharp stick. Sometimes they were forced to dance, 'by means of a Cat of Nine Tails'. 'The Men could only jump up and rattle their chains.'[6] Sometimes, in spite of the huge odds against them, the captives succeeded in mutinying. One slaving captain gives us a touching picture of the charity shown by Igbo captives to each other. 'Their mutual affection is unbounded, and . . . I have seen them, when their allowance happened to be short, divide the last morsel of meat amongst each other thread by thread.'[7]

In the New World, the Igbo did not take kindly to servitude, and were unpopular among planters for this reason. Some, preferring death to captivity, tried to commit suicide, although, in the words of one planter, 'if their confidence be once obtained, they manifest as great fidelity, affection, and gratitude as can reasonably be expected from men in a state of slavery.'[8] Another source gives us a glimpse of Igbo slaves in Haiti, 'excellent for work in the fields yet difficult to manage'. They kept a strong sense of their Igbo identity, and gave 'help, care and instruction' to new arrivals from Igboland.[9]

It is only rarely that the sources allow us a glimpse of Igbo communities in the West Indies or the Americas. In general, their history becomes merged with that of the Afro-Americans, a history full of heroic episodes, and triumphs of the human spirit against great odds. Doubtless, for instance, there were Igbos among the gallant slaves who won their freedom, and established the independent African republic of Palmares in north-east Brazil, which kept its independence from 1605 to 1695, despite many attempts to conquer it. But in general, the eyes of the historian strain in vain to follow them, and the student of the Igbo past must redirect his gaze to those who remained behind.

THE EFFECTS ON IGBOLAND

It is important to realise that the slave trade's impact on Igbo society was greatest in the eighteenth and nineteenth centuries, that is, in the years when the trans-Atlantic slave trade reached its height, declined, and came to an end. It may seem paradoxical to suggest that the trans-Atlantic slave trade affected Igbo life most after it had come to an end. Nevertheless, it is true. As we shall see, Igbo societies had grown used to collecting slaves. When the export outlet disappeared, men were still sold into slavery, and the slaves were kept within Igboland itself, imposing many distortions in the process.

The slave trade robbed Igboland of many of her members, in the prime of life, and of the children they would have had. We can only speculate as to the contributions they would have made to Igbo life had they remained. But its effects went far beyond this. In order to understand them, we must first ask ourselves how the slaves were obtained.

The available evidence all points to one conclusion – that the most important source of slaves was kidnapping, and the second most important, war. A trader who visited the Delta many times between 1862 and 1896, and made a practice of asking slaves how they had been captured, wrote,

> On questioning them how they became slaves, I have only been told by one that her father sold her because he was in debt; several times I have been told that their elder brothers have sold them, but these cases would not represent one per cent of the slaves I have questioned; the almost general reply I have received has been that they have been stolen when they had gone to fetch water from the river or the spring, as the case might be, or while they have been straying a little in the bush paths between their village and another.[10]

In the mid-nineteenth century, a missionary questioned five Igbos who had been sold to slavers, rescued by the English naval squadron and brought to Sierra Leone. One had been sold by his relatives, and one had been sold as a punishment for adultery but the other three had been kidnapped. The first was from 'Isiele' (a northern Igbo group – Ishielu?), the second from 'Naki', in Agbaja, and the third from the Isuama area. These are their stories.[11]

1. 'He had a child three years of age when he was kidnapped and sold to Igala, whence he was at once brought to the sea.'
2. 'He . . . married two wives and had a child about twelve years old when he was kidnapped by a treacherous friend and sold into slavery.'
3. 'Born in Isoama country, whence he was stolen and brought to Aro when a little boy. He was brought up in the little village Asaga of the Aro country, and lived there till about his twenty-fourth year, when he was sold to the Portuguese in Obane [Bonny].'

At the end of the nineteenth century, another victim of the slave trade described his experiences. He was from 'Isuama, in the interior Ibo Country.'

> As now, so then in those parts men roam about to steal children and even adults from their homes, and sell them as slaves in places quite distant, and to prevent my being dealt with in such a manner, my father took the precaution to remove me from my native land to the care of his father-in-law . . . But whilst playing about one afternoon, with others of my companions mindful of no danger, 12 of these manstealers rushed out from the forest near by and single me from my mates and away they go dragging me along with them. Proceeding along they were met with three slave-dealers, which class of men are to be seen daily in these parts; these by agreement unhesitatingly collected some hundreds of cowries and bought me.[12]

He was sold at Ohumbele, where he remained for a year, after which he was sold to a Bonny merchant to meet a debt in 1860.

Igbo communities tried to limit the practice of kidnapping. Equiano relates how slave traders would be questioned as to how they obtained their slaves, and kidnappers were sometimes sold into slavery themselves, as a punishment. But the ineffectiveness of these precautions was clearly shown by the fate of Equiano himself, who was kidnapped, together with his sister, and sold to European slave dealers on the coast.[13]

The second source of slaves was war. War and kidnapping were closely connected, for many wars were fought as a reprisal for an act of abduction. Sometimes wars were fought with the intention of obtaining captives; the traditions of some Igbo states, such as Ossomari and Arondizuogu, are explicit on this point.[14] Perhaps a greater number followed the policy of Obi Ossai of Aboh, who did not initiate wars for the purpose, but if he was at war, took all the slaves he could.[15]

There were other sources of slaves. Communities tended to punish their criminals by selling them into slavery. Sometimes, it seems, parents sold their own children, either coerced by poverty and hunger, or in order to rid themselves of a ne'er-do-well.[16] Nothing bears stronger witness to the corrupting effect of the slave trade, for Igbos are passionately attached to their children, and regard them as the greatest of blessings.

In other areas of life, too, the slave trade bred a disregard for human life. One example is to be found in the practice of human sacrifice. This almost certainly antedates the slave trade – several slaves were buried with the dead ruler of Igbo-Ukwu. In the years of the slave trade, the practice of human sacrifice expanded vastly (a process, incidentally, which is very well documented in the history of Benin and Bonny). In the nineteenth century, the loss of external outlets for slaves led to an unprecendented escalation of the practice. Forty slaves were killed at the death of Obi Ossai of Aboh,[17] in *c.* 1845, and greater numbers were sacrificed at the death of Delta rulers. In the Nsukka area, the going rate was ten slaves for a horse[18] a rate rather more flattering to humanity than that described by Leo Africanus in sixteenth-century Bornu, where it was fifteen to twenty slaves to a horse.[19] At Uburu, in the 1880s, a horse was exchanged for four to six adult slaves.[20] The practice of human sacrifice came to be a way of disposing of sick and disabled slaves. In Ohuhu, such slaves were called *ovulabo* because they were carried in long baskets to Uburu, to be sacrificed to the spirit of the brine springs.[21]

Another institution which underwent similar distortion and corruption was that of *osu*, cult slavery. As we have seen, the service of a god entailed many arduous and difficult conditions, so the practice developed of delegating the service to a slave. Henceforward, the slave and his descendants belonged to the god. The evidence suggests that originally *osu* were regarded with respect and honour. In the nineteenth century, their numbers expanded and their status deteriorated dramatically, so that they became outcasts, feared and despised.[22] (There is however some evidence that the association of reverence and abhorrence, as in the word 'dreadful', is basic to Igbo religious thought. Henderson draws parallels between *osu* and Onitsha kingship, the latter being 'the object of attitudes of mingled awe and revulsion . . . simultaneously revered and abhorred'.[23] Traditions recorded in Akokwa, in Nkwerre Division, reflect the same attitudes to the ritual specialists of Nri. 'Are you asking me what we learnt from these people? What should we learn from Nri people who buried people who died of bad diseases . . . or people who hanged? In our land these were abominations. People even found it difficult to eat with them. In fact we isolated them.'[24])

The nineteenth century was one in which the shadow of the trade in slaves overshadowed every aspect of Igbo life. We have noted some of the aspects – the cheapening of human life, the fundamental insecurity. A former slave noted the disintegration of social bonds and the constraint on productivity; 'how the whole population was continually in a state of excitement and fear . . . how their fields were neglected . . . how every one was afraid of his own neighbour.'[25]

The crisis of the nineteenth century had many aspects. The strain imposed by the slave trade merged into the new crisis of the spread of alien rule. But before we explore these themes, we must examine another theme of the middle years of Igbo history – the theme of economic and political change.

4 Political and Economic Change: The Middle Years

Up to this point we have looked at the slave trade from the point of view of the victims, and of its impact on the quality of Igbo life. But there is another aspect we must consider. The slaves exported were, of course, paid for, by the European traders at the Delta ports. This meant that there was a great influx of goods into the Delta and Igboland, an influx which was unprecedented, for the goods which were imported previously, across the trans-Saharan routes or direct from other West African states, must have been quite limited in quantity.

We must now consider these questions – what goods were imported and what changes they made in Igbo economic life – and examine their relationship to the rise of certain states in Igboland.

It is still painful for an Igbo to reflect on the price that was paid for his predecessors. The price of a slave varied, of course. At one time, in the late seventeenth century, when prices were higher than usual, a man was sold for thirteen iron bars, a woman for nine iron bars 'and proportionately for boys and girls according to their ages.'[1] What was an iron bar worth? It was worth half a gallon of brandy, or one bunch of beads, or four copper bars, or 'one piece of narrow Guinea stuff' (i.e. textiles).[2]

In the late seventeenth century, imports to the Delta included

> iron bars, in quantity, and chiefly; copper bars, blue rings, cloth, and striped *Guinea* clouts of many colours, horse-bells, hawks-bells, rangoes; pewter basons of one, two, three and four pounds weight; tankards of *ditto* of one, two and three pounds weight; beads, very small and glazed, yellow, green, purple and blue; purple copper armlets . . .[3]

Another trade list mentions 'strong spirits, rum and brandy' and cowries. Guns and ammunition were not yet imported on a large scale, though individual items were given as presents to Delta rulers.

A hundred years later, in the late eighteenth century, another slaver[4] gives us another list of imports, with some illuminating comments on the quality which was deemed appropriate for Africa. Brandy and rum, adulterated with water and pepper, are important items. Gunpowder is listed (the author adds that 'much of a very inferior description has been sent from England') and also Dane guns and muskets (he notes, 'the greater proportion of the muskets taken to [Bonny] during the existence of the slave trade have been of a bad quality.'). Lead (used for making ammunition), iron, copper, salt and beads are listed, also hardware and earthenware. Cowries, he states, are not much in demand. Textiles are a major item on the list, often made originally in India.

All of these items were what one might call consumer goods. Many of them were items that the Igbo had already been producing for themselves. Extensive textile imports rivalled and probably weakened the indigenous textile industry (for an example see p. 31 above). Others were clearly beneficial; the salt produced by local sources was clearly inadequate to the demand (as witness the repeated references to vegetable salt substitutes in Igbo oral traditions). The iron imported, while it undermined traditional smelting industries, clearly stimulated agriculture and encouraged an expansion of smithing. Thus the smiths of Ohuhu, it seems, based their industry exclusively on iron imported from Bonny, an industry which, Ohuhu's historian suggests, may have developed independently.[5] Imported spirits, obviously, contributed little to Igboland's development, especially since palm wine, her traditional beverage, had a lower alcohol content, and was an excellent source of the vitamin B complex. The significance of firearms will be considered later on, when we turn to the militarisation of Igbo life, in the nineteenth century. The extensive imports of currency caused an inflation which probably had both negative and positive effects. Initially, it stimulated trade; ultimately it was carried to a point which undermined the currency's usefulness, for it was debased to an extent that made it too bulky for large-scale transactions.

Political change: the formation of states

An expansion in the volume of trade has often led, in African history, to changes in political institutions, the evolution of new states, and, within those states, the development of new types of government. This process is also very evident in Igbo history, where we can see, in the sixteenth and seventeenth centuries, the growth of new states with the following characteristics:

1. They grow up on the fringes of Igboland, at cultural meeting places with other peoples, often as a result of a migration from elsewhere.
2. They have distinctive types of political institutions.
3. They are closely linked with trade routes, and with the expansion of the slave trade.

The classic instance of the development of new states, and of new types of government can be seen in the Ijo states of the Delta and the Efik state of Calabar. These were closely linked with Igboland, and replenished their populations largely with accessions of Igbo slaves, but their history, which has been studied by others, lies beyond the scope of this book. The institutions to which we must now turn our attention fall into two main categories – the states of the lower Niger, and the states of the Aro network.

THE NIGER MONARCHIES

In the sixteenth century, a number of new states were established on the Niger, some of which rose to a position of great wealth and power, as the slave trade rose to a climax in the seventeenth and eighteenth centuries. These can, in their turn, be classified according to their place of origin.

States which claim an origin from Benin

Onitsha and Aboh, and a large group of western Igbo towns have traditions which claim that they were founded during a migration from Benin, led by China, during the reign of the *oba* Esigie (*c.*1517–*c.*1550). The exact details of the tradition vary, in different versions.[6] Some state that Chima and his companions were sons of the previous *oba*, Ozolua. This seems unlikely. Others state that Chima and his companions were Igbo slaves or hostages at the *oba*'s court – Chima's name seems to reflect an Igbo identity. The third, and most plausible version, is that they came from a homeland in western Igboland, an area that had been conquered by an earlier, expansionist *oba* in the fifteenth century. Onitsha tradition calls this homeland Ado na Idu. A tradition recorded over sixty years ago locates it between

Igbodo and Onitsha-Ugbo.[7]

Onitsha tradition, which preserves the *oba*'s name, but attributes it to a Queen Mother, Asijie, tells of a dispute between this Queen Mother, and Chima. The *oba* sent his war general, Ogbunwala, to avenge an insult, and Chima and his followers fled. This tradition is probably not literally true – perhaps the group left the Benin empire as a result of some more extensive and fundamental political disturbance. We know that early in Esigie's reign there was a major crisis – Benin was invaded by an army from Idah, which Esigie successfully repulsed, with the aid of a slave general, perhaps the one referred to in the Onitsha tradition.[8] This war with Idah was in its turn one of a whole chain of political upheavals in sixteenth-century Nigeria, 'upheavals which established a great Nupe state, and broke the power of Oyo for almost a century.[9] Perhaps the Idah war created disturbances in western Igboland, from which a number of communities chose to flee.

The tradition relates that Chima, in his migration, 'founded' a number of western Igbo towns, which still preserve a sense of common identity, as Umuezechima. Finally the group reached the Niger, at Illah (according to some versions of the tradition, Chima died before reaching this point). Here the group divided. One section crossed the Niger to found Onitsha, at a site which was several miles inland, because of the dangers of a riverain site. One section, possibly led by Chima, returned to Agbor in the extreme west of Igboland. Another section travelled south led by Esumai, 'founding' a chain of western Igbo towns – Ossissa, Obetim, Ashaka – before finally reaching Aboh. They crossed an intervening river, which they could not ford, with the assistance of an obliging manatee.[10] (Another version of the tradition puts the leader's name as Ogwezi, and states that the migration took place in the reign of the *oba* Ozolua, *c.* 1480–*c.* 1517.)

These migrations may, of course, have taken place over a considerable time period, and in fact a study of the Aboh and Onitsha king lists would suggest that they were founded at a date rather later than the early sixteenth century. Probably they were the work of a group – known collectively as *umuezechima* – rather than of a single remarkable, and peripatetic, individual. Neither Onitsha nor Aboh was founded in an unoccupied area. Onitsha was inhabited by the Oze people, who still retain a separate identity nearby. Aboh was inhabited

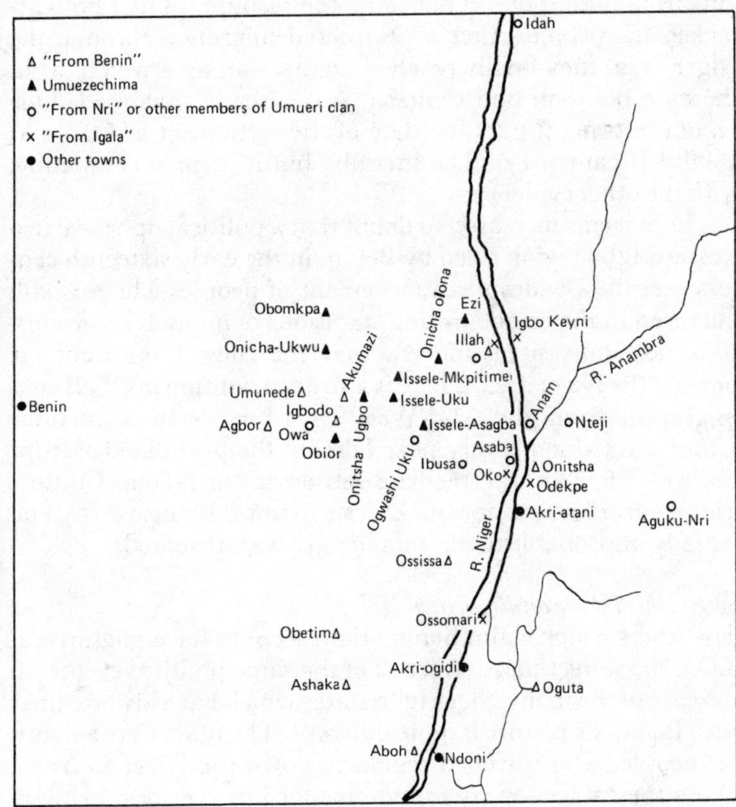

Map 3 The Niger Valley states

by the Akri Igbo. At first they co-existed peacefully, but after a time there was a dispute. The Akri fled north, to found Akri-ogidi and Akri-atani; one group returned to settle near Aboh. The antiquity of their settlement on the Niger is reflected in the name given them by other Igbo groups, 'children of the Niger', *umu otimili*.

Oguta was apparently founded after a migration from Benin – or an area ruled by Benin – at the same time as the Onitsha migration, and because of the same political upheavals. Her people settled first by the Niger, near Illah. They were forced to flee because of a betrayal of trust by their ruler. He was asked to arbitrate in a dispute between Aboh and Igala; he accepted gifts from both, but did not settle the dispute, so that both attacked his people. After a protracted migration through the Niger area, they finally reached Oguta – an area which, as in the case of Aboh and Onitsha, was already inhabited. One Oguta informant puts the date of the settlement at Oguta as 1600.[11] It cannot be taken literally, but it is quite compatible with the other evidence.

There seems no reason to doubt that a political upheaval in a western Igbo region ruled by Benin, in the early sixteenth century, set up a widespread movement of peoples which is still mirrored in the corroborating traditions of many Igbo groups. It is not impossible, indeed, that the migrations went far beyond the Niger area. There is a strong tradition in Ohafia of a migration from the Mid-West[12] – some versions mention Umunede (which is very near Igbodo, the postulated starting point) – after an intermediate settlement at Ndoni. Cultural and geographical factors make it seem improbable, yet it seems equally improbable that it should have been invented.

States which claim an origin from Igala

The states which claim Benin origin seem to have migrated at much the same time, as a result of the same political events. In the case of the many Niger Igbo states which have historic links with Igala, the picture is quite different. The Igala were a nautical people, who travelled regularly down the Niger to trade. Often they stayed away from home for long periods, living in their large covered house-boats, or in temporary houses. An account written in the 1920s notes that every large sandbank has 'a settlement of the lightly constructed huts of these river nomads.'[13] From this it was but a short step to a permanent settlement. A whole chain of Niger Igbo towns claim Igala origins, or have quarters which trace their descent from Igala. Illah – a cultural melting pot of different peoples – has Igala quarters, and Igala is still spoken by its masquerade.[14] Oko and Odekpe also claim Igala origins, but the most important state founded in this way was Ossomari. The earliest version of its traditions, recorded almost a hundred years ago, state that 'it is said to have been peopled by the Igaras originally as a trading station or market.'[15] Like Illah, it preserved Igala as the language of its masquerade, and the title of its ruler, Atamanya, reflects, perhaps, that of the Atta of Igala (Atta 'Gala). Like Oguta and Aboh, it was located at a strategic site, which was to have great influence on its later history. It, too, was founded as a result of an agreement between the Igala and the original Igbo inhabitants.

The process of Igala settlement was still going on in the nineteenth century. We have several well-documented cases in the Ibaji area, a transitional zone where both Igbo and Igala are spoken. One was Adamugu, founded by an Igala chief shortly before 1830, which by the 1850s was rivalling the commerce of Igala itself. Another was Igbokeyni, founded originally as a halting place 'by the late Ogabidokun Anaro during his piratical voyages down the river', and built up by his ambitious son, in the 1870s.[16] Today Igbokeyni people speak Igala, plus imperfect Igbo, and are closely associated with their Igala-linked neighbour, Illah, across the river. This is a well-documented example of the process of Igbonisation which obviously occurred, at an earlier period, in Ossomari.

States claiming an origin from Nri

A number of riverain towns, and towns in western Igboland, claim a founder from Nri, or from another member of the Umueri group to which Nri belongs. Asaba traditions tell of a man from Nteje called Nnebisi, who joined a pre-existing settlement, perhaps in the early seventeenth century, and became rich through elephant hunting and agriculture, using slave labour, and finally became Asaba's king. It was he who introduced human sacrifice.[17] Anam traditions relate that their area was uninhabited until a man from Nteje settled there in the late eighteenth or early nineteenth century.[18] Ibusa and Ogwashi-Uku are two western Igbo towns which claim a founder from Nri. These settlements are doubtless connected with the travels of Nri ritual specialists, who were in a good position to note the steady expansion of Niger economic life.

Trade on the lower Niger

In the seventeenth and eighteenth centuries, as the slave trade expanded, the volume of trade on the Niger expanded likewise. Practically all riverain towns had some share in this trade, serving as a gateway between the channel of commerce on the Niger and the towns that formed its hinterland. Thus we read of the little town of Utchi, 'The people here command the trade of all the tribes behind, so the gathering in the great market day used to be unusually large.[19] Onitsha's market regularly attracted visitors from Obosi, Nkpor, Obba, Nnewi, Nsugbe, Nteje, and from the Agbaja towns of western Udi division, and even from further afield.[20] The Niger was both a source of danger and a source of opportunity, and different towns reacted to it differently. We have noted how Onitsha was located on an inland site, and Illah, perhaps a generation later, moved from a waterside to an inland site, to avoid piracy.[21]

Ossomari and Aboh reacted to the challenge of their situation by becoming major naval powers. This was to be expected of Ossomari, founded by the river-going Igala, but for the people of Aboh, from an inland home, and lacking nautical skills (this is reflected in the story of the manatee) it was a major creative adaptation. A seventeenth-century geography book, compiled from about sixty-eight studies of Africa, tells us something about Aboh a century after its foundation. Like many later European accounts, it emphasises the influence of Benin. 'Gaboe', it states, is eight days journey from Benin, by canoe. It is a source of jasper and acori beads, and of many slaves. The inhabitants are friendly, and rather like those of Benin.[22] By the second third of the nineteenth century – when we have a number of first-hand descriptions – Aboh was a wealthy and powerful kingdom, which could muster a fleet of three-hundred war canoes. Her king, splendidly dressed in scarlet cloth, gold lace, and coral, was treated with the greatest respect by his own people and by visiting princes, who prostrated themselves before him. Her power was based partly on firearms; her canoes had cannon lashed in the bow, and her crews were armed individually with muskets.

Aboh was perhaps the best situated of all the lower Niger kingdoms, from a trade point of view. It stands at the apex of the Delta, where its many waterways join into a single channel. Ossomari, too, was strategically sited, at the mouth of a waterway leading to Oguta, and thence, via the Orashi river, to the Delta. Ossomari was the Niger port for the populous hinterland of the Isuama area, a connection which nineteenth-century observers always emphasised.

The potential economic rivalry between the two states could easily develop into war. Both tried to avoid this, and linked themselves, for instance, by numerous marriage alliances. On several occasions, however, war did take place. The most celebrated conflict – which Ossomari's local historian places in the 1820s[23] – was when Aboh made an unsuccessful attempt to invade Ossomari, but lost both its general, the Odogun, and its main war canoe. The treaty which followed is embedded in a proverb:

> *Aboh welu ife*, Aboh takes a share.
> *Igili welu ife*, Ossomari takes a share.
> *Aninta gba ubu*, small states scramble for what remains.[24]

To prevent conflicts of this type, the states of the lower Niger developed a set of diplomatic and marketing conventions. There were two boundary markets: one, south of Aboh, where Aboh traders exchanged goods with Delta traders, and one on a sandbank between Asaba and Onitsha, where Aboh and Ossomari traders exchanged goods with the Igala. To prevent clashes, Aboh and Ossomari visited the market on alternate weeks, Aboh on Eke Ukwu and Ossomari on Eke Nta.[25] (Ossomari tradition claims that the traders who kidnapped the Lander brothers at Asaba in 1830 were from Ossomari, and that the name 'Kirree' which the Landers used is really Igili, the name of the Ossomari people.) Delta traders who came direct to this market had to pay tolls to Aboh. The furthest permissible limit for an Igala trader was Aboh, for an Aboh trader, Idah.[26] These conventions did not prevent all wars – there was an outbreak of fairly minor conflicts in the late 1850s and early 1860s – but they did much to contain potentially destructive rivalries, an example which could have been studied with profit by many much larger states elsewhere . . .

This is how the exchange of goods is described in the 1830s, when the external slave trade was giving way to trade in palm oil:

> The Eboe [Aboh] people take up the river, powder, yams,

beads, cloth, iron bars, and knives. These articles are conveyed to Bonny by the palm-oil traders, and thence pass through the hands of three or four merchants into the possession of the Eboe dealers. They receive in return, slaves, rice, goats, fowls, calabashes, mats, country beads, horses of a small breed, and elephants' teeth; they also trade in Goora [kola] nuts. Cowries are the best medium of exchange . . .[27]

AROCHUKWU AND THE ARO SETTLEMENTS

Like the Niger monarchies, Arochukwu was founded at a meeting place between different peoples – in this case, the Igbo and Ibibio. Like them, it was previously occupied by small-scale communities engaged in subsistence agriculture, and like them, its political life was transformed as a result of a migration and conquest (in the case of Arochukwu, in the early seventeenth century).[28] It too rose to great power and wealth during the years when the impact of the trans-Atlantic slave trade was greatest in Igboland.

In the early seventeenth century, a crisis occurred in the Arochukwu area. Different traditions give different versions of this, but it is clear that there was a war between the Igbo and Ibibio inhabitants.[29] During this war, a third group, the 'Akpa', using firearms, entered the scene, either invited as mercenaries, or seizing the opportunity to fish in troubled waters. The origin of the Akpa has never been identified with certainty. One version states that they came from Okoyong, near Calabar, which would fit in well with their early access to firearms and their ancient trade relationship with the Delta. Another suggests that they came from higher up the Cross River, from the area now inhabited by the Akunakuna and Ugep.

Other neighbouring peoples, such as the Edda, have traditions of an invading people, equipped with firearms, from whom they retreated. British officials, recording these traditions, described the people rather enigmatically as the 'white-eyed Ukwa'.[30] '*Anya ocha*', white-eyed, is simply an Igbo idiom for aggressive. '*Ukwa*' was used by other Igbo groups to refer to the prosperous market towns of southern Asa and Ndokiland.

Aro traditions make it clear that, whatever their origins, the Akpa had been trading with the Delta communities before the

Europeans arrived, exchanging smoked meat, camwood and plantains for salt, fish and shrimps.[31] The advent of European trade gave them both access to firearms (a few pieces were introduced in the seventeenth century, though they were not imported on a large scale until the eighteenth) and a powerful means of conquering groups which did not possess them. At the same time, the trade in slaves gave them a motive for such conquests. After their settlement at Arochukwu, 'The other sections of the Aro soon emulated the Akpa and learnt the art of long distance trading.'[32]

The Aro seem to have developed their trading network with great rapidity. Their famous oracle – one of the essential bastions of their prestige – developed out of a small Ibibio shrine. Its expansion to the greatest of Igboland's regional oracles is attributed to the generation following Arochukwu's foundation.[33] Regarded from one point of view, it was profoundly exploitative: eight hundred western Ijo went to consult it in the 1890s, and only 136 returned.[34] Yet the possibility of an appeal to an impartial external arbiter was of the greatest value, and undoubtedly prevented innumerable local wars. The prestige and authority which Chukwu's oracle conferred on the Aro is clearly mirrored in the first recorded interview between a European and Aro representatives, which took place at Aba, in 1896.

> He announced in broken English that he was an 'Aro man' and a 'God boy'. Motioning them to a seat on the box, I told the interpreter to tell the Aros that I was very pleased to see them, but, before I could talk to them, the man with the hat on must remove it; to this he replied that he was as good, and would not take his hat off to any white man, saying in broken English, and with an air of giving satisfaction, as he looked at me, 'Me be "God boy" – me be "God boy". You be white man; me be "God boy".'[35]

On a number of occasions, Arochukwu's sons settled in colonies abroad – the most important being Arondizuogu, and the group of settlements known collectively as Ndieni – which have been regarded as the oldest of the Aro colonies, and which probably date from the late eighteenth century.[36] Local historians have given us a detailed account of the foundation of Arondizuogu, and of Ndikelionwu, one of the

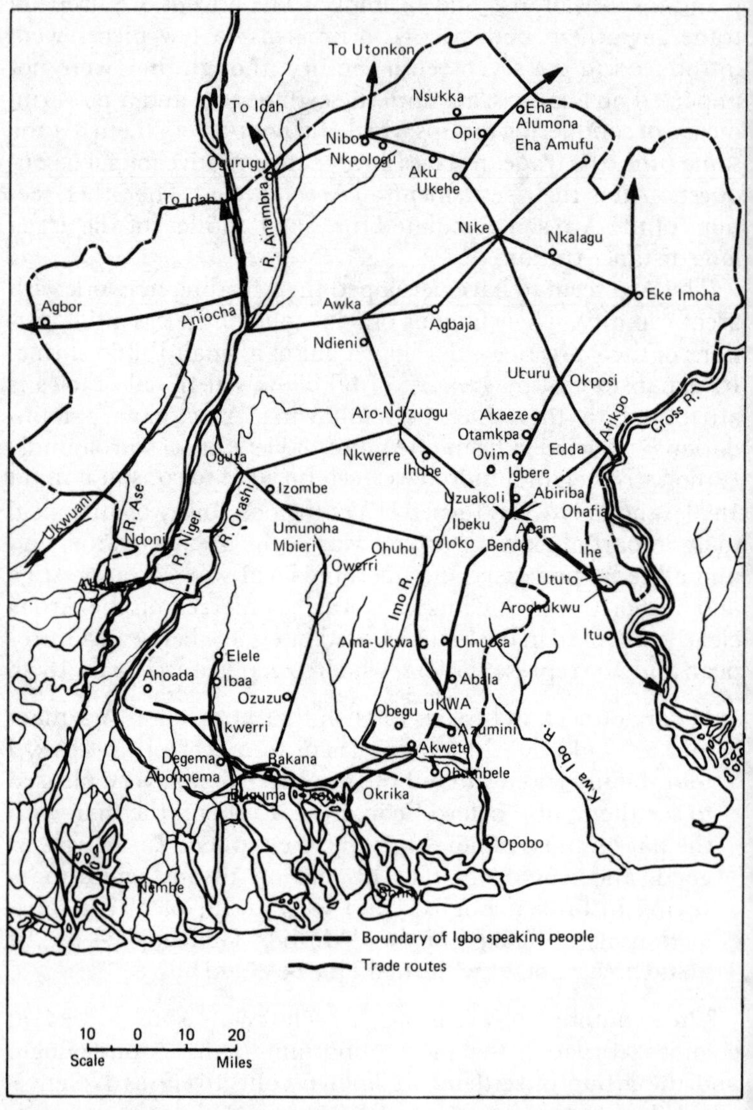

Map 4 The Aro and their neighbours, with some nineteenth-century trade routes:

Ndieni settlements. Each was founded by a slave – reflecting the great mobility open to trusted and gifted slaves in the Aro economy. Ikelionwu was originally a slave from Awka, who was adopted by a wealthy Aro trader. He decided to settle in a densely populated area which was well suited for slave dealing, and obtained permission to settle by taking part in a local war, playing a decisive role through the use of firearms.[37] Ndizuogu, too, was founded by a slave, Iheme, who was joined by his master Izuogu, at a well-chosen site, watered by tributaries of the Imo River, and, similarly, close to dense clusters of population. These included 'Anaocha' – the Awka area – and 'Igboadagbe', south of Onitsha.[38]

Slave trading was the basis of the Aro economy. Aro youths went through a long trading apprenticeship, with the trade in slaves as its pinnacle. This is how an Arondizuogu historian describes it:

> The people of Izuogu were trading on slaves, and they traded with Ibo's near and far. These places had no good water for drinking, scarcity of food and no fertile soil for cultivating their crops . . . they thought it wise to sell some of their children to feed others.
>
> There were three ways of capturing these slaves. One way of doing it was to go into a woman's house whose husband died and captured them. Another way was that brave men hid by the bush side so that any weaker person passing along might be seen by him and then he would jump out and capture the weaker person. The last way of capturing slaves was by capturing small boys and girls during heavy rain. These slaves captured were sold to the people of Aro-Ndizuogu.[39]

In the 1890s, up to six slave troupes of a hundred to two hundred each left Ndizuogu for the monthly fair at Bende.[40] And when a linguist was studying Igbo dialects in Sierra Leone among those who had been sold as slaves but rescued on the high seas by the British anti-slavery squadron, he found that he could not find a single native Aro speaker . . .[41]

Ndizuogu was only one of the most famous of the Aro settlements – an Aro historian has estimated their total number at ninety-eight – which stretched as far as Ibagwa, in the Nsukka area, in the extreme north of Igboland. There were Aro settlements at Afikpo, and early European visitors to Ezzaland, further north, described the Aro domination of economic life, and the trade routes known as 'Aro roads'.[42] To the south, their spheres of influence ended in the hinterland of the Delta, and to the west with the Niger and its hinterland, served by such powerful commercial states as Ossomari and Oguta. Wherever they lived, both Aro at home (*Aro ulo*) and Aro abroad (*Aro uzo*, or *Aro enugu*) retained an over-riding sense of their common Aro identity.

The rise of the Aro was marked, not only by great commercial acumen, but by a brilliant talent for diplomacy. This was remarked on by many European observers, who, typically ethnocentric, suggested that they must have been descended from Portuguese, or even wandering Carthaginians! In the words of an Aro historian, 'Izuogu came into Ibo land with peace and sword'. Wherever possible, they gained their ends by peaceful negotiation. If this failed, especially in the recovery of bad debts, they resorted to war. Nothing bears more striking witness to their astonishing talent for inter-group relations than their relationship with the warrior peoples of the Cross River – the Ohafia, Edda and Abam. We shall look at this more closely in a later chapter; suffice it to say now that the culture of these groups hinged around prowess in war, so they were constantly on the look-out for legitimate wars in which to take part. The Aro harnessed this warlike spirit to their own diplomatic purposes. They established a similar relationship with agricultural communities – such as Ututo and Ihe[43] – which grew the foodstuffs for a community engaged in full-time trade. To transport their trade goods they depended, not on the unwilling and unreliable services of slaves, but on Igbo groups which made a professional speciality of contract porterage, such as Ibeku and Igbere.[44] They established an equally mutually satisfactory relationship with the host communities at their great monthly fairs.[45] The host communities profited by the fairs in a variety of ways. The Aro 'owned' the fairs and could – and on occasion did – transfer them elsewhere.

The greatest of the fairs was Bende, which by the mid-nineteenth century was a familiar name to British visitors who knew no more of Igboland than the lower Niger. It had two seasons, a major and a minor, colloquially named after two Aro families, Abbagwu and Bianko. The major season lasted for four days, at 24-day intervals. Further to the north was the twin Aro fair at the salt centre of Uburu, one of Igboland's main gateways for imports from the north. It too had a major and a minor season, following a 24-day cycle, dovetailed into the cycle of Bende, so that traders could attend both. In the nineteenth century, Uzuakoli developed as a rival fair to Bende. It was the last stopping place for the 'Aro abroad' travelling from the Aro settlements further west. The Aro encouraged the rivalry between the two, from which they could only profit, and in the 1890s, after a dispute with Bende, they transferred their patronage to Uzuakoli, with dramatic consequences. The Bende market dwindled to insignificance. Uzuakoli enjoyed a glowing Indian summer of prosperity, before the advent of colonial rule once more rewrote the economic geography of Igboland. There was a similar rivalry between Uburu and Okposi in the north, from which the Aro likewise profited.

Traditions recorded among the neighbours of these Aro settlements reflect an attitude which was basically ambivalent. 'There was mutual understanding between us and the Aro. If the Aro were to fight any towns around they had to notify us. . . . But there was mutual suspicion between Akokwa and the Aro. We feared them for their wit and craftiness.'[46] On the one hand, Aro traders brought an economic stimulus which amounted sometimes to an economic revolution. In the case of Akokwa (situated near Arondizuogu) the Aro brought firearms, cloth (the textiles used previously were made from the bark of the *aji* tree) and new types of cassava. The Aro introduced long-distance trade. The Akokwa traders began to trade at Eke Agbaja, Oguta, Uzuakoli and Bende; 'it was the Ndizuogu traders who took us to these markets.'

Ohuhu traditions[47] show a similar picture of rapid economic change. The Aro introduced guns 'brought in parcels from Ukwa market by Aro people or traders who went there from Ohuhu.' They introduced coco-yams (known appropriately as *ede-aru*) and the type of matchet called *akparaja*. 'Cassava was introduced in Ohuhu via Akwete and Uzuakoli'. The Ohuhu sold slaves to the Aro, but also engaged in long-distance trade themselves, travelling to Uburu, and Bende, and the markets behind the Delta, such as Azumini.

The Aro brought a rapid impetus to economic expansion. They also did much to expand the slave trade; the traditions of various groups relate that it was in travelling to oracles, such as Ibinukpabi, at Arochukwu, that they first learnt that men could be sold . . . The total impact is well summarised by Ikwuebisi Ejiofor, a seventy-five-year-old elder of Aguinyi.

> We were told that external trade brought many good things into the clan but that its evils were perhaps greater. Before the external trade, we were told that the clan was comparatively quiet and that everything moved orderly. We were told that everything turned topsy-turvy with that trade. Traders from Awka, Umuchukwu, and Uzuakoli brought new articles like cloth, ivory, mirror, iron rods, bangles, etc. Later they also brought in *njenje* [gin] . . . and *utaba* [tobacco] . . . It was these traders that first brought guns into the clan . . . At that time it was very unsafe for any child to go out alone from its father's compound even in the day time. . . . So that the trade with those foreign traders brought many new things into the clan but it also brought wars and chaos.[48]

INSECURITY AND THE GROWTH OF TRADE

Before we leave the theme of economic expansion, we must consider two problems. The first is this: is there not an apparent contradiction between the assertion, repeatedly made in this book, that the slave trade generated chronic insecurity, and the picture just given of economic growth and long-distance trade routes.

The contradiction is only apparent. All the traditions agree that long-distance trade was a perilous affair. 'The paths through which people travelled were full of danger but what made them to be all that dangerous was not wild beasts or something of the sort but our fellow human beings instead.'[49]

The danger of long-distance trade was a variable which the Aro, and other long-distance traders, fully accepted, and which they developed techniques to overcome. The most obvious of these techniques was travelling in convoy; a trader would pay a commission to join a group of traders, the commission being used to cover the expenses of overnight accommodation and so on. These troupes were well armed – as was the ordinary citizen. A traveller in Ngwaland in the 1890s observed that 'not a man apparently moved a step without carrying a naked sword in one hand and a rifle at full cock in the other.'[50]

Judicious marriages were a way of cementing good relations with other towns, and extending the protecting bonds of kinship over a wide geographic area, though multiple marriage was a technique available only to the wealthy. Obi Ossai, the ruler of Aboh in the 1840s, married a wife from his trading partner, Brass. Ja Ja of Opobo was to cement his trading empire with well-planned marriages. The founder of Ndikelionwu married a wife from Ohafia, the source of the warriors on which he depended so largely. 'Women are the linking factors in the society. They are the string with which peoples are tied together.'[51] (Another aspect of this was the role which a town's daughters, married abroad, often played in resolving inter-community conflicts.)

Blood covenants, *igbandu*, were another technique, universal in Igboland, by which the bonds of kinship were simulated and expanded. Leading traders in towns through which a trade route passed would form these bonds with each other, guaranteeing each other's safety while they were within their sphere of influence. Lesser men, travelling, made use of such a wealthy and powerful patron's protection.

Certain groups of individuals, protected by religious sanctions, were immune from attack wherever they went. They included ritual experts of Nri, or men holding high titles. These were protected not only by the divinity which hedged them, and which made any attack on them an abomination, but by more mundane considerations. 'An eye for an eye' was the basic principle of all Igbo inter-group relations. Anyone who killed a titled man would have to provide an enormous amount of compensation, or involve his kin in a long war of retribution.

Long-distance traders overcame natural, as well as social barriers. In some parts of southern Igboland, the Okonko society levied tolls in return for maintaining the roads – a system of financing public works which obtained in England, for centuries. The important commercial centre of Obegu was approached through 'a broad, well-kept, beautiful avenue of trees.'[52] The Imo River and its tributaries were crossed by a series of brilliantly executed suspension bridges. An account from the 1890s describes one of them, and gives us a shining glimpse of one of the many natural beauties of Igboland.

> There was a wonderful floating bridge, by which we crossed over, that extends for quite half a mile, winding in and out among the dense undergrowth, out of which the water, clear and limpid, comes gurgling – so clear that you can see to a depth of forty feet and count every speckle on the white stomachs of the fish as they swim lazily about.[53]

THE SCALE OF TRADING TRANSACTIONS

The historian of Igboland must inevitably concentrate on a few major themes. Thus we have looked at long-distance trade on the Niger, and in the Aro network, and concentrated on what might be called macro-economic institutions. But in the total picture of Igbo economic life, markets were more important than trade routes, and local small-scale exchanges were vastly greater than the specialised long-distance trade in imported goods and slaves. An anthropologist, writing in the 1930s, writes of the impression obtained at Igbo markets 'that thousands of people are buying and selling minute quantities of the same things.'[54] Eye-witness accounts of nineteenth-century Igbo markets, such as the following account of a market on the lower Imo river in the 1860s, mainly emphasise the exchange of local agricultural products. 'Their market consists of corn, fish very little, and palm-wine in abundance, yams, raw and cooked, palm-oil, pepper, country pots, bowls and mortar, plantains, fowls, eggs, snails, cocoa-roots [coco-yam], palm-nuts, ropes, mats and many other products.'[55] The market was less than four hours by water from Opobo, yet not a single imported product is mentioned. The great bulk of Igbo economic transactions consisted of exchanges, over short distances, of products which were locally produced.

The macro view of Igbo economic history probably leads to an over emphasis on the role of the Aro.[56] Ohuhu, for instance, is not even mentioned in the existing accounts of Igbo trade, but the researches of Mr Esobe have revealed the extent of its involvement even in long-distance trade. Professor Afigbo, in a brilliant study of the economic history of the Nsukka area, has established the vitality of this local economic life – manufacturing cloth, which was exported to the north and south, smelting iron, and making a wide range of metal implements, importing horses and salt and exporting slaves to at least three different outlets, and later, exporting palm products to the Anambra river. Although the Aro were active in the area, many different communities engaged in trade – Awka, Igala, Agbaja, and the Aku of southern Nsukka division, who made a determined effort to oust the Aro from the slave trade. The relatively small area was criss-crossed by trade routes – less 'crowded imaginary highways', than, to use Professor Afigbo's imagery, a dense network of tiny capillary veins.

OTHER TRADITIONS OF MIGRATION

In a general survey of this kind, one can mention only a few striking elements from Igboland's myriad traditions of migration. (We shall mention the traditions of origin of two other important groups, the Ezza and the Cross River Igbo, in a later section of this study.) But if one narrows one's focus, and looks, for instance, at any small section of Igboland one finds a detailed and complex story of small-scale and local migrations. Many such traditions in the Owerri area, for instance, describe migrations taking place within a radius of about five miles.

Some Igbo village groups – such as the riverain towns of Illah and Aguleri – had ample land, and were able to give a generous welcome to successive groups of strangers, seeking a refuge. But in the more densely populated parts of Igboland, such as Owerri or Mbaise, the traditions reflect a constant struggle to balance the unequal elements in Igboland's ecological equation – her dense and expanding population, and her limited land – limits often made worse by the land's infertility, and scarcity of water. When the pressure on land grew too great, a section or village group would migrate a short distance. As population pressures increased, this kind of migration became less feasible, and increasingly, village groups attempted to extend their boundaries by war – a theme to which we shall return. Within its own boundaries, a village would sometimes shift its location. Often this was due to portents, to a series of misfortunes, which made a site seem unlucky. Mr Iheagwam's case-study of the Naze village group, near Owerri, gives an interesting example of this. 'We move from each settlement for fear of accidents, from unexpected crash of dry trees.'[57]

5 Igbos Abroad in the Era of the Slave Trade

OLAUDAH EQUIANO

The vast majority of the Igbos who fell victim of the trans-Atlantic slave trade have been forgotten. They lived lives of toil and suffering, and their children rapidly lost a sense of their Igbo identity. One of them, however, by his courage and ability, won his freedom, and went on to a remarkable career which he described in an autobiography which is one of our most valuable sources of knowledge of the Igbo past. He was the first of many Igbos who have achieved distinction in Europe, and the first of a series of notable Igbo authors in English. His name was Olaudah Equiano, and he was born in about 1745, and died in 1797.[1]

In modern Igbo, his name would be, perhaps, Ude, or Uda, Ekwuano. We are not sure which part of Igboland he came from. He states that he is from 'Essaka', which was subject to the *oba* of Benin. This would, of course, suggest a western Igbo, possibly from Ashaka. But there are difficulties with this identification – there were no rivers in his home town, but Ashaka is on the Ase River – and many of the details in his narrative suggest an Igbo from the east, possibly from the Awka area. Equiano left Igboland at the age of eleven, and wrote his book when he was forty-four. Probably he supplemented his own memories with details from other Igbos, for there were a number of Igbos in London at the time. Alternatively, he might have drawn his reference to Benin from literary sources.

At the age of eleven, Equiano and his sister were kidnapped. They were taken south to the Delta (being separated en route), where Equiano was sold into slavery. He was taken to the southern states of America, surviving the appalling hardships of the Middle Passage. In all probability he was doomed, either to an early death, or to a life of misery and servitude. Later he was sold to a planter in the West Indies, and then worked – still a slave – on slave ships. But Equiano was a youth of exceptional courage and determination. He learnt to speak, read and write

English, he studied arithmetic, and even mastered the difficult science of navigation. Despite many obstacles, he managed to save money, and bought his freedom at the age of nineteen.

For some years after that, Equiano led a life of constant travel. Working sometimes as a valet, sometimes as a merchant seaman, he made trips to the West Indies and to central America, and even took part in a scientific expedition to the Arctic. He took an active part in the struggle to abolish slavery. In the 1780s, he was given a position of responsibility in a philanthropic scheme to send black settlers to Sierra Leone, but he criticised the corruption of a white colleague, and the way in which his fellow-Africans were 'plundered and oppressed', and so lost his job. The experience did not prevent him from continuing to take part in the abolitionist struggle. He settled in England, where he became a popular platform speaker in the abolitionist cause, and wrote his autobiography, which became a best-seller. Like many later Igbos who have lived abroad, he married a European, in his own case an English lady from Cambridge. He was a fervent Christian, an evangelical, who went through an experience of conversion which changed his life. He ends his book with these words: 'What makes any event important, unless by its observation we become better and wiser, and learn to "do justly, to love mercy, and to walk humbly before God?"'

AFRICANUS HORTON, AND THE IGBOS OF SIERRA LEONE

When the British passed a law in 1807, forbidding their own nationals to take part in the slave trade, they did all in their power to persuade other nations to commit themselves to do likewise. To enforce their own commitments, and those of others, they placed a naval squadron off the West African coast, to intercept illegal slavers. It was impracticable to return their captives to their original homes, so they took them instead to the colony of Sierra Leone. It is difficult to imagine the colossal difficulties which these recaptives, as they were called, faced and overcame. They landed in Sierra Leone destitute, exiles from their homes and families, with no knowledge of English. With the help of C.M.S. and Methodist missionaries they learnt English, became Christians, and mastered a variety of skills. Through hard work and determination they soon turned into a wealthy élite, educating their children to a high standard.

By the middle of the nineteenth century, they had produced lawyers, clergymen, merchants and doctors. Like the modern Igbo middle class, they followed a way of life basically similar to that of their counterparts in Europe, synthesised with a number of African customs, such as elaborate funerals, generosity to the extended family, and African styles of food preparation. The largest ethnic group in Sierra Leone was Yoruba; the second largest, 'the Igbo race, who are in Freetown both numerous and wealthy.'[2]

Like their Yoruba counterparts, the Igbos in Sierra Leone retained a strong interest in their homeland, and especially in its Christianisation. In the early 1850s, a hundred Igbos petitioned the bishop of Sierra Leone to establish missions in Igboland, and a party of three Igbos, led by the first black American college graduate (the Reverend E. Jones) visited Nigeria, but were prevented by circumstances from penetrating Igboland.[3] The Igbo community in Sierra Leone was not discouraged by this failure – 'We believe, that in the Igbo country also, as in other parts, the Lord has "much people."'[4] Several years later the project came to fruition, and the first Christian mission in Igboland was established at Onitsha, in 1857, under the leadership of the Reverend John Christopher Taylor, a Sierra Leonian of Igbo parentage.

One of the most outstanding members of the Sierra Leone Igbo community was James Africanus Beale Horton.[5] He was born in Sierra Leone in 1835. Both his parents were Igbos; we know that his father had been enslaved and liberated in adult life, and earned a modest livelihood in the colony, as a carpenter. Despite his parents' poverty, Horton was enabled to go to secondary school, through the generosity of a black West Indian, the colony's Chief Justice, who financed the education of a number of poor boys. Just when he was finishing secondary school, the British government decided to award scholarships to three outstanding pupils to study medicine in England, because it was so difficult to recruit white doctors to serve in the British army in West Africa. One of the three boys chosen was Horton.

He qualified in medicine at King's College, London, and then went on to do an M.D. at Edinburgh, winning a number of distinctions and prizes. He then had a distinguished career as an officer in the British army, serving in different parts of West Africa, and finally rising to the rank of lieutenant colonel, and head of the Army Medical Department in the Gold Coast. He was a man of dynamic energy, who found time amid his professional duties to write a number of books, both on tropical medicine and related sciences, and on politics. He drafted schemes for the government of the West African colonies when they became independent – a day he thought was close at hand – and put forward plans to turn the many little states of Igboland into 'an independent united Christian and civilised nation.' He was proud of his African identity, and of his Igbo and Sierra Leone inheritance. He added the name Africanus in Edinburgh, and usually stated on the title-page of his books that he was a native of Sierra Leone.

Like many later Igbo professional men, he was also a daring and enterprising businessman. His business enterprises were both personal investments and patriotic schemes to develop the resources of West Africa. They included the establishment of a bank in Freetown. He had hoped to finance the education of some Igbo boys from the Niger, in England, but practical difficulties arose, and so he helped another Sierra Leonian Igbo intellectual, the poet Christian Cole, to study law in London instead.

Africanus Horton was a man of small stature and large heart. He died in 1883, having crowded more achievements into his relatively short life than most men who live the allotted span can dream of.

III The Nineteenth Century

6 Igbo Warfare in the Nineteenth Century

The increasing militarisation of life is one of the most striking features of nineteenth-century Nigerian history. In the north, it was the century of the *jihads*, and in the west, the century of the decline of the Oyo empire, and the long and bitter struggles of the successor states. In Igboland, too, it was a period of almost continuous war, wars which emerge, in the oral traditions of its many little states, as perhaps the dominating fact of their nineteenth-century history.

We cannot be sure whether internal warfare was becoming more extensive and more bloody in nineteenth-century Igboland, possibly through the increasing use of firearms. Many oral traditions suggest that this was the case, and that new techniques of warfare – such as elaborate trenching techniques – were evolved to meet the new crisis. But if the oral traditions of different groups are taken at their face value, one would have the impression that the most important wars of their history were fought in the 1890s. The explanation of this, of course, is that soon colonial rule was to intervene, and put an end to these internal wars. The wars fought in the 1890s were the last of their kind, and thus appear unique and unforgettable. Their uniqueness preserves all the attendant details, like a fly in amber. They are remembered, not because they were the most important wars, but because they were the last.

THE TECHNOLOGY OF WAR: FIREARMS

A key question in the history of Igbo warfare concerns the role of firearms. When were they introduced, how effective were they, and when did various Igbo groups develop techniques to repair and maintain them?

It was not until the eighteenth century that European traders began the systematic import of arms and ammunition to the Delta. In the seventeenth century, items had sometimes been given to Delta rulers as presents. The 'Akpa', who used blunderbusses in the wars which led to the foundation of Arochukwu, in the first half of the seventeenth century, obviously obtained them exceptionally early.[1] Firearms were probably most decisive in wars at the time when they were first introduced and their practical effect (not always, as we shall see, very devastating) was reinforced by their powerful psychological impact. Their successful use by the Akpa is a case in point. So is the tradition concerning the foundation of Arondikelionwu, whose eponymous founder intervened decisively in a local war with a single gun, in the late eighteenth century.[2] Obviously the Aro obtained and used guns much earlier than most of their customers, as did other powerful groups of middleman traders, such as the people of Aboh.[3]

It seems that it was not until the nineteenth century that the use of firearms became widespread in Igboland. In Onitsha, the introduction of firearms is associated with the reign of Ijelekpe, in the early nineteenth century. For a short time, their use of firearms gave the Onitsha much success in their wars with neighbouring towns. But retribution followed. Their chief rival Obosi obtained 'many guns which were newly bought from the people of Aro-Chuku' and ambushed them.[4]

The German doctor, Köler (in a work which has been neglected by Nigerian historians, for it is written, not only in German, but in Gothic type), gives us an interesting description of the transition in weaponry which was taking place in Bonny and Igboland in 1840.[5] He states that the weapons used in Bonny were manufactured partly in England and partly in Igboland. He describes the variety of knives, swords and spears used, and states that the flint-lock was becoming the standard weapon, and hence losing its psychological impact among the Igbo.

Köler suggests that the practical effect of these weapons was minimal. The cannon used in the Delta and on the Niger, to arm war-canoes, were lashed fast, so could be aimed only by the slow and inefficient procedure of manoeuvring the whole canoe. Both guns and ammunition imported were, as we have seen, of poor quality, and the Bonnymen, never having been taught to aim the guns they bought, were poor shots, using them like pistols.[6] Mr Nzewunwa's interesting case-study of a war between several Owerri village groups in *c.* 1888–90 points in the same direction.[7] One of the combattants, running out of ammunition, experimented with ersatz gun powder, and with a variety of replacements for bullets – palm kernels, cowries, and finally, maize grains. In a later war, they used goat droppings. The fact that they fought wars successfully with these presumably non-lethal projectiles would seem to suggest, in general, that firearms were of greater psyhcological than practical effect in Igbo wars.[8]

In parts of northern Igboland, firearms did not come into general use until the second half of the nineteenth century. Professor Shelton's fieldwork in the Nsukka area suggested that forges for the repair of dane guns in the area were not established until the 1870s, 'and that guns were extremely scarce before the 1850's.'[9]

In the second half of the nineteenth century, further south, a second firearms revolution was already occurring. The older type of weapon, dane guns (smooth bored and muzzle loading) were giving way to superior weapons of precision. King Ja Ja of Opobo armed his men with breach-loading rifles. Inevitably, the prosperous trading groups such as the Aro and the Awka were the first Igbo communities to follow suit. In 1894, a British official described the weapons of the Aro communities trading in Ibibioland: 'They are brave and have plenty of guns, chiefly cap and flint-lock, although I saw a few Snider and old revolvers.'[10] A visitor to Awka at the turn of the century was surprised to note that many of the men were armed with Snider rifles.[11] At much the same time, in a town close to Onitsha, a missionary described the equipment of a typical Igbo warrior, in an account which holds true of many other parts of Igboland as well.

> When the natives here go out to fight, they wear platted [sic] banana leaves, sling native bags over their shoulders containing ammunition, hang charms and medicine round their waists, stick matchets in their loin cloths, and carry guns from Long Danes (trade flint-locks) to Snider rifles; a splendid fighting kit.[12]

A problem which is rather difficult to solve concerns the proportion of the population which possessed guns. Some early European descriptions of Igboland give the impression that much of the adult male population went armed. But guns represented a major capital investment, and only the relatively prosperous could afford the initial purchase, and the subsequent ammunition. Mr Nzewunwa's study of Obibi warfare shows that in this Owerri village group, guns were the preserve of the wealthy. Visiting gun dealers from Nkwerre would settle temporarily in their homes, and conduct their transactions there. In Obibi warfare, there was a special élite group, *ndi ukwu egbe*, each of whom controlled five guns, which engaged in guerilla raids by night. 'Since the distribution of wealth was very limited and uneven a greater majority could afford only bows and arrows and at times knives.'[13] This is confirmed by evidence from Ezzaland: 'Not every soldier was able to afford a gun but the possession gave the warrior a moral and combat superiority.'[14]

To the Igbo, religio-magical protection was at least as important as conventional weaponry in preparing for war. No war preparations were complete without the *dibia* who arranged religious protection both for individuals and for the whole town. One Item village group carried these techniques to extreme lengths, inviting a whole clan of distinguished *dibia* from Okposi to live with them. 'Item Okpi sons depended more on the strength of their gods than on their own personal strength.' The techniques it appears were successful, and the group of *dibia* – Ndi-Agwu – still live as part of Item.[15]

THE SOCIAL ORGANISATION OF WAR

Igbo communities were almost constantly at war, but the destructive effects of war were held in check by an elaborate set of military conventions, which many larger and more 'civilised' states might have done well to emulate. There were two basic categories of war. The first was that between several members of the same village group. Here, the loss of life was forbidden. No formal declaration of war was needed. Sticks, stones and matchets were used, but those wielding matchets took pains to avoid a fatal blow. Sometimes these civil wars escalated to more serious dimensions – indeed there is some evidence that, like other types of war in Igboland, they were becoming more bloody and less restrained as the nineteenth century progressed. In Awka, for instance, several quarters fought a bloody civil war in 1903–4, apparently occasioned by an infringement of the prerogatives of the blacksmiths.[16] It greatly facilitated penetration by the British, and by missionary bodies, and was finally suppressed by the British.

A more serious type of war was that fought between village groups, called *ogu egbe*, because guns were used. Typically, they were caused either by a land dispute, or by the desire to avenge an injury suffered by one of the village group's members. Oral traditions suggest that as the nineteenth century progressed, and population pressures increased, wars over boundaries became more frequent. Thus an elder of Aguinyi:

> The wars were fought mostly over land issues. We are told that in the early days, there were very few people in the clan and these had no need to quarrel over land. When the population of the clan grew, land became more scarce. And as no one could be told to build his home in the air, the people of the clan began to share the available land more equitably . . . Soon, however, this honest and peace-loving generation died off and the few that remained either got confused about the actual boundaries or were overwhelmed by the majority who preferred the might-is-right approach. This was the main reason for the wars.[17]

The role of land disputes is very marked in the history of warfare in the Owerri area. Obibi, for instance, was surrounded by no less than nine other village groups. If her land became inadequate for her needs, she had no alternative but to endeavour to extend her boundaries by war.

The law of 'an eye for an eye', which was the cardinal principle of Igbo inter-group relations, had both good and bad effects. It greatly limited the loss of life in wars, for the combattants knew that at the end of the war, a balance sheet would be drawn up, and the side which had the lower casualty list would have to give the other side victims to equalise. But the principle led to many wars. An insult or an injury to a son travelling abroad, the mysterious death of a son visiting another town, all this could and did lead to wars. The practice of exogamy was a fruitful source of disputes. Every village had a large group of daughters married in other towns. If any of them was mistreated, in life or in death, the resulting dispute easily escalated into war. A missionary noted in the 1850s that 'the inhabitants of Onitsha, especially the chiefs, were afraid to venture out of their town, not knowing but some one might waylay them to avenge the death of some one killed by the people, either accidentally, maliciously, or in war.'[18]

Some states, whose prosperity rested mainly on slave trading, made wars specifically to obtain slaves. Arondizuogu traditions record this, and so do those of Ossomari. 'In the olden times Ossomari people used to call all the villages around them "Aninso", meaning forbidden people. I am told that Ossomari nearly wiped them out in those early days of piracy. In the same way . . . they did a lot of havoc in the Anambra.'[19] To avoid reprisals, Ossomari sometimes raided 'as if in the name of Aboh', and Aboh, not unnaturally, reciprocated.

Typically, wars between village groups were regulated by many conventions. They were preceded by negotiations, which endeavoured to prevent conflict, and by a formal declaration of war. Women and children were unharmed. Markets and those visiting them were left in peace, in theory, though not always in practice. Shrines and places of religious significance were similarly left alone, and during religious festivals, such as the New Yam festival, the land was at peace.

War was regarded by the young – and this is not true only of nineteenth-century Igboland – as a glorious and exciting sport. It was the reverse of total war. As we have seen, the thought of the final balance sheet tended to keep casualties down. Sometimes wars dragged on for years, but agriculture and other forms of economic life continued, and feasts and festivals were still held. Combat was restricted mainly to the farming off-season.

> In the olden days wars were not fought continuously or daily and *Ogu Mkpuru Oka* was no exception. Fighting was resumed by any side whenever it felt it had the means . . . Each side knew when the other observed its religious festivities and refrained from attacks . . . Sorties and raids dominated the other periods when war was strictly speaking not forbidden. Any side could also send a delegation for a truce whenever the occasion called for it. An example was at the death of a priest of a cult or an important personality or a disaster like fire.[20]

The desire to capture enemy heads as trophies, however, was a factor militating in the opposite direction. The practice of beheading a fallen foe was very widespread among Igbo communities east and west of the Niger. The skull was valued as a souvenir, and as a concrete and unequivocal proof of personal valour. In Cross River Igbo communities, as we shall see, head hunting became of supreme importance, but elsewhere in Igboland too, the trophy was a proof of a man's courage, and brought him different types of honour. In north-eastern Igboland, they formed a title society, *ogbu isi*. In Niger communities, they wore the eagle plume of courage, and they alone could dance when a special war drum played.

When a community desired to make peace, it sent a delegation carrying the palm fronds which symbolise peace and innocence. Typically, women played a key role as a pressure group for peace, because of their unique role as daughters and sisters in one community, and wives and mothers in another. Those whose parents came from the two contesting parties the *nwanwa*, again had a special role to play. When peace was made, the balance sheet of the dead was adjusted, and the victor often adjusted a boundary to his advantage. But just as there was no total war among most Igbo communities, similarly, there was no total conquest.

> Among the Owerri Igbo conquerors are not known to impose themselves on the conquered. This is forbidden by the religious belief of the people since the gods would not wish to be involved in imposing themselves on fellow gods . . . no conqueror pressed the vanquished to the wall. Every effort was made to normalise relations as quickly as possible.[21]

Not all Igbo wars followed this ideal type, though most did. We shall now turn to a more detailed examination of a number of exceptionally large-scale nineteenth-century conflicts, which did not.

ABAM, EDDA AND OHAFIA WARFARE

All Igbo communities honoured courage, and gave marks of esteem to the daring and successful warrior. But for certain Igbo clans in the Cross River area, the love of military glory became a consuming passion, and the focus of all social values. These included two related clans, the Abam and Chafia, who believe that they migrated to their present homes from Ibeku, near Bende, and the Edda, who believe that they came from an original homeland east of the Cross River to their present territory in the Edda hills.

The Aro and these Cross River warriors established a remarkable symbiotic relationship. The Aro, as we have seen, came to the rest of Igboland with 'peace and a sword'. They sometimes made use of force in inter-town relations – to recover a bad debt, for instance, or, increasingly, to raid for slaves. They sometimes fought in these wars themselves,[22] but also called on the services of their martial and widely feared allies from the Cross River. They also acted as middle-men, hiring Cross River fighters for other towns, sending an emissary on the long journey across Igboland, sometimes using corn cobs to indicate the number of fighters required.[23] They took pains to avoid unofficial wars on the journey, for if they were attacked by another group, the hired warriors regarded their contracts as fulfilled, and went home.[24]

These fighters are generally referred to in the literature as mercenaries, and the groups which hired them always use this kind of terminology,[25] but traditions collected in Ohafia by Mr Oji Kalu Oji insist that the Ohafia, at least, fought for glory and not for pay. The substantial tribute offered by the groups requesting their services was used in the religious rituals which preceded war. The Ohafia sought only the concrete symbol of military prowess – human heads. Ohafia adult male society was divided into heroes, *dike*, and cowards, *ujo*. *Ujo's* life was full of humiliations and civic disabilities, to which death seemed preferable. It is much to the credit of the Ohafia that they did not obtain these heads by kidnapping stray travellers. They obtained them only in a legitimate war – crossing the length and breadth of Igboland, if necessary, in search of such a war.

There are signs that the Aro–Cross River alliance was under some strain as the nineteenth century progressed. Aro traditions recorded that the Edda were not too scrupulous about the sources of their heads, so that the Aro came to dispense with their services.[26] Ohafia traditions record that towards the end of the nineteenth century, the Aro began to enslave certain of their Ohafia allies. For this reason, Ohafia men did not engage officially in the Obegu war, which was fought by the Abam and

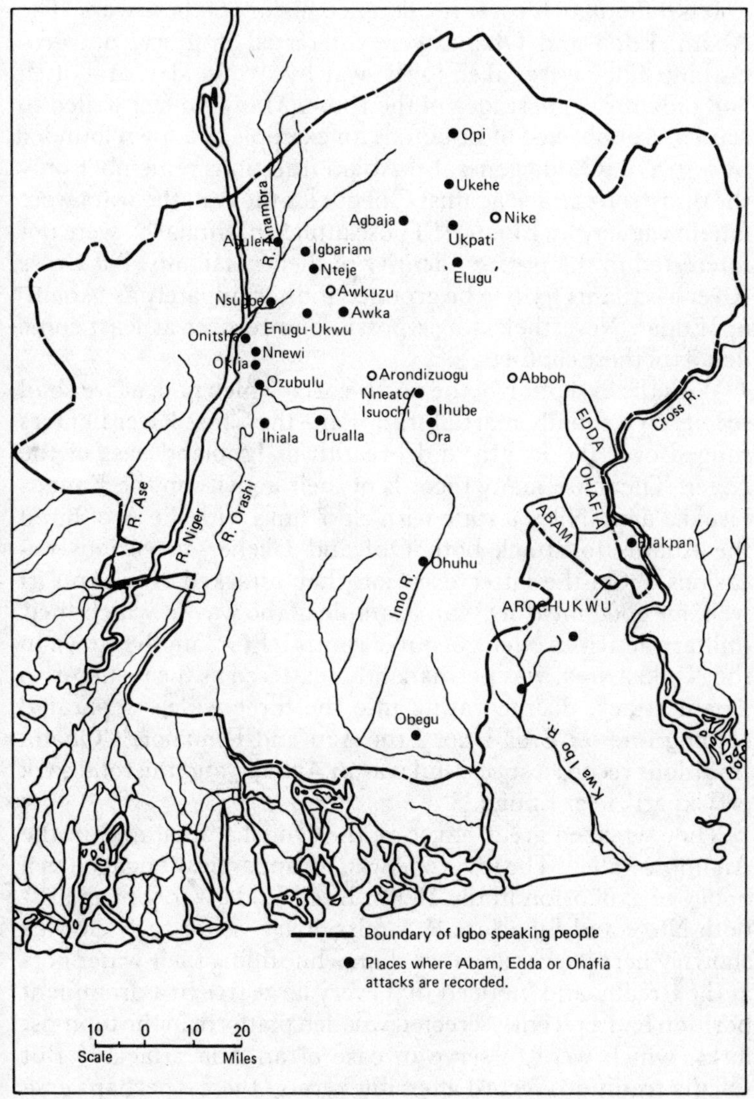

Map 5 Abam, Edda and Ohafia warfare

one clan from Edda.[27]

It is difficult to recover the detailed history of these wars. The Abam, Edda and Ohafia were interested in glory, not geography. They were taken to the war by Aro guides, and often had only the vaguest idea of the route. Many, in fact, failed to return. Abboh, east of Enugu, is an example of a town founded by a straying Edda general.[28] Abam traditions remember only the disastrous attack against Obegu; for the rest, the wars were fought vaguely 'in Elugu'.[29] Those attacked, similarly, were not interested in the precise identity of their assailants. All Cross River assailants tend to be grouped indiscriminately as 'Abam' or 'Edda'. Nevertheless it is possible to recover at least some details of these conflicts.

With the exception of the north-east – which had, as we shall see, its own equally martial tradition – the Cross River fighters ranged over the length and breadth of Igboland east of the Niger. There are many records of their activity in the Enugu-Nsukka area. Nike, a state with close links with the Aro, hired the Abams to attack both Opi and Ukehe, on various occasions.[30] On the latter occasion they attacked Ngalakpu as well, for good measure – an example of the way in which their military activities often got out of control. Eror, another town in the Nsukka area, was permanently scattered as the result of an Abam attack, disintegrating into the three widely separated communities of Eror Uno, Eror Agu and Umualor.[31] Ohafia traditions record a successful war in Agbaja, and the total sack of 'Ukpati', near Enugu.[32]

They wreaked great havoc in the Onitsha area, and in the Anambra valley. The town of Awkuzu, apparently engaged in a policy of expansion in the 1890s, hired Edda warriors against both Nteje and Igbariam.[33] A missionary visitor to Nteje was shown where its women were slain while filling their water pots at the stream, and 'noticed that every large tree in a prominent position had a recently-erected wooden platform in the topmost forks, which were to serve in case of an Ada attack.'[34] But Ohafia traditions record a terrible reverse there – perhaps on a different occasion.[35] The nearby town of Nsugbe was defended by a strong wooden gate, framed with thorn bushes.[36] Another missionary, visiting Awka, was begged by his carriers not to whistle, for 'our way now lay through the dreaded Abam country.'[37] In Awka, they found each compound surrounded by high walls, with loopholes for firing, and a number of high watch towers, 'intended for defensive purposes against the dreaded "Abam"'.[38] We have several eye-witness accounts of Edda attacks on Aguleri, in 1891 and 1892.[39] In the first instance, warned by messengers from the Elugu area, the people fled; in the second, helped by Catholic missionaries armed with guns, they put up a successful resistance. The people of Igbariam, fleeing from the Edda, spent some time at Aguleri as refugees. On occasion, they threatened the people of Onitsha.[40]

Further south, they were hired in the internal struggles of the Achalla clan, by Ihiala, against Uli.[41] Missionary visitors to the Okigwi area in 1910 described it as desolated by continual wars, and by raids from slave-dealing Aros.[42] Aro traditions relate the total destruction of Ora, near Okigwi, by Ohafia.[43] Ohuhu's historian states of the Abam that 'Next to Ohuhu slavers, they were the greatest single factor responsible for terror and insecurity in pre-colonial Ohuhu.'[44]

They were not always victorious. An Ohuhu village won a crushing victory over the invaders by the grim expedient of setting a trap, which involved sacrificing 'the wretched, the dunces and the incapacitated.' The mass grave of the slaughtered Abam soldiers can still be seen in Ohuhu.[45] Enugwu-Ukwu, a village group on the main road between Onitsha and Awka, enjoyed a similar triumph over the Edda. A certain Okoli Ijoma of Arondikelionwu had hired Edda warriors to attack the Udi area, and decided to attack Enugwu-Ukwu as well. The people, again, set a trap for them by leaving out poisoned water, wine and provisions. When the invaders were incapacitated, they were killed by the Enugwu-Ukwu people, who suffered only a single casualty, and took the praise name, 'Ike Melu Edda'.[46]

The map on p. 83 indicates that most of their attacks took place in the Nsukka, Awka, Onitsha and Anambra areas – which are, of course, suprisingly distant from their Cross River homes. It is not clear if this represents a real concentration, or distortions imposed by the evidence (we have European eyewitness accounts of the Onitsha-Anambra area at the end of the last century, but none, of course, of, for instance, Okigwi). Some of the places recorded as attacked in Ohafia tradition cannot be identified. But some of these wars are recorded, not in European records, but in local traditions, and it seems that there was a real concentration of military activity in the area. Probably it became a tradition in the area to call in Cross River warriors. Undoubtedly, their services were often negotiated by the people of Arondizuogu.

We have seen how various Igbo communities developed elaborate defences against the Edda, Ohafia and Abam: watch towers, platforms in trees, trenches, walls, and so on. Another form of self defence lay in union – to form the scattered little states of Igboland into larger and more powerful units. The Isuochi and Nneato towns of Okigwi division successfully formed the Isumisu confederation for defence against the Ohafia, whom they defeated.[47] A number of towns in the Onitsha-Awka area formed the Amakwam confederation, to repel Aro mercenaries. 'The Aro mercenaries were badly slaughtered and defeated some fifty years ago [this was written in 1934] in a raid on Awka town.'[48]

To their victims, the Cross River warriors were usually a source of terror and dismay. As Ohafia traditions point out, they did not profit the Edda, Abam and Ohafia themselves. In an era of expanding trade, they were unable to participate, for fear of reprisals, and forced to rely on the produce of their flourishing farms.[49] Many did not return – either being killed in battle, or losing their way, or succumbing to hunger and exhaustion in their tremendous journeys where every man's hand was against them. Their long isolation is reflected in their dialects, which are practically unintelligible to the rest of Igboland. Like the whole of human history, this story bears compelling witness to the tragic waste and futility of war.

In the last major war in which they engaged, the Aro and their Abam and Edda allies suffered a grim retribution. In the November of 1901, they attacked the southern Igbo town of Obegu.[50] The aim of the attack was to enforce the repayment of a bad debt; underlying it, were anxieties about British encroachment (Obegu had signed a treaty with the British), and disputes about the Ndoki towns' claim to monopolise trade with the Delta. It so happened that the raid concided with the beginning of the Aro expedition. The neighbouring towns allegedly involved were razed by the British, and the Aro trader involved, Okori Torti, and his Abam ally Uchendu were publicly executed in the market place of Obegu. The Colonial Office minuted that the executions were illegal – 'They could fairly plead belligerency as their reason for killing the Obegu people'[51] – but these *post facto* scruples were not, of course, of much use to Torti and Uchendu.

THE NORTH-EASTERN IGBO: THE EZZA AND THEIR NEIGHBOURS

If the wars of the Cross River Igbo were inspired by a single-minded passion for glory, those of the Ezza and their neighbours were inspired by an equally single-minded passion for land.

The Ezza, Izzi and Ikwo trace their origin from three brothers,* whose father came from Afikpo.† A government official who studied their traditions in the 1930s stated that the migration had occurred twelve generations, or three hundred years, earlier. It is difficult to know how much literal truth this founding charter embodies; the official wrote that 'the writer concerned has become convinced that Noyo and his immediate descendants are not mere mythical benefactors but persons who actually lived and set up the administration with which they are credited.'[52]

According to these traditions, Noyo, the founder of the Ikwo clan, settled at Akpelu; Nodo (or Olodo), the founder of the Izzi, at Amagu; and Ezakuna, the founder of the Ezza, at Amana. From these original settlements, their descendants fanned out across the broad plains of north-eastern Igboland, in an insatiable quest for land which was inevitably to bring them into conflict with other Igbo and non-Igbo groups. The desire for land was to prove stronger than kinship, and by the late nineteenth century, the Ezza, Ikwo and Izzi were locked in bitter and protracted internecine wars.

The north-eastern Igbo did not suffer from land shortages in the conventional sense. An observer noted in the 1930s, 'Ikwo now possesses more than sufficient land both for present needs and for many generations to come.'[53] Their land hunger sprang from the unique ecological context of their agriculture,[54] and

* Various versions state that Ezekuna was the half-brother, nephew, or brother-in-law of the others.

† Ezza version; a varient, Ikwo, version states Item.

their single-minded and tireless dedication to farming. In most parts of Igboland the planting season is quite a short one, for

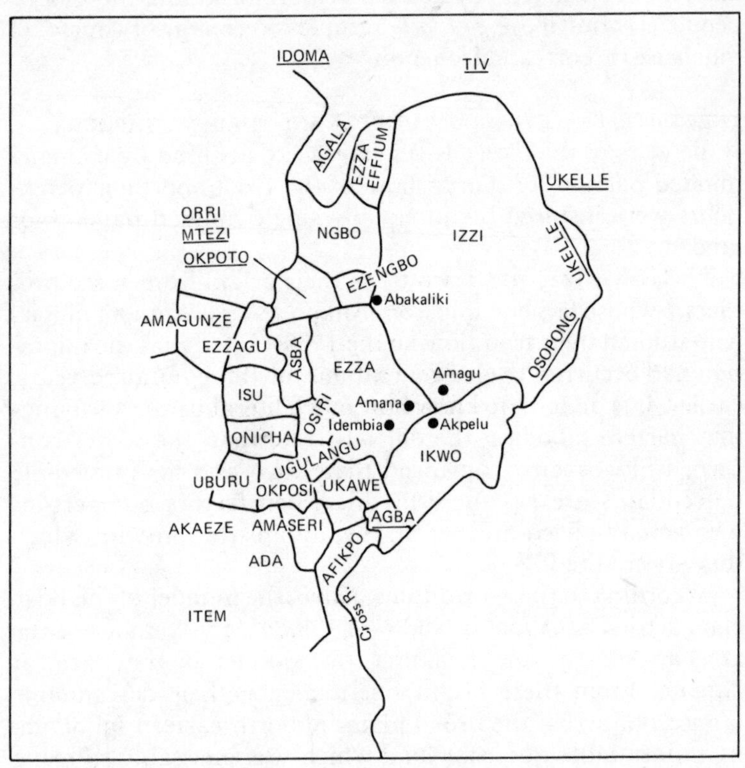

Map 6 The north-eastern Igbo and their neighbours

seed yams left too long in the ground rot there. When harvest time comes, the yams must be dug from the ground and stored in racks (called, rather misleadingly, barns). In the north-east, the climate is much dryer. The mature yams can be left in the ground till used, and the planting season can and does extend through most of the dry season, thus enormously expanding the number of yams a single individual can produce. The ground, of course, is of the consistency of concrete in the dry season, but this did and does not deter the north-eastern Igbo, wielding the giant hoes which no other Igbo group can use effectively, and piling the ground into enormous yam mounds of a cubic yard or more of soil. In modern times, the Ezza, having performed herculean feats of industry on their own farms travel as migrant labourers to work on the farms of others.

Like the Cross River Igbo, the Ezza and their neighbours engaged in total war. Military service, for age-grades of fighting age, was compulsory.[55] Defeated foes were beheaded, or offered in religious sacrifices. Enemy villages were often razed, their populations put largely to the sword. They expanded through a series of violent wars. The defeated groups were put to death, or moved to another site, or, in many cases, joined the victors and became assimilated with them. Amuda village is an example, founded by Okpoto who preferred to join their Ezza conquerors rather than migrate. The area thus conquered was called *ndiagu*, the frontier (literally, people of the field) where young men settled. The area that launched the attack was called *ndiazu*.

In the traditions describing these wars, it is interesting to note that the earlier wars are overlaid with a veneer of mythology. Thus on their southern frontier, the Ezza fought an early war with the 'Agalaga Okpa Ezea', a tribe whose military feats were handicapped by their unusually large heads. Defeated, they leaped together into the Abonyi river, where today their spirits disturb surrounding villages, at morning and evening, with the sound of food preparation.

Later, less poetic, and more convincing traditions describe a war with the Agba, who originally lived in an area now occupied by Idembia, the most warlike sub-group of a warlike people. Forced to flee, they covered their salt ponds with enormous stones. One section fled to the Cross River, another to the west, where soon they came into conflict with another Ezza group, Izo Imoha, expanding westward. This time they determined to stand their ground, and the Ezza bypassed them to settle in an unoccupied area, which became the colony of Ezzagu (Ezza farmland, or Ezza-in-the-fields).

The southern Ezza fought an interminable series of wars with the Igbo neighbour whom Ezza tradition generously describes as 'the gallant and indomitable Oshiri'. Gradually they were pushed south of the Abonyi river, which they regarded as a natural frontier, but which the Ezza, by the late nineteenth century, were determined to cross. Gallantly fighting a losing war against a much more numerous opponent, the Oshiri looked for help, first to the distant oracle of Igwe-ka-Ala at Umunoha, and then, when this proved ineffective, to the British. Like many other Igbo groups, they manipulated the British into attacking their traditional enemy, by describing them as slave traders and so on.

Another Ezza colony founded in the late nineteenth century was Ezza Effium. The inhabitants of Effium appealed to the Ezza for help in withstanding the aggression of the Ishieke Izzi. To win this help, they invited them to settle. Large numbers of Ezza – whose descendants now far outnumber the Effium – accepted the invitation. Not content with their gains in Effium, they were anxious to win territory from their northern neighbour, the Agala, an Idoma group. In the period of colonial rule, a war ensued, and the Agala fled further north. Nemesis ensued in the Nigerian civil war, when the Ezza were chased back to Effium, which they had left some forty years earlier.

When the British reached north-eastern Igboland in 1905, the process of expansion and warfare was still continuing apace. The north-eastern Igbo were trying to cross the 'natural frontiers' where they existed. A group of Ikwo crossed the Cross River in 1896. The Ezza were trying to cross the Abonyi, and various groups of Ezza, Ikwo and Izzi border villages were locked in combat. The north-eastern Igbo clans won their victories mainly because of their large size. The clans were vastly greater than their Igbo neighbours, or the small non-Igbo tribes they displaced. By the turn of the twentieth century, the main direction of expansion was towards the west, and the Ezza were coming into conflict with various Nkanu clans, such as Amagunze. They continued to press in this direction, until the British marked the boundary with concrete pillars in 1923. Had the British not intervened, they might well have reached Enugu and beyond. The history of Ezza expansion is really the history of a colonising power, assimilating or displacing rival groups, and constantly enlarging its geographical and demographic scale. One can only speculate as to how far this enlarging of scale would have gone.

It is fairly certain that they would not have advanced much

further to the north. Decreasing rainfall made the area ever less favourable for yam cultivation. And further north lay a truly redoubtable foe, the Tiv, whose poisoned arrows the British found much more alarming than Dane guns.

Like other powers which aggrandise themselves by violent means, the Ezza paid a price for their conquests. They lived in constant fear of reprisals. A visiting party of Presbyterian missionaries, early this century, observed 'that the Ezza towns were strongly fortified with ramparts and ditches. The Ezzas themselves were usurpers, and lived as uneasy conquerors in constant fear of attack.'[56]

The constant experience of war tended to brutalise Ezza life. Duelling, with wooden swords, or pointed metal daggers, was endemic (a practice which is not yet dead in north-eastern Igboland). Sometimes contestants would tie themselves together, so that the one who lost his nerve first had to cut himself free. Often young men ran riot in the market, fighting mock battles and plundering the market stalls.[57] Robert Cudjoe was a Ghanaian who worked as a government interpreter at Abakaliki from 1909 to 1929, and thus had ample opportunity to observe the north-eastern Igbo. This was his description:

> The Ezzas were brave, cheerful and above all truthful, and they would face death smiling and laughing. In those Provincial Court days you would be surprised to see one, two, three or more Ezzas, charged with murder, shouting, in spite of very weak evidence for the prosecution, that they were ready to die. Fools, eh? A stranger may regard them so.[58]

WARFARE IN THE NSUKKA AREA: IGBO-IGALA CONFLICT

The histories of many northern Igbo communities vividly reflect an episode, or series of episodes, called 'the great Igala raid'. According to one authority, these traditions encapsulate a long series of encounters, over perhaps as long as five hundred years.[59] Certainly, the states of the Nsukka area were for centuries closely linked with Idah by trade, importing horses, and later, European products in return for textiles and slaves.

These traditions lay great emphasis on the achievements of a semi-legendary Igala hero who made his capital at Ogurugu, a town on the Anambra, on the Igbo-Igala frontier. It seems that the wars associated with his name were due, not to conflicts of economic interests, but to his desire to carve out a kingdom for himself. Probably his career belongs to the late eighteenth or early nineteenth centuries, when the Igala kingdom was at the summit of its power, and before external and internal challenges brought about a sudden and disastrous decline. The hero, Onoja Ogboni, is mentioned in Baikie's account of his 1854 Niger voyage, and the traditions specifically state that firearms were not used – which would suggest an eighteenth – rather than a nineteenth-century date.

Onoja Ogboni was apparently a member of the Igala royal family 'who was compelled to leave Idda, being too fond of thinking and acting for himself.'[60] Some of the traditions linked with him similarly suggest a restless ambition and original and inquiring mind, such as the obviously mythologised interpretation that 'He was strong and brave, and he thought he could go to heaven all by himself, so he built a ladder and climbed very high, but he fell down to earth again, because he was not so strong as the spirits.'[61] He built a defensive wall around his capital, Ogurugu, and raided as far afield as Opi. Igala traditions ascribe Igala victories to their superior equipment – horses, spears, and bows and arrows – *vis à vis* the Igbo, who fought with matchets.[62] A series of forts, stretching from Nsukka to Ogurugu, provide a tangible memorial of these conflicts. One is situated on the university campus at Nsukka, attributed by various traditions to the Igbo and to the Igala.[63]

In tradition, Onoja Ogboni is given the various attributes of a man larger than life – a giant, with six fingers and toes. His death was as spectacular as his life, 'for having contracted a painful disease and growing weary, he ordered his people to dig a great hole in which a house was built. All Onoja's properties were then placed inside and having entered himself he ordered his people to seal the doors and fill in the holes. There is a mound which marks this spot, but no stranger may see it.'[64]

Probably, the traditions reflect a very long period of Igbo-Igala relationships, characterised by close economic links and periodic wars, in which the Igala, with their larger political unit and their superior arms, had the best of it. Onoja Ogboni probably belongs to the latter period of this conflict, in the late eighteenth century, dominating the traditions through a strikingly distinctive personality, and the scale of his military achievements. Professor Shelton, the student of the Igbo-Igala borderland, believes that the Igala introduced a system of Igala-dominated religious cults in northern Igboland to perpetuate this dominance, a hypothesis which Igbo historians tend to find unacceptable: 'the Hamitic hypothesis in miniature'.[65] The theory – which assumes considerable naiveté on the part of the Igbo – is inherently unconvincing, and should, at the very least, have been established rather than assumed.

It is clear, in any event, that the tide of political and cultural influences flowed in two directions. In Igala, the highest official after the king is the Achadu, the head of the nine kingmakers, who holds his own court, has his own palace retainers, and is responsible for relations with the Igbo of the Nsukka area. The office is said to have originated with an Igbo, who was captured while hunting in Igala territory, and who in a career reminiscent of Ja Ja of Opobo rose from slavery to the second highest position in the kingdom.[66]

7 Social and Economic Change: The Growth of Social Polarisation

The key social and economic change in nineteenth-century Igboland was the decline of the external slave trade and the vast expansion in the export of palm products. In 1807, partly as the result of humanitarian agitation, and partly as a result of economic changes which made plantation slavery less profitable, the British parliament passed legislation prohibiting its own nationals from engaging in the slave trade. The institution of slavery, in British possessions, survived unchanged until 1833, and other nations were not, of course, necessarily affected. It was not until the 1830s that the export of slaves ceased at most Delta ports; the last slave ship finally sailed from Brass in 1854.[1]

European traders to the Delta were able to switch their shipping and commercial experience to the trade in palm oil, and later, palm kernels as well. The export of palm oil began towards the end of the eighteenth century. It had a great variety of uses in industrialising Europe, first as a lubricant, illuminant and fuel, and later in the vastly expanding soap industry, and in the new industry of margarine manufacture. For Igboland the processing of palm products for export did not involve any new techniques – palm oil was one of the staple ingredients of the Igbo diet. It did involve an enormous expansion of the quantity of production, and a vast multiplication of laborious, tedious and time-consuming processes. Four-hundred palm kernels must be carefully cracked to produce a pound in weight. By the end of the nineteenth century, Igboland was annually exporting kernels which were measured in thousands of tons.

Not all of Igboland was in a position to participate in the new economic activity. Not all of Igboland was within the palm oil belt – oil palms diminish rapidly north of a line between Onitsha and Afikpo.[2] Palm oil was not, like slaves, self-transporting.

Local producers carried oil in calabashes for miles to the bulking centres on navigable waterways, but much of Igboland was prohibited by lack of transport from participating.

The palm-oil trade catapulted some Igbo states into great prosperity. Oguta was a case in point, linked to both the Niger and the Delta by navigable waterways, and lying to the south of a rich area of oil palms, which almost cover the rolling hills of Ihiala, Okija and Ozubulu. Towns in southern Igboland, like Azumini or Akwete, lying on the lower, navigable, stretches of its rivers, became major palm-oil markets. But it was not a prosperity that was widely distributed and shared.

The key to an understanding of Igbo social history in the nineteenth century is a realisation of the fact that the growth of the palm-oil trade, and the decline of the external export of slaves, did not mean that the slave trade ceased to exist in Igboland. The long centuries of the trans-Atlantic slave trade had created patterns of behaviour which did not cease to exist when the external stimulus which created them died. States such as Nike or Arondizuogu, which had grown wealthy by slave trading, were prevented by geography from switching to trade in palm oil. Capturing slaves was easier, more exciting, and more profitable than squeezing palm oil by hand or cracking thousand upon thousands of palm kernels. But the decline in slave exports meant that the slaves had to be absorbed, either in the Delta, or in Igboland. Slaves became cheaper, and their number increased vastly. Their increasing number worsened the social distortions which the slave trade had created. Paradoxically, the evil heritage of the trade in slaves became most evident after, internationally, it was abolished.

IGBO SLAVES IN THE DELTA

There was a tremendous influx of Igbo slaves into the Delta in the nineteenth century. The Kalabari states developed elaborate techniques for acculturating their new accessions,[3] but in the other Delta states the Igbo influx had a very marked effect on society. In Bonny, Ubani was almost replaced by Igbo, and most foreign observers assumed the state was Igbo in origin.[4] A visitor to Calabar in 1853 'was informed by the missionaries that more than half the population were Ibos.'[5] In the island state of Okrika, on the southern fringes of Igboland, 'only a few of the free-born' were ignorant of Igbo.[6] In 1895 it was stated that 'The Brass tribes are a mixed race, recruited largely by the purchase of slaves from . . . chiefly the Igbo people, living inland, and by domestic slaves born in their families.'[7] And in 1905 a missionary wrote of 'the members of the Igbo tribe, who form the chief inhabitants of the Niger Delta.'[8]

In Bonny, these slaves carried out the work involved in collecting palm oil from the inland markets. They were the 'pulla-boys' who paddled the great trade canoes, and transferred the oil from calabashes to casks. Some of them were responsible for the actual bargaining – an occupation in which a man of ability could rise, in time, to real prosperity and power.

After the C.M.S. established a post at Bonny in 1865, many became Christians. Some were persecuted for their faith: they include Nigeria's first martyr, Joshua Hart. Like the early Christians, they combined their secular avocations – trade in the markets of southern Igboland – with the preaching of the Gospel.[9] They were the first evangelists of southern Igboland.

Köler commented on the economic distinctions among the Bonny slaves. Those employed as traders by their masters had a higher standard of living, and a real opportunity to accumulate wealth. But the majority – those employed in manual labour, such as paddling – lacked these opportunities. Köler describes their pathetic attempts to accumulate capital, selling pineapples or bananas to a European trader, or collecting the occasional dash.[10]

The slaves of Calabar were largely engaged in the plantation cultivation of oil palms, and thus cut off completely from even these meagre opportunities for betterment. 'The very lowest class is composed of those recently arrived from some interior country, or living continually in the "bush" without opportunities of raising themselves; cut off from European Intercourse and Trade.[11] Interestingly enough, when a revolutionary movement developed in the Delta, it was among these Calabar plantation slaves. It developed as a protest, not against their economic exploitation, but against the worst form of social oppression which slavery engendered, human sacrifice. When Delta rulers died, holocausts of slaves were expended at their funerals. (There is a photo in the Fombo papers[12] which mirrors this extreme form of social polarisation; it shows in the background King George Pepple's country residence, and in the foreground, Ikuba's temple of human skulls.) This was the form of exploitation which the slaves of Calabar united to combat.

In late 1850, and early 1851, they formed a society, the Blood Men, cemented by bonds of ritual, and designed to oppose 'encroachment and oppression' in general, and human sacrifice in particular. They came to the town in armed bands, alarming the ruling élite, who arrested some of their number. The slaves still on the plantations retaliated effectively by seizing their property there, until their comrades were released.[13]

The Blood Men did not seek the radical transformation of society, or the abolition of slave status. Theirs was essentially a peaceful movement with a clearly defined and limited end, which they were completely successful in attaining, and which enlisted the support of 'many free and half free people.' To their lasting discredit, the British trading community opposed it vehemently.[14]

The Blood Men won a victory over human sacrifice. The polarisation of Delta society into a westernised bourgeoisie, with a high standard of living and a proletariat of pullaboys and plantation workers, continued. Many observers commented on the high standard of living of the Delta élite in the nineteenth century, with their 'large wooden corrugated-iron-roofed houses . . . the rooms expensively fitted up with furniture of European manufacture; cupboards stored with decanters, glasses, etc., large pier-glasses on the walls . . .'[15] Rather fewer were aware of the social base which supported it. Here is a description of Calabar, written in 1904, by a Catholic missionary:

> I have visited a number of farms, or 'Pindis'. They are full of Ibos. These poor Ibos, so numerous, have furnished all the slaves of Calabar, Bonny, Brass etc. . . . And so all the chiefs have one, two or three storeyed houses, furnished like chateaux in Europe. Port, malaga wine, champagne, brandy, and elaborate pastries adorn the tables of these *gentlemen*. But on the other hand, how much misery there is among these unfortunate Ibos, who form two thirds of the population of Duke Town.[16]

JA JA OF AMAIGBO AND OPOBO

Several of the Igbos who were brought to the Delta as slaves showed an astonishing ability to triumph over circumstances.

Of these, the most celebrated, and the most outstanding, was Ja Ja of Opobo, who was probably the greatest Igbo of his time.

The man whom history knows as Ja Ja (his full name was Jubo Jubogha) was an Nkwerre man, born in Amaigbo village group, in what later became Orlu Division, in *c.* 1821. He was sold into slavery, apparently for cutting his top teeth first (a phenomenon which Igbo communities regarded as non-normal, and therefore sinister).[17] In Bonny, he joined the lowest rank of slave society, comprising those born outside Bonny. As a youth, he paddled the trade canoes.[18] It was unusual for such a slave to make the transition to trading, but Ja Ja managed it. Through his ability and honesty he prospered to such an extent that when his master died in 1863, he was elected the new head of his House. He reformed the finances of the House, but his success aroused jealousies, and he became involved in disputes with other Bonny Houses. Rather than involve his followers in a bloody civil war, he decided to leave Bonny altogether. He conducted a masterly and bloodless withdrawal, to a brilliantly chosen site at the mouth of the Imo River. At a stroke, he cut Bonny off from her commercial empire. His House followed him to a man in this venture into the unknown, and several European traders risked their livelihood to do likewise.[19]

For eighteen years, from 1869 to 1887, Ja Ja ruled the sovereign state of Opobo. In successive treaties, the British recognised both his sovereignty, and his exclusive rights over his trading empire. He built up excellent relations with his Igbo and Ibibio oil suppliers, which he strengthened with judicious marriages, and the use of religious symbolism.[20] He armed his followers with modern rifles. Deeply attached to traditional religion, he was hostile to missions, but not to education.[21] He sent one of his sons to Glasgow to be educated, and set up a secular school in Opobo, under the tutelage of a remarkable black American, Emma White. Emma White, born in Kentucky of slave parents, left the States to settle in West Africa, ultimately coming to Opobo, where she changed her name to Emma Ja Ja.[22] Ja Ja invited distinguished *dibia* from Igboland to his court, gathering around him, in Professor Dike's phrase, the illustrious Igbos of his generation.[23]

But in the 1880s the clouds of imperialism began to darken.

There was a trade depression in England, and white traders thought – mistakenly as it proved – that they would increase their profits by dispensing with Ja Ja's middle-man role. In 1884, like other Delta rulers, Ja Ja signed a treaty accepting British 'protection'. Unlike other Delta rulers, he first obtained a written assurance that his sovereignty was not diminished. 'I write as you request, with reference to the word "Protectorate" as used in the proposed Treaty, that the Queen does not want to take your country or your markets.'[24] But the pressure on Ja Ja continued. The acting Vice-Consul, Harry Johnston, egged on by the European trading community, was anxious to advance his career by the spectacular feat of overthrowing Ja Ja. Ja Ja sent a deputation to London – which was ignored – to plead his treaty rights. He would have gone himself, had he not been prevented by religious taboos. Finally he began to transfer his resources to the Igbo interior.[25] One can only speculate as to the way in which his well-armed followers and charismatic leadership might have transformed the history of Igbo resistance to colonial rule.

On 18 September 1887, eighteen years almost to the day after his withdrawal from Bonny, Johnston invited Ja Ja on board the gun-boat *Goshawk* for a discussion of their differences, promising him a safe conduct.

> I have summoned you to attend in a friendly spirit. I hereby assure you that whether you accept or reject my proposals tomorrow, no restraint whatever will be put on you. You will be free to go as soon as you have heard the message of the Government . . . If you attend tomorrow I pledge you my word that you will be free to come and go . . .[26]

Ja Ja never returned alive to Opobo. He was taken first to the Gold Coast, but such was the power of his personality, that Johnston still saw him as a danger to the British presence in the Delta, even in captivity.[27] At Johnston's insistence, he was deported to the West Indies, like so many of his Igbo fellow-countrymen in the past. He bore himself in exile with a truly kingly dignity and magnanimity. When he died in 1891, his people gladly paid the cost of repatriating his body, and spent his enormous fortune on giving him a royal funeral.

SOCIAL POLARISATION IN IGBOLAND: THE SLAVES

In Igboland, as in the Delta, the ending of the trans-Atlantic slave trade meant that slaves became cheap and abundant. The number of slaves owned increased, especially in communities which had played an important role in the slave trade. Slaves were accumulated, partly as a status symbol. Bishop Crowther observed in the late 1850s that 'Accumulation of slaves at Abo . . . to show how wealthy they are . . . is the prevailing ambition of the people.'[28] In Ossomari, the slave population far outnumbered the freeborn, and Ossomari's historian paints a grim picture of social oppression and human waste:

> Each trader used to possess a couple of hundred slaves. Sometimes those traders became so intoxicated with their possessions that two members of one family, nay, brothers, could pitch a battle between themselves for the purpose of wasting their slaves . . . At that time of the slave trade, very few Ossomari people, if at all, were farmers.[29]

In the early 1950s, Professor Horton carried out fieldwork in Nike, a village group which had had a large slave population, drawn apparently from the Agbaja area. He found that the surviving impact of slavery on custom was so great that the freeborn refused to engage in many of the normal operations of farm work, such as clearing the ground, preparing yam heaps, or cutting wood. They regarded these occupations as unsuitable for the freeborn, and delegated them to hired migrant labourers, although this meant that a substantial proportion of their income went on wages.[30]

A more sinister result of the increasing cheapness and abundance of slaves was the expansion of human sacrifice. *Haaba*, the oracle of the Aguinyi village group, was honoured initially with chickens and goats, but later, with sacrifices of human beings.[31] The expansion of human sacrifice is especially well documented in the case of Asaba, where each *Eze* had to sacrifice two men at his accession, and two more at his death. Originally Asaba had one *Eze*, and then half a dozen. In the nineteenth century, their numbers increased vastly. A missionary who came to Asaba in 1874 wrote in 1879 that the number of *Eze* title holders had increased during his stay from about 200 to about 500.[32] Strong men would pursue the slaves in the special slave camps each quarter possessed. The practice is still reflected in the ritual for the second burial of a titled man, as the iron gong, *akaja*, sings *choga ugwule, choga ugwule* (go for a slave, go for a slave).[33] Not all slaves lived in separate villages or quarters. It was a paradox, to which the history of the Delta provides parallels, that whereas slaves were subject to the ultimate disability of sacrifice, they sometimes enjoyed a standard of living little different from their masters, and a reasonable degree of economic mobility. 'Some of the old slaves', observed Crowther on the Niger in the 1850s,' have themselves become owners of a large property and many slaves.'[34] This economic mobility of slaves is strikingly illustrated in Mazi Igwegbe's history of Arondizuogu. But the civic disabilities always remained; for a slave there was no marriage with the freeborn, no titles, no second burial – and no forgetfulness, among those surrounding him, of his servile origins. The reality of his situation is reflected in a story told in Ibagwa:

> In Ibagwa there was once a man called Nju Olieme who owned a slave in Ugwogo. This slave was very rich, and in turn owned many slaves himself. One day he was sitting with Nju in Ibagwa when he challenged his master to a counting of possessions in order to see which of them was the wealthiest. After counting his own, he said to his master, 'Now do you count yours, and I am willing to swear that they cannot exceed mine.' Nju Olieme replied, 'There is no need for me to count: you have already counted three parts of my possessions for me, as all your own are mine.'[35]

Slave responses to social oppression

Like the Blood Men of Calabar, the slaves of the Igbo interior sometimes rebelled against oppression. The most obvious form of protest was flight, a mode of action which was more difficult than would appear. When I was conducting my fieldwork on the subject in Asaba, I asked my informant why the slaves waited to be sacrificed, and why so few attempted to escape. He pointed out the difficulty of escape to a distant homeland, the perils of inter-town travel, which we have noted before, and the social organisation of the slave camps. Slaves were organised by the 'trusty' system. They had their own headmen, whose status exempted them from sacrifice, and who therefore co-operated closely with the status quo. Conversely, a slave who tried to escape and was caught, was certain to be next on the list for sacrifice . . .

But in the middle years of the nineteenth century, a number of Niger slave communities voted against their status with their feet. It seems that the ideological stimulus for protest came from the British members of Niger expeditions, who made a point of telling slaves that their brethren in other lands had been emancipated. In the western Igbo town of Abarra Uno, 'many of the domestic slaves became restive and began to assert their independence.' A large body of them left the town, and founded an independent settlement at Abarra Ogada, a move in which their former owners acquiesced, aware 'that the task of recapturing a large and united body of slaves would be one of magnitude.'[36] The same thing happened in Ossomari: 'Ossomari people never forget how some of their slaves rebelled when the British came and announced the abolition of slavery.'[37] There was a whole series of slave migrations from Ossomari, in the nineteenth century. The first groups, in about the beginning of the last century or earlier' migrated to Okpolodum Creek, and to a site three or four miles south of Ossomari, respectively. A later group, interestingly enough, crossed the Niger to Abarra. Finally, in colonial times, there was a catastrophic migration of slaves from the town, in 1928, which permanently reduced Ossomari to the shadow of its former self.[38]

THE OGARANYA

'All persons of some property', wrote Crowther in the 1850s, are called *Ogaranyan.*'[39] *Ogaranya* was not a title, it was a description of a social and economic class. The name was not universal in Igboland, but the social reality was.

The *ogaranya* was distinguished by his many wives, children and slaves.[40] He could afford guns for the defence of his compound. As in other societies, money generated money. He could afford to establish the links which made inter-town travel and trade possible. Lesser men travelled and traded under the umbrella of his protection. Inevitably, he attracted clients, young men who would serve him, and be ultimately rewarded with a wife, yams, or capital for trade. In an age of economic expansion, this bourgeoisie expanded, equally. All local histories describe them. Thus, in Item,

> a man's wealth depended on the number of his slaves. There were three important slave owners in Item. The first was Igwe Okpo of Okoko who had over four hundred slaves. Another person was Mpo Oriaku of Amokwe Item. Mpo was a well known native doctor who made war charms. He who obtained his charms paid for them with captives who became the doctor's slaves. He also had over four hundred slaves. The third person was another doctor, Ofia Egbichi of Amokwe Item, who also made war charms and received war captives in return. He also had more than four hundred slaves.[41]

Slave dealers in Arondizuogu would keep the strongest slaves for their own service, and sell the rest. They, too, had all the trappings of affluence: 'Some important men in Aro-Ndizuogu used to marry 20–40 wives . . . The important personalities from Aros are recognised by their high robes and usually have in their Company four orderlys and each with a double barrelled gun.'[42]

Their wealth and prestige meant that the *ogaranya* tended to acquire strong informal political power. In Naze, near Owerri, the *ogaranya* 'wielded great influence internally and externally. They acted as the generalissimo in wars because they provided the bulk of the money with which the wars were prosecuted.' One of them, Nnodim Odu Obashi, acquired such prestige, by bearing the cost of a successful war with Egbu, that he became accepted as Naze's king.[43]

The economic expansion of the eighteenth and nineteenth centuries meant that the number and wealth of the *ogaranya* apparently increased. The technological limits of the society, and its restricted imports of consumer goods, meant it difficult to divert this prosperity into productive investments, or into luxury. Therefore, the prosperous tended to value wealth largely as a source of prestige and influence. Hence the accumulation of clients and dependents, and hence the expansion of the custom of purchasing titles. The purchase of titles was valued both as an investment and as a way of formalising and legitimising the link between wealth and political influence. We have already noted the expansion of the title system at Asaba. G. I. Jones describes the same process at work elsewhere:

> The title societies of the Northern and Central Ibo can be seen as a development of this principle of awarding titles on the basis of wealth in response to the increased wealth of the area. More people in a community were able to obtain titles and they formed themselves into associations to regulate the taking of these local titles.[44]

He points out that groups which lacked title societies tended, nonetheless, to evolve in the same direction. Some secret societies, like the Okonko society, involved the payment of heavy fees. Even the Izzi, who have neither secret societies nor titles, and are ruled by their eldest men, adopted the same principle, for only the elders who have killed a cow, and thus become *Isi Nze*, speak with authority. The Ekpeya, and other Ikwerri groups, were ruled by their senior age-grades, but admission to the age-grades depended on the payment of heavy entrance fees.

THE NEW MEN

One of the most strikingly recurrent themes in the history of various Igbo communities in the nineteenth century concerns the emergence of New Men. Outside the inherited structures of Igbo political life, they seize eminence and authority, either in consequence of their wealth, or sometimes in consequence of their military exploits and bravado. It is difficult to know to what extent this is truly a nineteenth-century phenomenon – the result of circumstances such as the insecurity bred by the slave trade, and the increasing circulation of wealth in the society – and to what extent it had existed earlier in the past. The recent past always looms large in oral traditions, and the figures of Igboland's nineteenth-century history doubly so, for the imposition of colonial rule was destined shortly to shatter that history's continuity.

Probably, each period of Igbo history produced men of this type. Agave, the founder of Aguleri's first royal dynasty was possibly an example. Nnebisi certainly was – a man of the seventeenth century from Nteje, who overcame the handicap of slave descent, enriched himself by trading in slaves and ivory, and overcame all opposition to become the ruler of the new state of Asaba.[45]

The traditions of almost any nineteenth-century Igbo community provide examples of careers of this type. One tradition states clearly that it was a time of changing political forms, when the rule of elders was undermined by the rule of the wealthy and powerful.

> Before the whiteman came, the people of the clan themselves started to make political changes within the clan. The lineages were formerly headed by the *ony'isi*. These lost much of their political power at this period. What mattered more to the people were wealth and influence.[46]

The pattern developed in every part of Igboland, among states that were rich, and states that were relatively poor. Alor, for instance, is a village group fifteen miles from Onitsha, which struggles with the problem of inadequate and eroding land. In pre-colonial times, its people eked out an income by wood carving, trading and palm-wine tapping. A section of the community, however, grew rich by trading in slaves. One of them, Okwunanne Udogu, progressed from slave trading to slave raiding, in alliance with an Aro man who arranged for the slaves' transport from the area.[47] The history of the wealthy state of Arondizuogu provides similar examples of robber barons:

> Nwankwo Okoro was the first son of Okoro Idozuka . . . At the age of 21 he joined his father on slave-trade . . . He killed anybody who came across his way . . . He once said 'I must visit any town that crosses my way and nothing will prevent me from attacking them with my great troops.' . . . By collecting slaves and war-captives he was able to build a very large family.

When the British came, they made him a Warrant Chief.[48]

Many men in towns on the Niger had careers of this type. In the middle third of the nineteenth century, they were exposed to a revolutionary situation. For the first time, they came into direct contact with representatives of a different culture – European and Sierra Leonian missionaries, traders, and so on. The situation encouraged the rise of the independent minded, courageous and enterprising. Ogbuanyinya Idigo of Aguleri is a classic example, but his career belongs rather to the story of Christianity in Igboland, and will be considered in that context. Another is Obi Igweli of Asaba. In theory, the only men who could take titles in Asaba were those who could establish their Asaba descent. Igweli came not only from outside Asaba, but even from outside Igboland; his father was a hunter from Ishan. Yet he succeeded in taking the *Eze* title, and built up such wealth and influence, in the first phase of European trade, that visitors to Asaba invariably regarded him as Asaba's king.[49]

The rise of the New Men was not necessarily linked with wealth. Njoku Chita was the greatest Ezza warrior of his day. Born of poor parents, he did not limit his energies to the wars of his own martial village of Idembia, but flung himself exuberantly into any Ezza conflict, and became famed for his daring and panache. Tall, fair complexioned and handsome, he was a splendid marksman. He never opened a gate into a garden, but always jumped the fence. His qualities had their own disadvantages in Ezza life, for he was turbulent and lawless, and often ready to disregard custom and convention. It is said that when he wanted to replace the leather scabbard of his dagger, he held a bull immobile and cut a new one from the living hide. The advent of the British was the first event ever to overawe him.

The story has rather a sad sequel. His son, Akirike Njoku, was put to death for his lawlessness, by his fellow clansmen, in the 1920s, 'a son who wanted to live the life of his father in an age that was increasingly turning its back to barbarism and destruction.'[50]

Aguinyi traditions, which repeatedly stress the violence and disorder of the nineteenth century, describe it as a time when bandits were praised as heroes. They relate that a man from Obeledu blamed his fellow townsmen for their refusal to 'swallow smaller snakes so as to grow richer'.

> Then he accused them of blocking his way when he tried to do so. Finally he pronounced his famous curse of equality on the whole people. 'I tried to grow rich, you refused. I told you to grow rich, you refused. From henceforth, all of you will be

equal.' Then he hit his *ofo* on the ground, packed his belongings, and went back to his mother's kindred at Igbo-Ukwu.[51]

IMPORTS AND EXPORTS

Igbo communities had very little control over the goods they exported or the goods they imported. Igboland's exports were determined by the needs of Europe. One man pointed out to the British that moral exhortations about the slave trade were inappropriate, for it had been imposed on the Igbo from without: 'If White people give up buying, Black people will give up selling slaves'.[52] Nguru traditions reflect how successive economic phases were imposed on Igbo communities:

> It was at Aro where we were told that slaves could be sold . . . People who could not farm either because they had no yams or because they hadn't enough land often started trading . . . The major trade then was to sell slaves or to carry mats to Igwenga and Igweocha for sale . . . Later on we learnt from our customers at Igwenga [Opobo] that we could bring oil and sell. Then we started preparing oil for sale to them.[53]

From the 1830s on, Igboland could obtain imports from abroad only in return for palm products. Palm products were of the greatest value in Europe's industrialisation. Had they ceased to be of value, she would have ceased to import them. This never happened, but sometimes other sources of edible oil became cheaper, and then the prices paid to Igbo producers fell accordingly. And the mechanical processes by which oil was produced were not of a kind to build up skills within the society.

Similarly, Igboland had little control over her imports. Without first-hand knowledge of Europe, African merchants were restricted in their choice to what Europeans chose to offer them. Often, as we have noted, the quality was poor. The arms were often obsolete (obsolete arms could often be bought up cheaply in Europe) and sometimes they exploded in their users' hands. Textiles were cheap and shoddy – and sometimes fraudulently mismeasured as well. The British themselves were well aware of these defects; the Niger Coast Protectorate Annual Report for 1896–7 observed 'I am afraid that during the year no marked improvement has been made on the quality of the goods in question, and as long as the native will take an inferior class of goods so long will the European merchants import them.'[54] This was in the Delta. The same observation was made of the Royal Niger Company: 'The Company import what manufactured goods they choose, and practically impose them upon the native, who has a very limited and inferior class of articles from which to select.'[55]

By the end of the nineteenth century, imports were overwhelmingly dominated by alcohol.[56] In Nembe-Brass, gin accounted for 90 per cent of all imports. In 1896–7, the Niger Coast Protectorate had an income of £151,244 from import duties; £116,320 of this was on trade spirits. In 1899, liquor accounted for 90 per cent of its customs revenue. Most of it was manufactured in Scheidam, Holland by the firm of Wilhelm Hasekamp and Co. A label from one of their schnapps bottles shows the exchange – ivory and palm products in return for gin.

The large scale of liquor imports is surprising. Many observers commented on the sobriety of the Igbo and other southern Nigerians, and a Commission appointed in 1909 accumulated a vast amount of evidence to confirm it. The depreciation of Igboland's currencies meant that liquor was a useful – albeit fragile – way of accumulating wealth. They were used in festivities such as second burials, but palm wine and locally made gin were equally suitable. Dr Ofonagoro makes the interesting suggestion that schnapps was valued because of the astonishing array of health-giving properties promised on the label (advantages still extolled, in much more moderate language, on bottles of Hasekamp schnapps sold in Nigeria today). Lacking medical services, Nigerians put pathetic confidence in these promises. The same spirit, in modern Nigeria, sustains an unbelievable number of patent medicine stalls. Anyone who lives in Nigeria knows members of an older generation who have an unquenchable confidence in the health-giving properties of schnapps, milk of magnesium, mentholatum, and epsom salts.

ECONOMIC TAKE-OFF – FOR WHOM?

We have noted how the slave trade helped generate capital for Europe's industrialisation, and how the markets it provided gave a valuable impetus to England's textile manufacturing.

The profits of the palm oil trade also made an economic take-off possible. It was not, needless to say, a take-off for the palm oil producer. The palm oil producers of the 1970s still cannot afford to send their children to secondary school, and die rather than go to hospitals whose fees they know they have no hope of paying . . .

But for the expatriate firms which bought palm oil on the Niger and in the Delta in the nineteenth century, the trade proved the means for an almost magical transformation of their fortunes. John Holt came to West Africa on a salary of a hundred pounds a year in 1862.[57] The firm he founded flourished enormously. Between 1901 and 1907, its capital multiplied 'five times or more'. Finally in 1969 it was absorbed in the Lonrho complex. The other firms involved turned to combination much earlier. The firms of the African Association, in 1896, paid a dividend of 3 per cent 'with difficulty'. They were badly undercapitalised, and some of them went bankrupt. In 1918, they were paying 20 per cent plus a bonus dividend, and founders' shares paid more. Then they joined with other groups to form the African and Eastern combine. In 1919, its turnover was over twenty-two million pounds, and it paid a dividend of 32 per cent on ordinary shares.[58]

But a more astonishing case of economic take-off can be found in the history of the Niger Company. In the 1870s, four small European firms were struggling to buy palm oil on the Niger. A shareholder in the smallest, which was in great financial difficulty, was the man whom history knows as Sir George Goldie. First he combined the competitors into a single firm. Then he obtained from the British government a Charter to govern, which enabled him to exclude all new competitors. This enabled him to offer the Niger oil producers what prices and what goods he chose. The Company paid for produce, not with cash, but with cheques usable only in the Company shops. If the goods the producer wanted were not available, he had to wait till they were – which meant that the local people gave the Royal Niger Company interest-free credit. Each year the company bought palm produce worth £200,000 in Europe at the cost of £35,000 worth of goods.* When it finally lost its charter,

* Administrative costs must be subtracted from the profit.

it received £865,000 compensation, plus valuable mineral concessions.[59]

Ultimately, both the African and Eastern and the Niger Company joined the gigantic Unilever complex.

The economic history of southern Nigeria reminds one irresistibly of Matthew 13:12, 'For to him who has will more be given, and he will have abundance; but from him who has not, even what he has shall be taken away.'

8 The History of Ideas: The Igbos' Perception of their Changing World

No aspect of Igbo history is more difficult to recover than the history of ideas.[1] Oral traditions tell us much about external events, but little about how events were perceived by the protagonists. Accounts written by foreign observers tell us much about their own responses, but relatively little about the attitudes of those they encountered, whom, in any case, they lacked the linguistic and other skills to understand.

In the middle years of the nineteenth century, Igboland was surrounded by an inexorably rising tide of alien encroachment.[2] One can isolate a few landmarks. In 1830, the Lander brothers travelled down the Niger, from Badagry to the Delta. Henceforward, Europeans knew that the Delta was the gateway to the Niger. In 1849, Britain appointed a consul to a large area of West Africa, including the Delta. Soon his sphere of action was narrowed to the Delta. He lived on the island of Fernando Po, but took an active part in Delta affairs, and increasingly undermined the sovereignty of its rulers. In 1854, a naval physician led an expedition up the Niger which, for the first time, escaped deaths from sickness due to the use of quinine. Henceforward, the Niger stood open to commercial enterprise.

In 1857, the C.M.S. established the first mission post in Igboland, at Onitsha, and a Birkenhead trader established the first trading posts, at Onitsha and Aboh. In the sixties and seventies, the number of mission posts grew gradually – a number of stations in the Delta and in a handful of Niger Igbo towns, among them Asaba and Ossomari. Several competing British firms struggled on the Niger for palm oil; by the end of the seventies, they had posts in nine Niger Igbo communities. All the missionaries, and almost all the Niger traders, were Christian Africans from Sierra Leone, often of Igbo origin. Missionaries and traders were, of course, strongly aware of their differences, but to the Niger Igbo communities there was little distinction to be made between them. 'To them as we are all book people and come from the whitemen's country, we have the same interest one with another.'[3]

From the middle eighties a number of important changes occurred; the process of colonial conquest began, and two quasi-colonial administrations were established, one on the Niger and one in the Delta. We shall see in the next chapter how the Igbo people resisted this conquest. The growth of colonialism was mirrored in other spheres. There was a white takeover in the C.M.S. Niger Mission, which darkened the last years of its saintly Bishop, Samuel Ajayi Crowther. There was a parallel takeover in the trading firms, as well as an amalgamation between them. Two new mission societies entered the field, both Catholic.

The question which confronts us now is, how did the Igbo regard these changes? A tiny handful of Igbo communities were directly affected, most were not. Ryder, in his learned and perceptive study of Benin history, suggests that the expansion of human sacrifice there in the nineteenth century was partly a response to 'growing hostile pressure from without', which encouraged 'a terrible elaboration of . . . supernatural powers.'[4]

How did the Igbo perceive and respond to the changes that were occurring in their world? The evidence is contradictory. When individual missionaries visited towns in the interior, they were given an urbane and hospitable welcome (until the eighties, they were men of African descent – *oyibo oji*, black Europeans, the Igbo called them – which reduced the extent of culture shock).[5] When John Christopher Taylor visited Nsugbe in 1857, a leading citizen 'thanked God that he saw what his forefathers had not seen. They had long *heard* of *Oibo*, but today they were satisfied with what they have *seen*.'[6]

But Igbo communities' recollections of the experience of military conquest mirror what was evidently a traumatic experience. The most horrifying element was the vast difference between the firearms Europeans had sold them and the firearms which were now used against them. The first encounter with strangers (the missionaries had visited only a handful of towns, near the Niger or the Delta) produced great culture shock. To the Igbo, their invaders lacked almost all the charac-

1 *a* Prehistoric pottery from Afikpo
b Manilla-shaped ninth-century object from Igbo-Ukwu
c Ninth-century bronze shell from Igbo-Ikwu, with a pattern of flies

2 *a* The first Igbo portrait: detail of a ninth-century bronze from Igbo-Ikwu. Note the *ichi* facial scars

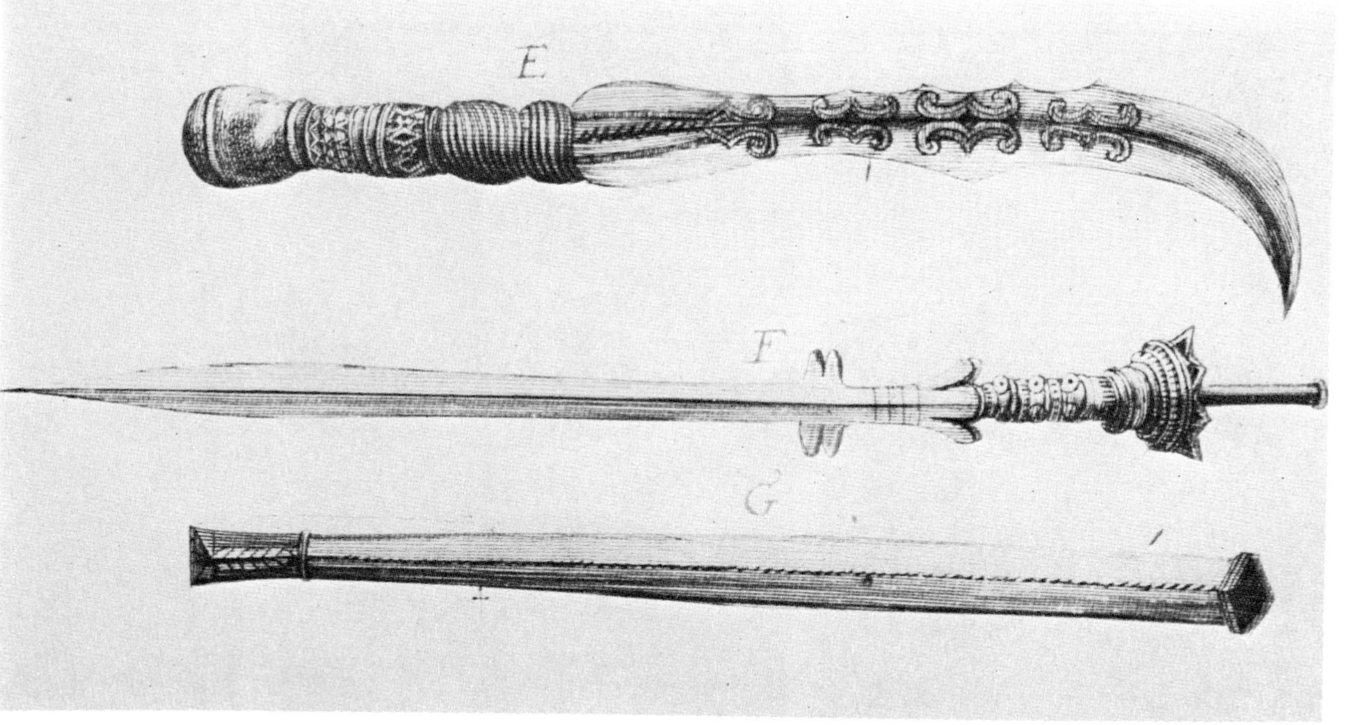

3 Seventeenth-century swords manufactured in Igboland

4 Pestle and mortar thought to have been used by Akumenyi and Ezekuna, at Amara, Ezza

5 *a* Nineteenth-century clay tower in Awka, photographed in the 1950s

5 *b* The coming of the white man: a symbolic representation from an Mbari house

6 *a* Eighteenth-century Igbo : Olaudah Equiano, c. 1745-97
b Nineteenth-century Igbo : King Ja Ja of Amaigbo and Opobo, c. 1821-91

7 Some pioneers of Igbo Catholicism: centre front, Bishop Shanahan; right front, the future Bishop John Anyogu; back row, second from left, the future Father Cyprian Tansi, O.C.S.O.

8 Exodus, 1966: one of a series of twelve paintings depicting the flight of Igbos from the north, by Uzo Egonu

teristics they regarded as distinctively human.[7] Some found white complexions repellent, because of the association with leprosy. The Ezza seem to have been particularly struck by the fact that they wore their toes in parcels! The British, of course, also suffered from this kind of culture shock, and reciprocated, but these attitudes are too well documented in the annals of colonial Africa to need exemplification here. The death of Dr Stewart, a white doctor travelling by bicycle in Mbaise in 1905, was a classic example of this cultural incomprehension. Before he was killed, the Ahiara people took him to their neighbours to show them *what* they had caught.[8] A village group in Okigwi relates that they fled when the British came, because 'Who knew *what* they were?'[9] Dr Stewart was killed because he lacked most of the characteristics the Igbo viewed as human. He was non-normal, and therefore, abominable. Before the Europeans first reached Akokwa, an Akokwa daughter, sold into slavery for cutting her top teeth first, 'came from her master and warned our father not to be afraid of the European. She described him as a man without toes, with entire body covered with clothes and was as white as a new born baby.'[10]

The response of Igbo groups to their first direct encounter with the invader is better documented than their concept of their situation when the Europeans were still at the frontiers of Igboland. The traditions, on the whole, reflect a growing sense of malaise and apprehension, becoming more immediate as the process of colonial invasion went on. 'There were often strange news in those days about whitemen coming majestically and victoriously with their soldiers policemen servants and fighting implements from the south eastern direction of the town.'[11]

In periods of rapid change, prophetic movements often arise. Several such movements are recorded in nineteenth-century Igboland, and further research may well bring more examples to light.

In 1864, some seven years after the establishment of the first Christian mission at Onitsha, a prophet arose in the Onitsha hinterland called Odesoruelu, which missionaries translated as Restorer of the Primitive Style.[12] We do not know where his base was, but his emissaries visited a number of towns within a ten-mile radius of Onitsha, including Obosi, Nkwelle, Nsugbe, Ogbunike and Ogidi,[13] though they did not visit Onitsha itself, because 'Beke is there'. Odesoruelu protested against the rise in food prices which the foreign presence on the Niger brought. The smallpox epidemic of 1864 gave an added point to his appeal for a restoration of the old way of life, and for a general rise in moral standards. Towns were to lay down their arms and give up their wars, and every village was to keep its pathways clean.

Ewenihi of Aguinyi was a mid-nineteenth-century prophet who attempted to understand events rather than to change them. 'We were told that he travelled to all places telling the people about the future. He was said to have foretold the coming of the whiteman, telling the people that he "saw them white and reflecting in the wilderness" and that they would usurp the children of the clan.' He foretold the colonial era's unprecedented escalation of land values, when those who were interested in land must look for 20,000 cowries. He foretold the loss of sovereignty, saying that those who were involved in internal political disputes were quarrelling over another's property. He foretold a revolution in religious belief and practice, and the decline of the old gods. The gods would be left to starve to death, and those that survived would have hot oil thrown in their eyes.[14]

CHANGES OF HEART

We have had occasion repeatedly to observe the various forms of social oppression, such as human sacrifice, existing in Igbo society, which were, in the view of the present writer, largely the consequence of the trans-Atlantic slave trade. Her colonial invaders used these injustices as an apologia for their own conquests. The British, in fact, established a colonial government in southern Nigeria in an endeavour to protect and defend their own economic interests. They preferred to interpret their actions, on occasion, as a crusade against slave trading, human sacrifice, and so on.

This suggests an interesting question: do we have any evidence that Igbo communities were contemplating the reform of these abuses from within? The history of social reform in most countries is the history of a progressive enlightenment of conscience. An early eighteenth-century English Evangelical sang hymns as he walked on the quarter-deck of his slave ship. His nineteenth-century successor devoted the best energies of his life to the abolition of slavery. To the early eighteenth-century Russian nobleman, his serfs were an inheritance and a form of property. To many noblemen of the middle decades of the nineteenth century, the ownership of serfs had become an intolerable affront to conscience.

There is some evidence that in the Igbo communities most affected by missionary teachings this kind of enlightenment was already taking place. We have seen how the news of the emancipation of the West Indian slaves gave some Niger Igbo slave communities the impetus to seek their own freedom. Similarly, Christian teachings of the love of one's neighbour began to undermine the worst forms of social oppression. Missionaries observed in Asaba, in the 1870s, that titled men were turning against human sacrifice, which was supported mainly by a powerful interest group, the *dibia*.[15] A little later a missionary interviewed an Asaba *Obi* who was willing to provide the acid test of sincerity – the readiness to waive these sacrifices in the case of his own funeral:

> Mr Phillips took me to see an old man, whom he considered the most sensible of all the kings. For a long time he had been urging his brother kings to listen to what the *oibos* were telling them, by giving up sacrificing men; and as a proof of his sincerity said he did not require the custom to be observed in his own case . . . I am of opinion that the death-knell of the system has been struck . . .[16]

At Obosi, in 1902, a group of young men were prepared to risk civil war to abolish the killing of twins, as well as certain other practices which missionaries condemned but which would appear to have been morally indifferent, such as facial scarification and title taking.[17]

Such enlightenment of conscience was not always the product of an external stimulus, such as mission teaching. Ewenetem (*c.* 1728–1820) was an Eze Nri who declared, at the height of the slave trade, 'that a slave was a human-being and to kill one was an abomination.'[18]

Perhaps further research will uncover more examples of this kind of internal change. In the event, Igbo society was not given the opportunity for peaceful renewal and reform. Instead, it was subjected to the violent and traumatic experience of colonial conquest.

IV The Colonial Experience

9 Igbo Resistance to Colonial Conquest

The same Arts that did gain
A Pow'r, must it maintain. *Andrew Marvell*

Colonialism, throughout the world, has always been an essentially violent phenomenon. It was imposed by violence, and maintained by its potential capacity for violence.

No Nigerian people resisted colonialism more tenaciously than the Igbo. The great Emirates of the north, once conquered, supported the British, with the minor exception of the Satiru rising. The conquest of Igboland took over twenty years of constant military action.

There is no obvious date to begin the story of Igbo resistance to the British. One could begin it in 1830, when the first European explorers on the lower Niger were taken captive. One could begin it in 1860, when the people of Aboh expelled a British trading factory. One could include a large number of desultory conflicts between expatriate traders and the Niger communities, in the sixties and seventies, when the expatriates sometimes reinforced their point of view with 'the moral authority of a man-of-war'. Those were the years which saw a British gun-boat shell Ndoni in 1876, a trade war between the United African Company and Atani in 1880, and, most serious of all, the sack of Onitsha in 1879, and its subsequent blockade.[1] The story gathers momentum after 1885, when the Royal Niger Company gained a Charter to govern, and began the systematic use of violence to maintain its economic interest.

The Royal Niger Company contrived to make war on all the cradles of Igbo Christianity. It blockaded Onitsha, which refused to cooperate with its policy of monopoly. It fought a fierce war with the people of Obosi – where it had placed its commercial installations – and destroyed half Asaba, which it had made its political headquarters.[2] (The attack on Asaba was partly motivated by the desire of several humanitarian employees to abolish human sacrifice, and in this it was successful, but no trace of such motivation appears in any of its other wars.) In 1892 the Company fought a 'terrible war' with Aguleri. Let us select the war with Aguleri for examination in greater detail.

Two years earlier, Aguleri had resounded with the splendid baptism celebrations of Ogbuanyinya Idigo, who had dismissed all his wives but one, and established a Christian village to avoid persecution. Two years later came the war. Its origins would have been comic had it not been for the grim sequel.

> One wet day in the Rainy Season, Onwurume of Ifite Aguleri, being much in need of oil with which to eat the yam which he had roasted, drew near to one of the barrels of oil belonging to the company and punctured it with his knife. He became alarmed when a stream of oil ejected with much force from the cask. The oil completely drenched Onwurume and in deep terror he quickly made his escape leaving his roasted yam and hoe behind.[3]

The Company's servants seized the culprit. The people of Aguleri, anxious to rescue their compatriot, attacked the factory and forced the Company's employees to flee. It was, as the missionaries said, a matter which could have been settled in an hour of discussion. The Company sent a military detachment from Asaba. They asked Idigo to lead them to Ifite, but Idigo refused to betray his people. The soldiers burnt and pillaged Aguleri, and demanded a heavy fine. Twelve chiefs, who had come to negotiate peace, were taken as hostages till the fine was paid. Idigo himself had his new-found Christian faith put to the bitter test of adversity, for he paid for his loyalty to his people by four years' imprisonment at Asaba. And Aguleri traditions relate a further detail. 'After the attack on Aguleri, the soldiers learnt of a town called Umuleri and concluded that, as the name indicated, Umuleri might have descended from the same

Eri. Therefore "if you did not your father did" followed. An attack was launched on Umuleri.'[4]

These wars formed the first phase of Igboland's military encounter with the British. The story of Igbo resistance to colonialism should probably end with the Udi-Okigwi patrol of 1918–19 (though there were patrols in the 1920s, and the Women's War of 1929, which we shall examine later, is basically in the same tradition). It would take a large book to write the full story of all the conflicts of those years – here one can isolate only a few themes, and examples. What is unquestionable is that the Igbo resisted colonialism, not for months, but for decades, with a courage and tenacity of purpose which were undeterred by disaster, and by the extraordinary inequality in arms and resources of the adversaries. In 1909, a British soldier, discussing campaigns in Igboland before a London audience, told them that Igboland 'is really quite a small portion of Nigeria . . . but it has been the most troublesome section of any.'[5] In 1909, ten years of conflict still lay before the British invaders of Igboland.

THE PROBLEMS OF RESISTANCE

Two central problems faced the village groups of Igboland in their attempts to repel the invader. The first was that of resources, and scale. With one notable exception – the Ekumeku movement, which we shall examine shortly – they never succeeded in overcoming their disunity. Even if they had succeeded, the British had behind them the resources, not only of a colonial government, but of an empire. Occasionally a village group managed to inflict a defeat on a British patrol, but the British at once poured in more troops, until the village group was conquered. For the Igbo, there were no more resources on which to draw.

The second problem which faced the Igbo was that of arms and ammunition. When the British invasion of Igboland began, they discovered, too late, that the British did not themselves fight with the weapons they had sold their Igbo customers. The Igbo fought with capguns, dane guns, or matchets, and the occasional rifle, and suffered from a chronic shortage of ammunition. The British fought with rifles and machine guns, and unlimited supplies of ammunition. To keep down their own casualties, they volleyed continuously into the bush as they advanced. From the time of the Aro expedition, they prudently prohibited all imports of arms and ammunition, and of materials from which armaments might be made. During their campaigns, they collected and destroyed the guns belonging to their allies, as well as to their opponents. During the Aro expedition, twenty-five thousand rifles and cap guns were collected and destroyed.[6] The British had previously sold the Igbo these guns – they represented a major investment, in a poor society. Now they made an arbitrary estimate of how many guns each village might be expected to possess, and lived off the village till the quota was handed in. What is astonishing, is not that Igbo resistance was unsuccessful, but that the Igbo, in the teeth of all these difficulties, resisted at all.

It is noteworthy that the communities which resisted the British most tenaciously were not, on the whole, those which had the most warlike reputation in pre-colonial times. The Ezza had eagerly awaited an opportunity to try their strength against the white man, but when he came, the power and noise of his artillery dissuaded them from the combat. A touching story is told of one heroic warrior, named Ogboji Agu Anyigor Ogodo, who picked up his dane gun and set out, alone, to repel the invaders from Ezzaland. As he went, a stray shell struck a tree in front of him, splitting it in two, and reducing the section still in the ground to ashes. He realised that at last he had met an adversary beyond his powers, and went home again.[7] Abam traditions relate that the Abam had worked out a plan of united action, in the face of the enemy, but the plan failed to withstand the traumatic experience of the British attack.[8] The Ohafia looked forward to the British coming, as a splendid opportunity to cut heads on their home ground, but they too were unnerved by their artillery. Eke Kalu was a man of Elu Ohafia who had worked in the Delta and knew a little English. He was in Calabar when he learnt that the British were approaching Ohafia, and hurried home, wisely dissuading his people from what he knew to be a useless struggle, and using his meagre resources of English to explain to the British that Ohafia favoured peace.[9]

I have been referring to the British, and the British were the ultimate beneficiaries of these wars. But as in other colonial wars in Africa, the actual fighting was done by Africans. The Royal Niger Company's forces consisted of five Europeans and 416 Africans from the Gold Coast, Yorubaland and Hausaland.[10] The British forces, in the Aro expedition, consisted of 74 white officers, and 3464 African soldiers and carriers.[11]

Most of this chapter will deal with the military response to colonial aggression. But other, non-military responses were also possible, and these, too, must be considered.

NON-MILITARY RESPONSES TO AGGRESSION: MAGIC AND MANIPULATION

The Igbos' implicit belief in the reality of the invisible world meant that many Igbo communities put their main reliance in supernatural modes of defence. The researches of Professor Afigbo have shown that many groups in the Onitsha, Awka, and Orlu areas, which apparently did not resist the British at the time of the Onitsha Hinterland Expedition of 1904 were, in fact, relying on the agency of *dibia*.[12] The traditions of Umuna, in Okigwi Division, relate an apparently successful example: 'The whitemen pitched their tents at Nkwo Okwe also, after a few months they were disturbed greatly by Uzowurus powerful medicines which were thrown to poison them. So they ran away after some had been infected somehow.'[13] After years of colonial rule, the soldiers' barracks at Abakaliki were accidentally destroyed by fire, and the local people drew the obvious conclusion. 'The Founder of the Ezzas is not asleep . . . he has begun to burn down the soldiers' barracks.'[14]

The modern historian is, of course, likely to dismiss such inferences as imaginary, but an early D.O. at Bende has left interesting descriptions of what it felt to be like on the receiving end of this type of magical or religious attack. At 'Isuingo',* in the Bende District, he tried to stay in a Rest House on which a local *dibia* had placed a curse, before committing suicide. He found a single night's stay there so terrifying that he burnt the Rest House down, and built a new one on a different site. He wrote, 'I can only say that I am relating exactly what I saw. I attempt no explanation – for to me the thing is unexplainable.'[15] (The same man had a similar experience in a non-Igbo area – at Obudu, near the Cameroons border – with a snake curse.)

* Probably Isingwu (part of Umuhu, in the Ohuhu clan).

Anyone who studies Igbo history cannot help reflecting on the real nature of the *dibia's* allegedly supranatural powers. Igbo traditions give many examples of *dibias* – some near-contemporaries – who were apparently able to perform feats for which there is no rational explanation. If there was as much evidence relating to any phenomenon which the historian regards as possible, such as rubber cultivation or elephant hunting, he would regard it as unquestionably true. I think that it is possible that Igboland's *dibia* were developing real skills – or sciences – in the sphere of what we would now call extra-sensory perception. The imposition of colonial rule has basically put an end to these skills, and deflected Igbo intellectual energies into such 'modern' spheres as medicine or physics. It is possible that in doing so it cut off a real and original advance of the human mind, and impoverished the total development of human knowledge.[16]

The second possible non-military response was the one I have termed manipulation. The British were incomparably the most powerful military element in Igboland, but they were, as the Igbo and their neighbours learned with great rapidity, one which could be manoeuvred into serving their own interests. The British military presence in Igboland often appears almost as a blind force manipulated by sectional groups, with great sophistication, to serve their own interests.

The British did not speak Igbo, and had little knowledge of the society they intended to rule. They were therefore very dependent on those who gave them information. The Igbo soon learnt that there were certain stereotypes the British regarded as reprehensible: 'stopping trade', levying tolls (the British waged relentless war on the Okonko society of southern Igboland), raiding for slaves, and offering human sacrifices. By accusing their local enemies of some or all of these malpractices, they were able to manipulate the British into fighting their local wars for them.

In the first British patrols to southern Igboland, in 1896, the Bonny and Opobo traders succeeded, not only in coercing their trade rivals, but even in securing British acquiescence in their capture of slaves![17] We have already noted how several Oshiri men made the long dangerous journey to Calabar in a successful attempt to secure British intervention against the Ezza. The

Nguru, in Mbaise, had been at war with Ahiara, so when the British attacked Ahiara, 'We helped the white men in the fight against Ahiara and captured many people whom we sold immediately.'[18]

At the turn of the century, two Nkalu towns, Akokwa and Obodo, were fighting a bitter and inconclusive war. When they heard of the destruction of the Arochukwu oracle, each side decided to seek British intervention. Obodo sent a deputation to Awka, and Akokwa sent a representative, Ukachukwu, to Bende. The Bende deputation was successful: 'The Europeans came and helped him to conquer Obodo . . . Akokwa was the only town in Mbanasa not conquered by the whiteman. Other towns like Uga, Ndizuogu, suffered terribly from the white man's guns. Through Ukachukwu's wisdom and early contact with the Europeans we never suffered any conquest from the white man.'[19]

Arondizuogu, after its initial conquest, rapidly became expert in the techniques of manipulation.

> But instead of just following the British people on the said crusade of massacre, the people of Arondizuogu who were employed, went as far as taking a lead in the crusade. They led the British people around the nearer and farther towns, burning houses, and doing all sorts of havoc and thereby realising big wealth. After some time the British soldiers and the Captains went back. The brave men of Arondizuogu who took part in this massacre mission were therefore disappointed, for they had lost their means of getting wealth; and they thought it necessary to continue this massacre mission by themselves. Then arrangements for this started:
>
> Imitation of British Raid.[20]

In the first decade of this century, there were imposters all over Igboland, pretending to be Court Messengers, or even British officers. Gradually, as British rule became more widely established, this kind of imposition became impossible.

The rest of this chapter will deal with the response of those Igbo groups which tried to repel the invader by force. The gallantry of the endeavour tends to make it more attractive to the later historian than the response of the manipulators. Yet the policy of diplomats such as Chief Ukachukwu of Akokwa was probably based on a more realistic estimate of circumstances, and brought more real benefit to the communities concerned.

INVASION FROM THE SOUTH: THE ARO EXPEDITION AND AFTERWARDS

In 1891 the British established in the Delta what was in fact, though not in name, a colonial government – the Oil Rivers Protectorate (rechristened in 1893 the Niger Coast Protectorate). In 1896, the officials of this government began the penetration of southern Igboland. In that year, two British officials visited Bende, to discuss free trade and the abolition of slavery with local Aro representatives. At the beginning of the discussion, the interpreter told the Aro to remove their hats as a sign of respect. Immediately, 'every Aro that had a hat put it on' and those that lacked hats borrowed them for the purpose, and an ancient Aro orator made a splendid speech of defiance: 'The white man may have come by the sun, they may have come by the moon, or they may have come through the clouds, but the sooner they went back from where they had come, and remained there, the better.'[21]

In 1896 the British attacked the southern Igbo towns of Obohia and Ohuru. These wars anticipate two of the commonest features of the conflicts of later years – the complete incomprehension of the people concerned, as to why they were attacked, and the plunder conducted by soldiers and allied towns: 'the houses burnt, a certain number of coconut trees cut down, and a quantity of loot taken by the soldiers consisting chiefly of cloth, goats, fowls, and manillas.'[22] In 1898, came the 'most severe and complete' punishment of Ehea, a southern Igbo town near the Ibibio boundary.[23] In the same year came conflict with Umukoroshe, an Ikwerri town near the present site of Port Harcourt, which was attacked mainly because it adhered to the traditional practice of levying tolls. 'The towns and surrounding farms of Omokoroshi were devastated, the houses being all razed to the ground and the palm and plantain trees cut down.'[24]

The Aro expedition of December 1901 to March 1902, was, of course, on a vastly larger scale than these local encounters. It represented the largest military force ever employed in the subjugation of Igboland, and the first major drive to the Igbo interior. Nevertheless, it has loomed too large in Igbo historiography. It affected only the southern Igbo – groups living south of a line from Oguta to Unwana, and east of the Orashi/Engenni River – though originally it was intended to

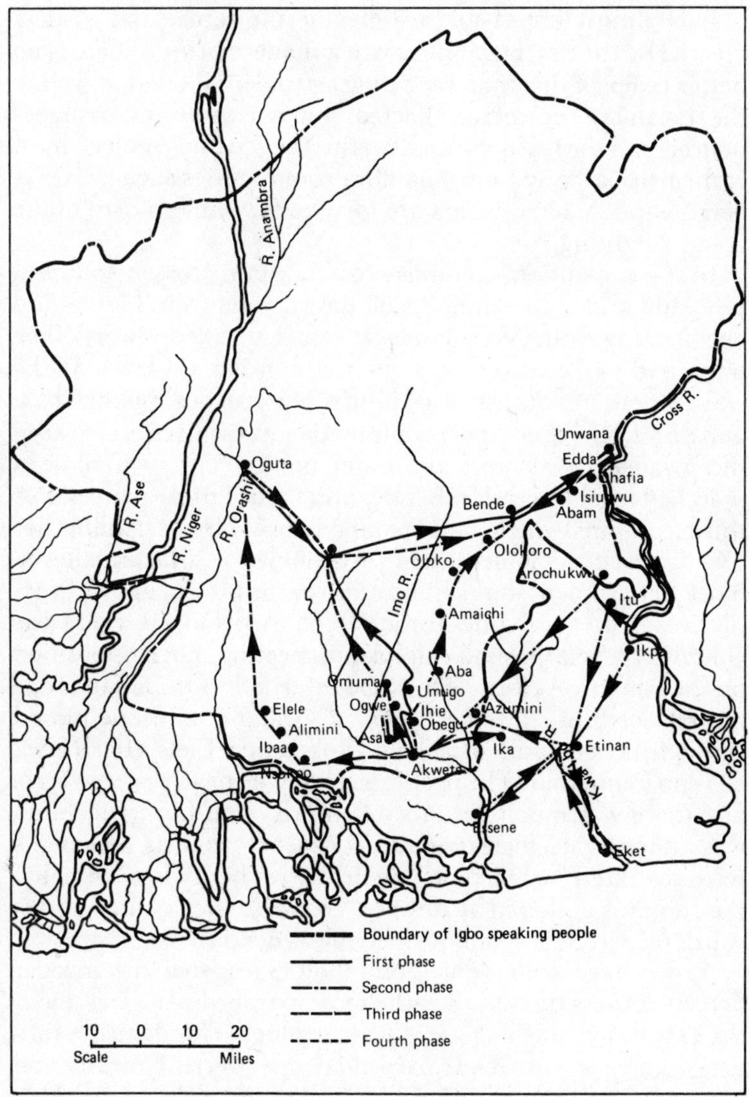

Map 7 The Arochukwu expedition, 1901–2

include areas further north.[25] And even in the area affected, the results were impermanent; war after war was to be waged in years to come, to subjugate the peoples allegedly subdued by the Aro expedition.

It is almost impossible to imagine the terror and dismay created by the first encounter with a modern army. There is no better index of this than the refugee problem it created well to the north of the areas affected. Fifteen thousand refugees poured into the Catholic missions at Nsugbe and Aguleri, most of them apparently from Anambra communities such as Nteje, Nando and Achala, which are forty to fifty miles north of the scene of fighting.[26]

In the expedition, columns crossed and recrossed southern Igboland and Ibibioland. A column starting from Oguta and one starting from Akwete met at 'a place called Oweri'. The latter had to face three days of bitter fighting at Ogwe, on the way, where resistance was ultimately crushed by machine guns, and where the local people made successful efforts to keep the invaders away from the water ponds. The two columns marched from Owerri to Bende, and thence to Arochukwu. A third column, which had marched through the Abam and Ohafia territory, joined them. Arochukwu was taken, after 'a most determined stand', and the oracle blown up with explosives. After ranging through the Arochukwu area, the columns moved through Ibibioland, meeting much opposition on the way, to Akwete. Then one returned to Ibibioland, one moved north of Akwete, through Ngwaland, and one moved through Ikwerriland, attacking Isiokpo and Elele. The Ngwa column found that 'The people were hostile nearly everywhere, and there was much desultory fighting.' The Ikwerri column was attacked at Ubele 'with great bravery', but its opponents were scattered by machine-gun fire, 'with heavy loss'. Finally, the columns gathered at Akwete, 'to sweep the country northwards on a front of 40 miles', meeting at Bende.[27]

As we have seen, some communities resisted the invader fiercely, others did not. But the most extraordinary fact about the expedition was its lack of lasting effect. The British established garrisons at Bende, Arochukwu, Owerri, Unwana and Oguta.[28] The District Officer at Bende was unable to go more than eight miles north of his post unless he 'had a numerous escort, and that was just then not available.'[29] The people of Mbaise, whose lands had been crossed by the columns repeatedly, were able to prevent the British from using the direct Owerri-Bende road, so that convoys had to make a sweep to the south.[30] The people of the Umuahia area, the Ohuhu, Olokoro and Ibeku, had realised that in the Aro expedition 'there were too many soldiers to give them a chance of success.' At the end of 1902, under the leadership of two *dibia*, they swore to expel the whiteman, and attacked an escort.

'I heard from Bendi and from all sides that the two tribes had given it out as their intention to remain hidden in the ravines and farms until we left the country, that they would never come in and we could destroy their towns if we wanted to.' It was during this expedition that Uzuakoli was first visited by the British.[31]

In the same year, 1902, the people of Ngor village group, near Owerri, chased the District Commissioner and his escort away, despite the proximity of the Owerri garrison. Like so many other resisters, they lost their homes, their food supplies, and their livelihood, for their trees were cut down, their houses razed, and their farms destroyed.[32]

The people of Afikpo, similarly, saw little point in attacking the Aro expedition, but when the expedition was over, they adopted an attitude of intransigent defiance, even making war on a local town which opted for peace with the British. At the end of 1902, the British sent armed forces to Afikpo. Learning that the Afikpo were expecting an attack from the river, they attacked from the rear. Despite 'the almost certain death which overtook any Afikpo who came within 200 yards', they attacked with dauntless courage. The area was covered with short grass, affording no cover, and as the Afikpo tried in vain to come to grips with the enemy, a machine gun mowed them down as they came within range. The British, for their part, lost one soldier.[33]

The British continued to have little control over Mbaise and northern Ngwaland. In 1904, another patrol was sent, but several months later it was necessary to report that the local people 'continue to give a great deal of trouble and are not yet under control'.[34]

The military encounters of the years that followed are

broadly of two types. The first consist of the initial conquest of areas previously unconquered. Each year, the British tried to move the boundary of advance further inland. No sooner was the Aro expedition over than Moor began to draft proposals for the conquest of areas further north. The end of 1904 saw the Onitsha hinterland expedition, which invaded the area between Ogurugu, Onitsha and Oguta, and established a new station at Awka.[35] The following year, a large expedition (700 rank and file) was divided into two sections which set out from Awka and Bende, respectively, with plans to meet at an unknown point called 'Z'. During this expedition, the news of Stewart's death arrived, and the expedition inflicted draconian punishment on Mbaise, which it had been intended to conquer anyway.[36] A new station was established at Umuduru, later moved to Okigwi. The same year, 1905, saw the first conquest of the Ezza, Ikwo, and other peoples of the northeast. The British did not reach Udi division until 1908 and Nsukka division until 1910, and the latter area, in particular, was not really subjugated until years later.

By far the greater number of wars, however, were what historians call 'secondary resistance' – wars fought after the initial conquest. Such wars demanded great courage, for the peoples concerned had first-hand knowledge of British military power. They resisted when they thought they had a chance of success, or when colonialism impinged on their lives in a way that seemed intolerable. Thus the Etche clan rebelled in 1907, in protest against the exactions of a corrupt court clerk.[37]

These risings continued, year after year. Every year, government records describe perhaps half a dozen or more of these local wars – wars of the greatest significance to the communities involved in them. In 1910, a missionary wrote, 'There has never been such a spirit of revolt throughout the whole country.[38] Another observed, 'Almost constant expeditions, which the papers never mention, take place in the interior of the country.'[39] In that year the British invited Bishop Shanahan to establish a mission at Okigwi.[40] He refused, because he felt that British control of the area was too slight.

It is impossible, in a book of this length, to record these numerous, and now forgotten wars; in the pages that follow I shall isolate three examples only, drawn from different parts of Igboland, at different times.

WESTERN IGBOLAND: THE EKUMEKU, 1898–1910

The Ekumeku movement is unique in Igbo history for two reasons. First, the length of time the movement endured, comprising military campaigns over a period of twelve years. Secondly, it is the outstanding example in Igboland of an attempt to unite previously disunited states to resist the invader. We have seen that one crucial reason for Igbo defeat was the great discrepancy of scale between the average Igbo community and the colonial invader. The history of some other parts of Africa reveals highly successful attempts to overcome this difficulty, by forming large-scale alliances, often united by religio-magical techniques. In western Igboland, over a dozen previously disunited communities spread over an area of some eight hundred square miles, succeeded in overcoming their traditional suspicions and antagonisms to oppose the invasion of their country.[41] (Nine of the towns were linked by a genealogical charter – the Umuezechima clan, cf. pp. 52–3 above. Others that joined them included Ogwashi-Uku, Akumazi, Ubulu-Uku, Ibusa and the two Idumuje towns. Asaba, the Royal Niger Company's headquarters, could only give passive support.)

The word Ekumeku is archaic, and different sources interpret it differently. One historian has written: 'The word Ekumeku in its indigenous meaning is onomatopoeic, conveying the idea of a whirlwind or something fast, devastating, invisible and yet forcefully real. It has a connotation of reality shrouded in fantasy'.[42] It grew out of secret societies of brave young men which most towns possessed, which combined the functions of a secret police and a guerilla army, and which formed, according to one source, the élite of the most capable young people.[43] After years of difficult negotiations, the leaders of the towns concerned decided to deploy the members of these societies in a rising to expel the hated Royal Niger Company.[44] Missionaries and Company officials fled to Asaba, and soon the Ekumeku controlled the entire Asaba hinterland except Asaba itself, a nearby small town, and Issele-Uku, where the Company had a garrison. Interestingly enough, their non-Igbo neighbours – from Ishan – hearing of their success, sent support. 'The bush was full of indigenous soldiers, who travelled by night and day to their guerilla attacks, and to their secret discussions.' After sending several unsuccessful patrols, the Company brought a gunboat, and bombarded all the towns within reach of its guns – not, as it happened, those which had been most actively involved in the rising. A missionary believed that if the movement had been united under a single able leader it could have expelled the Europeans from the west bank of the Niger. As it was, it failed. 'It was supposed at the time that the Ekwumekwu were finally subdued and that there would not be another rising.'[45]

In 1900 the Royal Niger Company was replaced by the Protectorate of Southern Nigeria, but the Ekumeku, rightly enough, thought that nothing essential was changed. In 1902 a Catholic missionary warned the government that a conspiracy was brewing 'which might equal the Indian Mutiny for the purpose of ridding the country of the white man.'[46] In particular, the local people were incensed by the malpractices of the native courts, which they began to boycott. The British decided on a pre-emptive strike, and in December 1902 sent a powerful expedition which systematically destroyed a number of towns and imprisoned their leaders.[47] This, it was assumed, was the end of the Ekumeku. 'The "Ekumeku" and other secret societies have been completely broken'.[48]

In 1904, the Ekumeku rose again. This time they changed their tactics – mistakenly, it would seem in retrospect, abandoning the united guerilla warfare of 1898 for the individual defence of each town. Predictably, the British overcame them one by one – first Ibusa, then Ogwashi-Uku, then Ubulu-Uku. The defence of Ubulu-Uku was the turning point. Naturally well located, on a hill, and well fortified, it succeeded in holding the British at bay for three days, and was taken only after they promised a bounty to their soldiers. When it fell, the other allies realised that further resistance was hopeless.[49] Heavy fines were imposed, and three hundred prisoners taken, of whom two hundred were ultimately sent to gaol in Calabar.[50] There they were decimated by epidemics, and some committed suicide. Incredibly, only five were alive a year later.[51] Colonialism, it is clear, did not lack its human sacrifices. The Ekumeku, it was plain to the British, 'has received a blow from which it is not likely to recover'.[52]

The last act of the Ekumeku drama began in late 1909.[53] The occasion was a succession dispute in Ogwashi-Uku. One of the claimants, Nzekwe, the son of the last Obi, feared that the

British would deprive him of his throne, and decided to fight for his inheritance. But the protracted gallant struggle which ensued was possible only because of his people's indelible opposition to colonial rule. In November 1909, the British sent an expedition to Ogwashi-Uku (which, even today, is a small town). They met with 'very strong opposition', and sent for reinforcements. After suffering heavy losses, both the original force and the reinforcements withdrew to Onitsha. The people were invited to surrender, but refused. In January, the troops returned. 'From 6 January to 4 April, the troops were consequently engaged by day and night without capturing Nzekwe and the ring leaders. The seriousness of the situation led to the despatch of heavy reinforcements of five officers, 160 rank and file and two maxim guns under Major Bruce, who left Lagos to take over command.' Their courage extorted the unwilling admiration of the missionaries: 'Notwithstanding their wretched old flint guns, these primitive sharpshooters had the bravery to attack an English column on the very highroad.'[54] At the end of May, Nzekwe and his men finally surrendered. The Divisional Headquarters was moved to Ogwashi-Uku, to prevent a recurrence. But the story had an epilogue.

The British perceived, in the whole Asaba hinterland, a sympathy with the Ekumeku, and 'a disposition to throw off government authority.' In 1911, there was a final round-up of Ekumeku leaders in the various towns, followed, once more, by imprisonments.[55]

The Ekumeku failed, but the western Igbo treasure their memory as an imperishable legacy. They included Dunkwu Isusu of Onitsha-Olona, Nwabuzo Iyogolo of Ogwashi-Uku, Awuno Ugbo of Akumazi (the youngest of the leaders) Nwoko of Ubulu-Uku, the Ekumeku trumpeter, and Mordi, of the same town, one of their outstanding shots.[56]

REVOLT IN UDI, 1914

Nothing shows the unpopularity of early colonial rule in Igboland more vividly than the spontaneous response, in perhaps a dozen different places, to the outbreak of the First World War.[57] Troops were withdrawn from local garrisons for the Cameroons campaign. Rumours developed – apparently spread in part by German traders in Nigeria – that Britain was losing the war and would soon leave Nigeria.[58] In the Cross River area, the sight of the bodies of soldiers of the Nigerian Regiment floating downstream, after a defeat in the Cameroons, gave these rumours a startling credibility.[59]

There was an almost total breakdown of British authority in the north-east – a theme to which we shall soon return. In 1914, there was a rising in Kwale, at the opposite end of Igboland.[60] In the same year, there were risings in Oguta and Elele, in Bende and Okigwi. In Aba Division, there was a rising in Obete and Abala. About 150 local people were killed when it was put down, and as many wounded.[61] There was a rising in Uli and Okija, which were undeterred by the harsh reprisals that had followed a revolt several years earlier.[62] In the November of that year, Lugard wrote to his wife, 'We have scotched the Kwale insurrection only to find that the Udi business is very widespread and no progress is being made . . . This evening I hear the Ogonis are up.'[63]

We must look now, in rather more detail, at 'the Udi business'. It involved a number of towns in a fifteen-mile radius of what is now Enugu (mainly to the south and east), among them Akpugo, Akegbe and Amagunze. It sprang in part from the reduction of soldiers locally: 'When our soldiers in Udi went out for Cameroons War then people at Akegbe [thought] there's no soldier again and soldiers are never coming back to Udi. Then they have to state that they are coming to capture the very small number of soldiers at Udi.'[64] Fundamentally, it reflected a number of intolerable grievances – among them the corruption and exactions of Warrant Chiefs and Court Clerks and Messengers. 'Court summonses have been refused in most of the towns, messengers flogged and the Chiefs . . . turned out of the towns, their compounds being destroyed.'[65] The Chief of Obinagu was killed, and the celebrated Chief Chukuani of Nkanu, who led the government troops to Akegbe, came within an ace of losing his life there.[66] It was a protest against forced labour on the roads (one informant brought me a stout cudgel, to show how labourers were flogged) where the unpaid workers, who were expected to feed themselves, often went hungry – 'sometimes they used to eat leaves.'[67] The survey of the railway line seemed to threaten their ownership of the land, and herald more forced labour. They had made only token resistance when the British first came.[68]

The British were anxious to suppress the rising 'so that both the Railway Survey through Udi and the operations at the coal-fields at Enugu can be proceeded with as soon as possible.'[69] They sent more troops to the area, but five weeks later they had achieved little. The Udi District Officer reported

> It is now quite apparent from the obstinate way in which the Akebes are holding out and by the opposition experienced from Apugu, that this is not one of the usual small fits of unrest to which these Ibo towns are subject but a most determined rebellion against the Government.'[70]

The Acting Lieutenant-Governor of the Southern Provinces sent an agitated telegram to Lagos: 'Whole country in above area . . . is in state of rebellion.'[71] Reinforcements arrived from Lokoja, and the British proceeded to a confrontation at Akegbe. I quote both the contemporary British account of the battle at Nkwo market, Akegbe and the account I tape-recorded, almost sixty years later, in the area; it is a striking illustration of the accuracy of oral tradition.

The British account:

> At dawn the following morning the Camp was attacked by about 800 of the Enemy, the Enemy approaching as close as 20 yards before being checked by rifle and machine gun fire . . . The casualties to the Enemy must have been heavy . . .[72]

The modern tradition:

> One certain morning all Akegbe people went and settled and had a meeting and then the soldiers were at Nkwo Akegbe . . . And one very early morning say by five or six o'clock . . . the prominent Chief Chukuani do lead them . . . He brought them (the British) in . . . And these people rose up [imitates gun fire]. Their [British] soldiers used their loose gun [imitates machine gun] and then the soldiers started firing. They killed so many people . . . They used to have a small machine gun.[73]

As in so many earlier and later wars, the villages were razed, quarter by quarter, house by house. They revisited the same places for good measure, when the villagers started rebuilding. The Chiefs of Udi division had chosen the right side; they were to make fortunes supplying labour for the mines, and become famous, in an era of rich and powerful Warrant Chiefs, for their wealth and unbridled power.

Those who fought lost everything. They had protested against Chiefs, and the Chiefs were more powerful than before. They had protested against forced labour, and the peace terms included supplying two thousand unpaid workers for the railway.[74] From 1915 on they were forced, against their will, to labour in the mines as well.

THE IKWO WAR OF 1918

The Ikwo first came into conflict with the British in 1905. They resisted the invader fiercely, and suffered many casualties.[75] In the years that followed, the British had little real control over the area. In 1913 the Ikwo began attacking travellers on the Abakaliki-Obubra road, so that government mail runners and carriers had to travel with an escort.[76] In 1914, the British suffered several defeats in the Cameroons, and the Ikwo observed bodies floating down the Cross River. It seemed a convincing demonstration of British weakness, and intensified their recalcitrance. It was not until 1918 that the British were able to send a patrol to Ikwoland. This is one of the few campaigns in Igboland of which we have a detailed description by a third party, in this case the Ghanaian interpreter, Robert Cudjoe. The extracts that follow are his eye-witness account.[77]

> Just as we had started the Ikwos leaped out from the belt of bush, yelling and shouting *Ikwo hayi, Ikwo hayi*! running and jumping towards the troops. Captain Wilton of the rearguard rushed up to the Major, gave the military salute and said 'Rearguard attack'. To this the Major replied 'No shooting'. All this time the Ikwos were coming on, and they opened fire when 150 yards from the troops. Of course I could not say how the order was given, but all of a sudden the whole column of soldiers knelt down and opened rapid fire in reply. The effect of the fire from the troops was a sad show, the Ikwo dropping down like flies. A few minutes later the Major sounded the cease fire and we continued our march back to camp by goose-steps. But these foolish brutes, not minding the heavy casualties, kept on coming but of course

> only with intermittent firing. We continued the slow-going until we reached a village square where the Major ordered the Officers' Cooks to prepare breakfast . . .

When they returned to their base camp, they found that a similar attack had been repulsed, with similar casualties: 'About 200 yards outside the camp we found scores of dead and wounded lying about the field. At the entrance to the camp we met Captain Collins, laughing with a report to the Major about what happened in the camp.' That night, to the sound of war drums and trumpets, the Ikwo attacked again, but were repelled by machine-gun fire. 'At about 8 o'clock in the morning the Medical Officer, Dispenser and medical labourers went out burying the dead bodies found lying outside the camp.'

Three days later the Ikwo attacked again, in daylight. The grasslands offered little cover, and they attempted to use branches as a screen for their advance. 'It was rather a fine show but a waste of precious lives.' After attacking for eight and a half hours, they dispersed. On the same day a detachment surprised an Ikwo army section near a stream, and mowed them down. 'It was here, as was known later, that all their determined war-leaders perished.' The British beheaded the corpses, burying the heads separately. A week later, the British received reinforcements – a light artillery battery. At last, the Ikwo lost heart. 'It now became our turn to chase them all over the fields and forests.' They were forced to pay a fine of £1500, enormous in terms of their resources.[78] The British did not suffer a single casualty.

THE SOCIAL COST OF WAR

It will be evident from the foregoing that the colonial conquest of Igboland was accomplished at great cost, both in human lives and in property. The many deaths, the looted farms and livestock, the houses razed, the trees cut down, are adequately documented even in British records, and are remembered with poignant emphasis in the traditions of the Igbo community concerned. The people of Ameke in Item still annually observe the day, in 1916, of conflict with the British – 'the blackest time of Item when one of the four principal villages was turned into a desert.'[79]

All these campaigns were waged in the dry season; in the early years of colonial rule the effectiveness of British authority depended on the weather. But the late dry season was also the planting season. One can only surmise what effect the looting, the wars, the uncertainty and disorder, had upon agricultural production. The price of food sky-rocketed. Contemporaries attributed it to the inflationary effect of the purchases of cash-paid groups such as the soldiers. It may well have reflected also the cost of war.

One of the most hated aspects of these wars was the conscription of carriers. Heavily burdened and defenceless, many of them were killed by accident in the wars, others died of sickness, or of exhaustion; 'a good number of them died owing to the wonderful gravity of the loads.'[80] We have an account of a carrier who was shot down trying to escape, and of others who were kept in gaol until their services were required. Often they served in wars against their friends and allies – like the bitterly unwilling carriers of Asaba and Okpanam, forced to serve in the Ekumeku war of 1904.[81] Near Owerri, in the same year, a village that refused to supply twenty carriers was punished with 'a brisk fusillade . . . the loss of several killed and wounded, and the place destroyed.'[82]

The building of roads obviously facilitated both the preservation of British authority – for the movement of troops became easier – and the extraction of the country's products, which was, of course, the reason for instituting that rule in the first place. The building of roads brought, as we shall see, many benefits to Igboland, but they were constructed by forced unpaid labour, which was bitterly resented by those concerned. Here are two contrasting comments on H. M. Douglas, the first District Commissioner in Owerri. The first was by the High Commissioner (later Governor), Egerton: 'Mr H. M. Douglas has now constructed over 200 miles of road in his District. These roads are nearly all 40ft wide . . . Mr Douglas has done wonderfully good work in his District.'[83] The second is a letter to Douglas, by a missionary: From what I heard from the people as I passed through your District, and from what I heard subsequently from those who accompany me, your administration appears to be well nigh unbearable. The people complained bitterly of your harsh treatment of them. . . .[84]

One of the grimmest and least known aspects of these wars was the condition of the prisons to which many resisters, and other offenders, were consigned. The sufferings of prisoners form a grim leitmotiv in the records of colonialism. The quarterly report from Aboh, in 1906, records that a dysentery epidemic had raged among the prisoners for four months, and seven had died.[85] Much later, a visiting doctor made the following report on Awka gaol:

> There are no means of ablution within the Prison. Prisoners never get meat or fish in their diet as it is practically unobtainable . . . [There is] a death rate of 222 per thousand . . . *I saw two prisoners with intractable ulcers on their buttocks, the unhealed effects of flogging administered by the Native Court some three weeks previously* . . . The two who had been flogged were obviously still suffering very acutely, so much that they were endeavouring to eat their mid-day meal as they rested on their hands and knees on the floor . . .[86]

Their offence? They 'were charged with harbouring Igbo rebels and property'. In terms of their own values, with succouring friends and neighbours in misfortune.

The wars fought to establish colonial rule in Igboland were fought in the name of the abolition of slavery, yet the regime they introduced was marked by the large-scale exaction of unwilling and unpaid labour. They were fought in the name of the abolition of human sacrifice, but no historian will ever be able to count the number of the human sacrifices they exacted.

10 Colonial Government and its Critics

'Immediately white men came justice vanished.'

An elder of Okigwi[1]

THE BOUNDARIES

From the beginnings of colonial rule until the present, different sets of essentially artifical administrative boundaries have been imposed on Igboland. None of them has ever been conterminous with Igboland. The maps that follow show some of the successive administrative units imposed during the period of colonial rule. Map 9 shows the boundary between the Royal Niger Company and the Oil Rivers Protectorate (it should be noted that the boundary was delimited only in the Delta; it did not run through Igboland, because Igboland was as yet unexplored and unconquered).

In 1900, the Royal Niger Company lost its Charter, and the Protectorate of Southern Nigeria, as it was now called, was divided into four divisions – at first centred mainly in the Delta, but, as time passed, gradually extending inland. In 1906, the Colony of Lagos and the Protectorate of Southern Nigeria were amalgamated, and the new unit was divided into three provinces. Igboland was divided between the Eastern Province, with its capital at Calabar, and the Central Province, with its capital at Warri.

In 1914, the administrative units were changed once more, and the Eastern and Central Provinces were divided into six smaller units. Most Igbos were in Onitsha and Owerri provinces: many of the north-eastern and Cross River Igbo were in Ogoja province, and Arochukwu was in Calabar province. The western Igbo were divided between Warri and Benin provinces. The system was to survive until the creation of Regions, by the

Macpherson constitution, in 1951,* which belongs to a later section of this study.

Just as the provinces did not correspond with linguistic or ethnic groups, the smaller sub-divisions did not correspond with clans. Each Division comprised a large number of clans, and most Native Courts served more than one clan. Thus Okigwi Native Court served the Otanchara, Otanzu, Isuochi, Nneato and Umuchieze clans.[2] The system of Divisions and Native Courts forced clans and village groups which had often been at enmity to act within the same structure. Sometimes this meant that the town where a Native Court was situated practised a kind of miniature imperialism at the expense of her neighbours. As time went on, the artificial units – the Divisions – came to acquire emotional reality and loyalties of their own, – like the American States. Owerri Division is a striking example, and so is Mbaise, which is an entirely artificial creation, going back to the Native Authority formed in 1941.[3] Her component towns were, in pre-colonial times, frequently at war. But in time Mbaise too became a unit for local attachments and loyalties.

THE SYSTEM

Much ink has been spilt in a discussion among historians as to whether the system of local government which was introduced into Igboland conformed to an abstraction called Indirect Rule. The fact that historians have for so long ordered their thoughts within this category is an extraordinary example of the remarkable tenacity of the Lugardian myth – a myth which the writings of I. F. Nicolson have now probably laid to rest.[4] The debate is not a debate about historical realities but about definitions. Like most discussions of definitions, it is not very interesting.

The system of government which the British introduced in northern Nigeria and the system which they introduced among the Igbo differed in degree, but not in kind. The Emirates were more suited to the needs of a modern bureacratic state, mainly

* It came into effect on 1 January 1952. The background to the creation of Regions lay ultimately in the division of the southern provinces into an eastern and a western sector, in 1939, a division perpetuated in the Richards constitution which came into effect in 1947.

because of their centralisation and relatively large size. For a variety of reasons the British found them emotionally attractive. Yet the Emirates too were radically changed by colonialism, for the imposition of an overlord transforms the position of any ruler, both in essence and in a host of practical details.

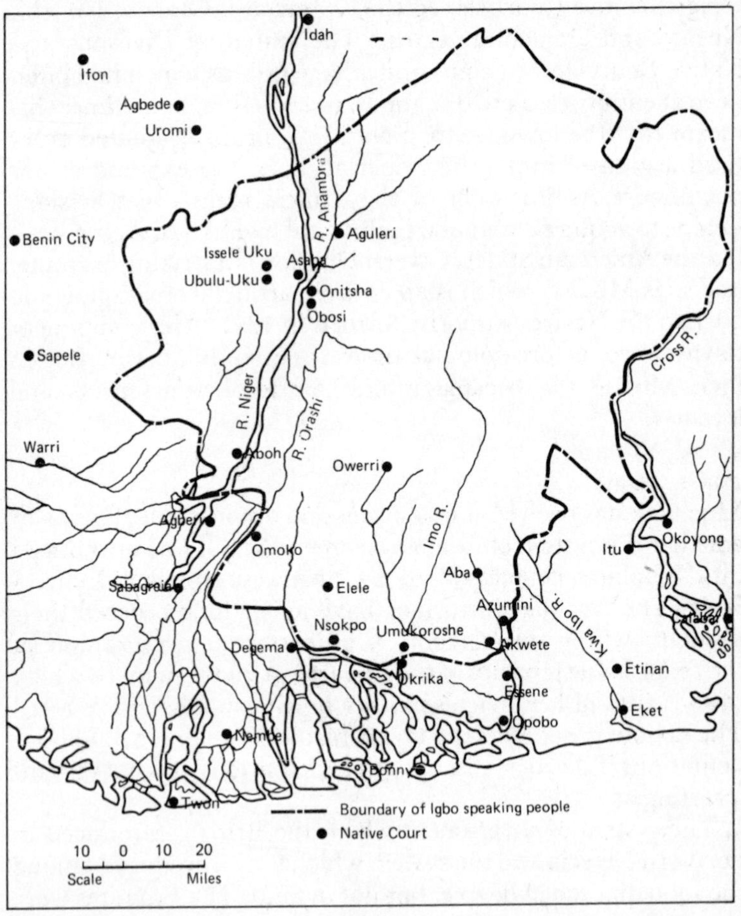

Map 8 Native Courts, 1903 (not all non-Igbo courts are shown)

The patterns of traditional Igbo government were hopelessly unsuited to the needs of the colonial state. Its system of checks and balances, its pursuit of consensus by protracted discussion, its use of religious sanctions, and especially, its small scale, rendered it impracticable.

The British introduced a system of Warrant Chiefs originally because they assumed that all Africans were ruled by chiefs, if not kings (the early records of colonialism are full of such fictional entities as 'the King of Ngwa'). But even had they perceived the nature of Igbo government more clearly, the British were almost bound to modify it.

Like all colonial governments in Africa, the British regime depended primarily on the agency of Africans, just as the wars which conquered Igboland were fought primarily by Africans – 'imperialism makes its victims its defenders'. The British could not have ruled Igboland in any other way. White officials expected high salaries, frequent leaves in England, and a variety of fringe benefits. Any colonial budget could only afford a limited number of them.

As the British established their rule, first in the Delta, and then in Igboland, they established a series of courts, called Native Courts. They were widely established by 1903, as Map 8 shows.[5] Individuals were given warrants to sit on them. The holders of these warrants came to be called Warrant Chiefs.

The Warrant Chiefs' selection was extremely haphazard. Sometimes the man chosen was already the possessor of real authority and wealth in his community – Chief Njemanze of Owerri and Chief Ukachukwu of Akokwa were examples. In such cases, the selection of Warrant Chiefs legitimised the careers of the New Men of the nineteenth century, which we have examined earlier, though they were given an authority to which the New Men of earlier times could not have aspired. The traditional elders were seldom chosen: they were too numerous, and they were too old. They were too old for the mental adjustments which the new role acquired, they were often surrounded by religious taboos which would have made such participation difficult, they were physically too old for the frequent long journeys from home to Court.[6] The elders of Onitsha Olona refused Warrants when they were offered to them.

The experience of colonial conquest was not of a kind to encourage the Igbo in confidence in the good intentions of their victors. Not knowing what the government had in store for the

Warrant holders, they often put their more expendable members forward. 'At first and for some time afterwards he was not usually the real Chief of the town, but some poor townsman who was pushed forward, the real chief keeping well out of the way in case there was a catch somewhere.'[7] Or as another version puts it, 'When asked who was their Chief, the people sometimes put forward a man who, so far as the system permitted, was the most important man in their village; sometimes (most often) they just looked blank; and sometimes they put forward the village idiot, to see what happened to him.'[8]

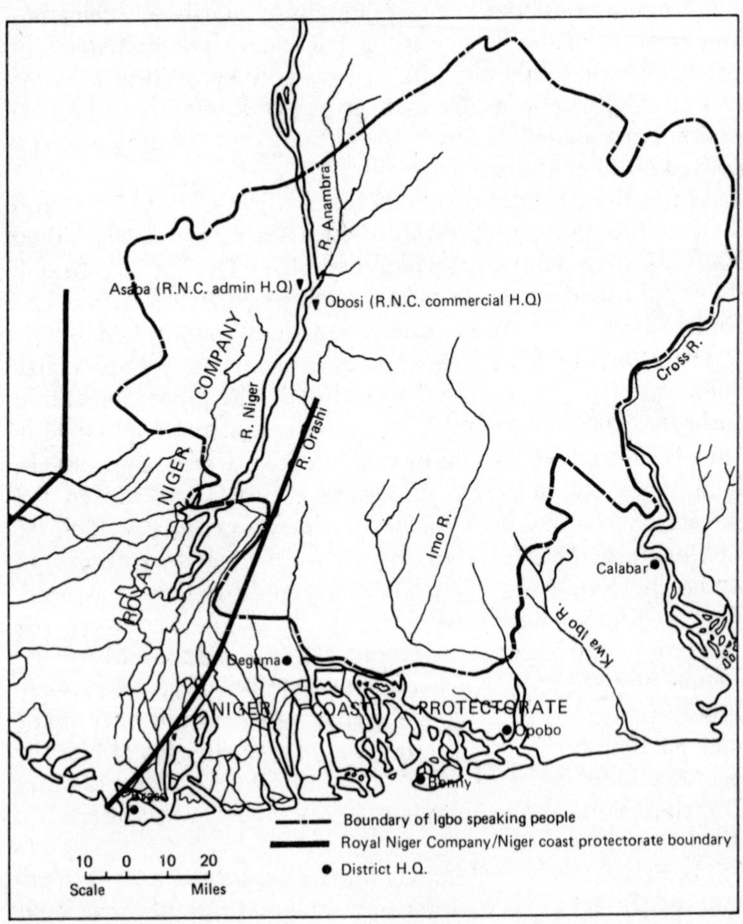

Map 9 British administrative centres and boundaries, 1896

The Women's War of 1929–30 broke out when a young man was conducting a local census, under the aegis of a local Warrant Chief, Okugo of Oloko. In the investigation which followed, complaints were made about his illegitimate exactions of cash and kind. Then Okugo was asked what his position had been before he obtained a Warrant. 'I was', he replied, 'an ordinary young man.'[9]

The Warrant Chiefs became notorious for their corruption and exploitation. In the words of Professor Afigbo, 'nearly every Warrant Chief of the time was guilty of corruption, extortion and oppression.'[10] This corruption is overwhelmingly documented in the traditions of local communities and in the records of British officialdom. The British realised from an early date that the Warrant Chiefs were both non-traditional and corrupt. They made many minor adjustments in the system, but did not change it until they were forced to do so by the Women's War. Why was there this reluctance for change? Partly because men who had worked the system for many years could not throw it overboard without appearing to condemn their whole life's work. More fundamentally, they were few in numbers and ignorant of Igbo. They depended on their Igbo collaborators, and did not know how to govern without their aid. In the words of an elder from Okigwi, 'the people gained nothing from the Warrant Chief System but the British did since it helped them to rule the peoples of the Eastern Provinces.'[11]

The Warrant Chiefs grew rich in many ways. They grew rich through the sale of justice in the courts. They abused their right of levying forced labour, for their private ends. Frequently, they engaged in money-lending to needy litigants. A report written in 1921 stated, 'The chiefs are undoubtedly anxious to give decisions for large amounts against poor defendants. They then advance the amount to liquidate the payment on security of the defendant's land.[12] They invented the device of *Akwukwo Nwannunu* (bird summons) – a summons as baseless as air – so that 'some innocent people went to prison without guilt; and some also forfeited their properties, without any just cause.'[13] This local history of Umuna gives a vivid picture of the system:

> The chiefs . . . made much money by sending their subjects in great numbers to work for the whitemen on the roads and

bridge constructions . . . The chiefs were the worst set of people who defrauded the labourers from their wages and got supreme control over them. In this way and by slavery too X accumulated much wealth and became the greatest man who

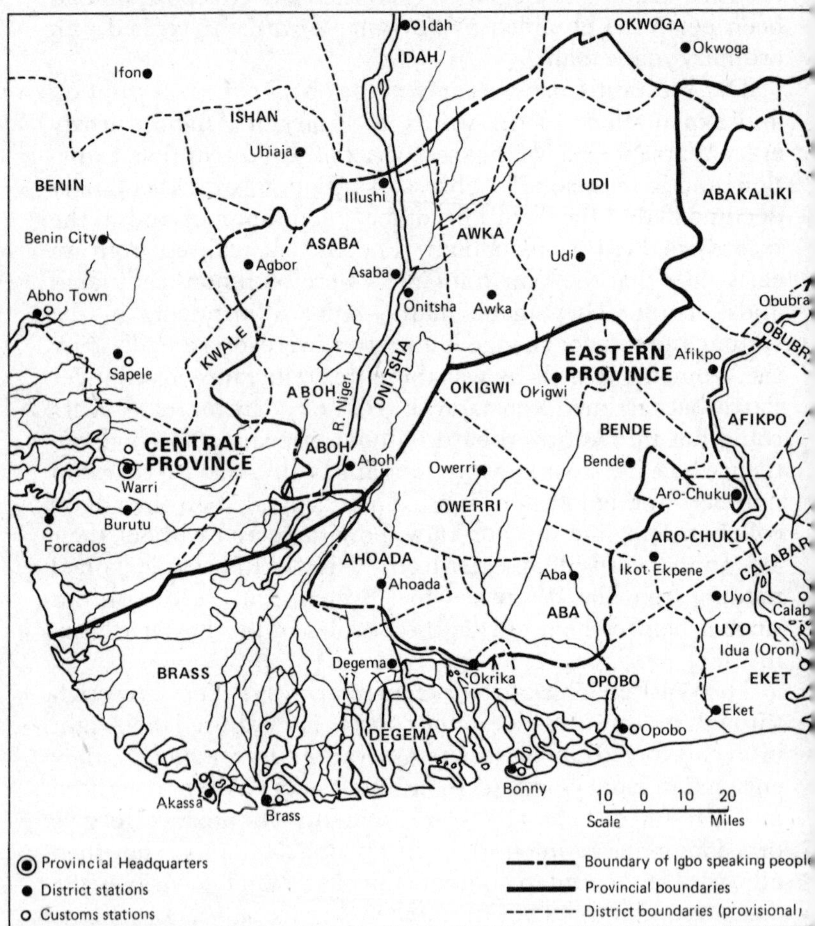

Map 10 British administrative centres and boundaries, 1909

lived in those days. He had the most famous zinc house by then and could entertain all classes of big men with food Palm wine and some imported drinks. He married over forty wives . . .[14]

In the early 1960s, a former Warrant Chief from Okigwi was asked how the Warrant Chiefs grew so rich. He replied, '*Ma ukpara erigh ibe ya o nagh ebu*' (to grow fat an insect must feed on other insects) and would say no more.[15]

The Court Clerks often attained a power and wealth greater even than that of the Warrant Chiefs especially after 1914, when European officers no longer sat as the Court Presidents. Only the Clerk had the education to understand the esoteric mysteries of court procedure. He kept the records on which any later review of the case would be based. Like the Warrant Chiefs they grew rich through corruption, through the use of prisoners' labour, and through money lending. 'Some of them own pretentious houses and possess motor cars, in which they have been known to be driven up to the court.'[16] Frequently they were expatriates from Ghana or Sierra Leone, or natives of Onitsha or of the coastal areas, so they were not restrained by the fear of public opinion, in an area where they were strangers.[17] The Court Messengers, similarly, who had the duty of serving summonses, built up the same grim record of exploitation and corruption.

It is easier to see the circumstances which made this abuse of power possible than to understand why it in fact occurred. At the heart of the colonial situation lies a problem of communication. The British officials almost never spoke Igbo. They were further divorced from the people they ruled by frequent leaves and changes in posting. Their fewness of numbers limited their contact with the people even more. Their version of events was that created for them by the Clerks and interpreters – who normally worked in close concert. Just as the manipulators of an earlier time ensured that the British fought their private wars, these intermediaries used the power and authority of the colonial regime for private ends.

Why did they in fact abuse their power? No single simple answer is possible. One answer lies in the basic locality of loyalties, which tended to mean that members of one town looked on members of another town as legitimate prey. The basic situation of the Warrant Chief was not one to attract a patriot. Too often they were forced to betray their people's interests – as Chief Njemanze was coerced, in Owerri, into giving the British a large tract of fertile farming land. In traditional society, duties and obligations were clearly defined. Decisions were made in the presence of the community, accordingly to universally acknowledged precedents and customs. But the Warrant Chiefs operated within a new and dimly comprehended system. There

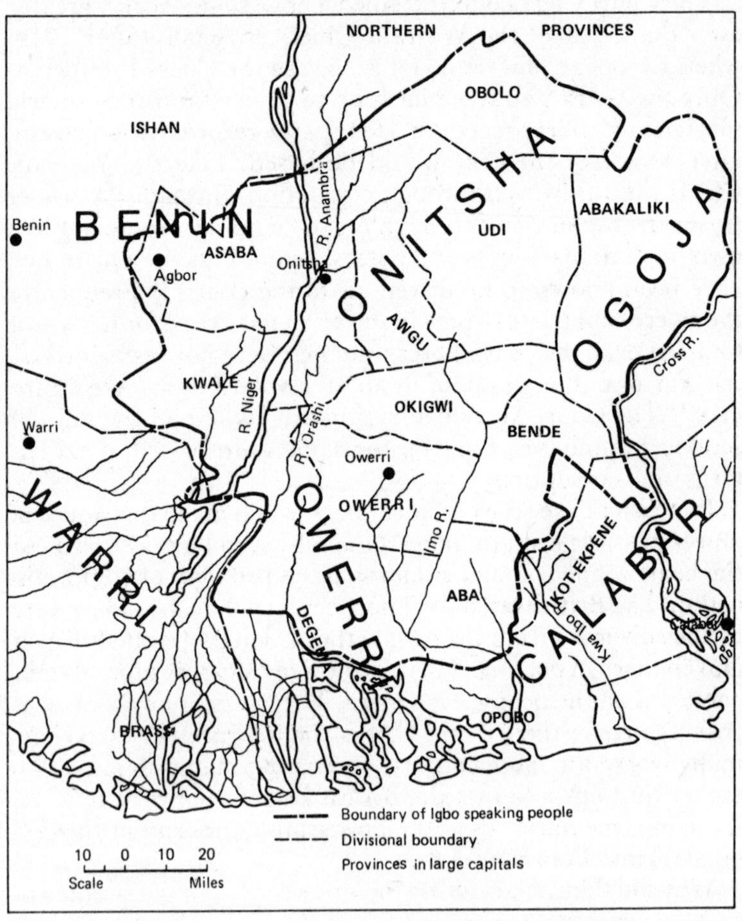

Map 11 British administrative centres and boundaries, 1924

were no precedents to guide them, and they were responsible, less to public opinion, than to the white official who had the power to take away their Warrants. In the words of a former Warrant Chief from Bende: 'Warrant Chiefs feared the Government more than the people. The latter could not unseat a chief but the Government could.'[18] It is proverbially difficult to serve two masters. . .

More fundamentally, colonialism created a new set of attitudes towards material wealth. The expatriate community, even the missionaries, enjoyed a standard of living much higher than that of Igboland. The great power of the District Officer, his 'zinc house', his car, his servants, all seemed manifestations of the one phenomenon. Success, authority, prestige, and material wealth seemed inextricably intertwined. At a later time, the legitimate aspiration towards the European's Senior Service grading was inevitably also an aspiration towards his car loan and his house in the Government Residential Area. Colonialism created a privileged élite, living in a way which was quite different from that of the impoverished villagers around them. It has left no more damaging legacy.

Times of great uncertainty and change seem to encourage materialism. Men try to attain the psychological security which the social context of their time denies them by creating a little charmed island of affluence for themselves. The Warrant Chiefs, living when 'Things fall apart, the centre cannot hold' sought security in a 'zinc house', a 'storey building', in the multiplication of wives. And education, the *summum bonum* of the new era, could be acquired only with money. Of the first Igbos who studied abroad and fully mastered the skills of the Western world, a notable proportion were the sons or close relatives of Warrant Chiefs . . .

Any system rapidly creates its own mores, which become difficult for the individual to renounce. In an age of corrupt Warrant Chiefs, an honest Chief would be stigmatised by his relatives and townsmen as a fool, a blameworthy neglecter of his and their interests. In such circumstances, those who disapproved stayed aloof. Inevitably, they seldom appear in the records, but Mr Okorah's history of Uratta contains an interesting section on 'men of Good Will'. One was Emmanuel Ewurum, a devout Christian, an adherent of the Faith Tabernacle. 'Because of his good behaviour, he was once unanimously elected chief of Orji. He attended court for a few days and discovered the amount of injustice, bribery and corruption going on . . . and unhesitatingly resigned.'[19]

The Warrant Chiefs were corrupt, but they were often also

generous. Chief Njemanze, who died in 1920, ruled Owerri with a rod of iron, but in later years one of his grandchildren recalled him with glowing affection, 'rich, strong and generous', giving yams to the poor, and shillings and corncobs to children, and comforting a child in disgrace with little presents, 'whispering to it not to tell its mother.'[20]

One of the most remarkable of the Warrant Chiefs was Chief Onyeama of Eke,[21] who enjoyed almost legendary wealth and power. He paid for the education of the first Igbo doctor, (visiting England himself at the same time), and sent many children to mission schools (he had seventy-eight children of his own). But he wielded a power which a missionary compared with 'an Arab despot', and which it was extremely dangerous to disregard. Even now, some forty years later, informants on his regime often ask not to be quoted. When I asked them why the British allowed him to continue for so long they replied, first that no one dared give evidence against him, and secondly that his authority suited the British very well. One informant was an eye witness of a conversation between the Resident and Onyeama, in which he was reminded that he was a chief over men, and not a chief over forests, and trees.

He died with the panache with which he had lived. In Agbaja, his power was waning. Two powerful men from Owa joined forces to form a band, *agadogu*, which defeated his henchmen, *ogwumili*. *Vis-à-vis* the British, the era of the Warrant Chiefs was coming to an end. He committed suicide, apparently to avoid an inquiry, having first taken care to procure – and display – a suitably resplendent coffin.

THE CHALLENGERS

There were several ways in which those who suffered under the Warrant Chiefs could challenge their regime. The most fundamental was that of education. We have an interesting case-study of the process in Ohafia.

> There was in Ohafia one Vincent, a Seirea Leonian, who was the Native Court Clerk. He was extremely wicked in his dealings with Ohafia people. On one occasion he locked several of them in the prison yard for a trivial cause. They broke out

and were intent on beating him when he instantly reported the matter to Major Cobham. The later [sic] promptly despatched policemen to his rescue. Later fines were imposed on the people.

My people wanted a way out of such persecution and my advice to them was to open a school, educate their children who, knowing what the clerk knew, could better challenge him and his successors.[22]

Frequently, great antagonism developed between the Warrant Chiefs and the educated elements. In Enugwu-Ukwu, a Warrant Chief persecuted schoolboys until a Catholic missionary rescued them. 'If those Warrant Chiefs had had their way they would have destroyed all of us. They found that because we went to school we learnt to oppose them.'[23]

What brought the system toppling, however, was a challenge of quite a different nature – the movement which the British called the Aba Riots of 1929, but which Igbo traditions, with much greater accuracy, call *Ogu Umunwanye*, the Women's War.

Our examination of armed resistance to British rule ended in 1919. Occasional small pockets of armed resistance occurred in the 1920s, but essentially protest movements came to take a different form, more akin to religious revivalism. The first of these movements, which anticipates the Women's War in many ways, began in Okigwi late in 1925. It purported to carry a message from God, heralded by 'a miraculous birth'. It swept through much of Igboland east of the Niger, following the same ritual pattern. A band of women would appear before the house of a Warrant Chief, symbolically sweep his compound, and deliver a message through a song and dance. They would then demand money, and ask that he should send the message further.[24]

The demands they made fall basically into three categories: for social reforms, for a return to the customs of the past, and for what one might call an extension of women's rights.[25] Some of the measures were protests against social abuses – exhortations to keep houses and compounds clean, and especially the area round food-bearing trees, to limit the bride price, and show greater honesty in bride-price disputes, to fix market prices, and to boycott native courts 'as poor men were often punished in native courts at instance of rich men.' One plank which accords a little oddly with their feminist proposals was that prostitutes should moderate their charges! Some were sheer conservatism: pregnant women should avoid foods known to encourage the birth of twins, roads built by the British should be abandoned, young girls should go unclothed (though this last seems to have been inspired less by conservatism than by anxieties about venereal disease), and English currency should be replaced by cowries. Some were feminist in tone – men should not plant cassava, but leave it for women, or (in a different version) 'That man must not go to market but women, that women must not do farm works but for men.' The British took the movement very seriously, and fined the participants, and it collapsed as suddenly as it had started. But for a moment, those whose views are not usually recorded in history comment on the changes of their time, with a clear voice.

The background to the Women's War lies in the decision which was taken in 1926–7, and implemented in 1928, to extend direct taxation to the Eastern Provinces. To the British administrators who took the decision, it was a matter of elementary justice. The rest of Nigeria paid taxes, and it was an anachronism that the south-east should remain exempt. Moreover it would liberate the peoples concerned from the hated imposition of forced labour. The proposal, however, aroused the strongest opposition among the Igbo and their neighbours. The Warrant Chiefs opposed it as strongly as they dared, until reminded by the British of the steel hand within the velvet glove of consultation – for their power, as they reminded the Chiefs, rested on conquest. 'I am not going to admit that the first gun boat or the first District Commissioner was here by your invitation . . . you are not in the position to say that the Government is your guest and they can go tomorrow.'[26]

The reasons for opposition were largely economic. The Igbo protested against a background of world depression and inexorably falling prices for palm oil. The chiefs pointed out the chronic problem of Igboland – which is still with us – the difficulty of obtaining paid employment. In the words of Chief Amobi of Ogidi, 'At present I have about five boys who have passed Standard VI, and they have nothing to do, will you kindly assist me to get them something to do? This is our main trouble.'[27]

No matter what their economic difficulties, the Igbo were and are prepared to contribute to a sacrificial extent to communally chosen and approved projects, such as a local Improvement Union's decision to build a school or cottage hospital. There was a great difference between this, and money extracted without real consultation for unknown and uncontrollable objectives. And who is to say that they were wrong? As the clan head of Otanzu told Professor Afigbo in the early sixties, 'The government promised us development; but tell me what development there is in Umulolo today after more than thirty years of taxation?'[28]

And there were other reasons for their reluctance. Taxation seemed like a reminder of their subjection, a rent levied on their occupancy of their own land. It was necessarily preceded by a rough population count, and by assessments of the value of land, livestock and so on. The assessment of the land seemed to herald a threat to their ownership of it. The counting of human beings had sinister overtones – which have still not entirely disappeared – for to count a numerous family seemed to be inviting the attention of death, or a jealous spirit.

In 1928 the tax was collected in an atmosphere of resentment and protest, especially strong among the Ezza and Izzi, but without a major confrontration. In 1929 the resentment erupted into violence. Several factors were responsible – the falling prices of palm oil, the over-assessment of some areas (where Warrant Chiefs had exaggerated the population to add to their own importance), and, especially, the rumour that women, too, would be taxed.

The spark that ignited the conflagration was struck in Oloko, in Bende Division.[29] A young British officer decided to check the accuracy of local population returns. He delegated the task to the local Warrant Chief, who, in his turn, delegated it to a local schoolmaster. He came in due course to a woman called Nwanyeruwa, who was processing oil in her compound. She took his questions as an affront, and a scuffle ensued. (She said later that her feelings had been exacerbated by the recent death of her only son's wife.) Nwanyeruwa rushed to a gathering of women, who as it happened were holding a church meeting near by. The women joined her in indignant protest, and the alarmed British officer gave them the local chief's cap of office, and imprisoned both the schoolmaster and the Warrant Chief after a summary trial.

The effect of this apparent victory over the British was electric. The women of Oloko sent delegates armed with symbolic palm branches to neighbouring towns. In a number of centres in both the Igbo and Ibibio areas of Calabar province, and in Owerri Province, the women responded with enthusiasm. They sent money donations, which Nwanyeruwa, who displayed considerable statesmanship, used to finance further delegations. Basically, it was a protest against taxation and the extortions of the Warrant Chiefs, which escalated into a total rejection of the whole colonial presence. The women of Ohuhu declared that 'they would go to Owerrinta to demolish the Native Court; that they did not want the Native Court to hear cases any longer; and that all white men should return to their country so that the land in this area might remain as it was many years ago before the advent of the white man.'[30]

As the map following shows, the movement covered quite a small area – it embraced western Ibibioland, the Igbo-speaking town of Opobo, and that area of Igboland lying between Owerri and Aba, and south of Aba to the Imo River. The limited communications facilities available to the women meant that it spread slowly. Before the message had reached areas further north and west, the news of the shootings had spread equally, and made participation seem obvious folly.

It is not easy to see how the women conceptualised their movement – it was a spontaneous protest against oppression, rather than a carefully thought out campaign. They wore chalk markings and carried palm fronds, which can symbolise both peace and war, and were armed only with sticks. They attacked the Native Courts, destroying a number of them, and attacked the Warrant Chiefs. After an accident at Aba, they attacked the European factories as well. A British doctor accidentally knocked down two of the women rioters in his car, and took refuge in a Niger Company factory. The furious women attacked the factory. Hearing of this, other women elsewhere, not to be outdone, did likewise.[31]

The women seem to have had a strange confidence in their invulnerability. They compared themselves with the vultures in the market, whom no one ever harms.[32] This confidence seems to have been rooted less in a misplaced confidence in British traditions of chivalry – of which they were probably unaware – than in a strange mystique of immunity, notable in many other risings in colonial Africa, such as the Maji-Maji war of southern Tanzania. Their confidence, in the event, was rudely shattered. Troops fired on the women in eight different places. The official casualty list was 55 women killed, 32 of them at Opobo, and 50 wounded, 31 at Opobo.[33]

Unplanned, spontaneous, disastrous, the rising gave outward expression to a deep inarticulate desire to turn back the clock of change, not only to remove specific forms of oppression, but to realise again the happier society *in illo tempore*. Half remembered, half understood, unrecoverable, the world they had lost beckoned them with a compelling attraction.

I once asked an old man from near Enugu if he thought that, after the first abuses of the colonial regime had been eradicated, people were better off than they had been before. He replied without hesitation, 'They were more progressive, but they were not happier.'

THE SEQUEL

Like the Brassmen's war on the Royal Niger Company in 1895, with which it has certain affinities, the Women's War was a disastrous failure on one level, but a complete success on another. It forced the British, as no earlier reports or criticisms had done, to re-examine the nature of their government of the Igbo and their neighbours. Belatedly, they decided to investigate what the traditional forms of government actually were. Clan by clan, village group by village group, British officials conducted an inquiry into the history and traditional government of the people they ruled. The quality of the Intelligence Reports they produced in the early thirties is very variable – some are perfunctory, others are detailed and well informed. It is a reflection of the underdeveloped state of Igbo historical studies that today, in the 1970s, these hastily prepared Reports are practically our only source of information about the pre-colonial history of many Igbo communities.

In the wake of this inquiry, the British introduced a new system of local government. Its basic characteristic was that it was an attempt to restore the political system of pre-colonial times. In practice, to restore this in all its complexity and subtlety was impossible, and they concentrated on one aspect – the role of lineage heads. Clan councils were created, attended by unwieldy numbers of elders. 'Authorities could and did consist

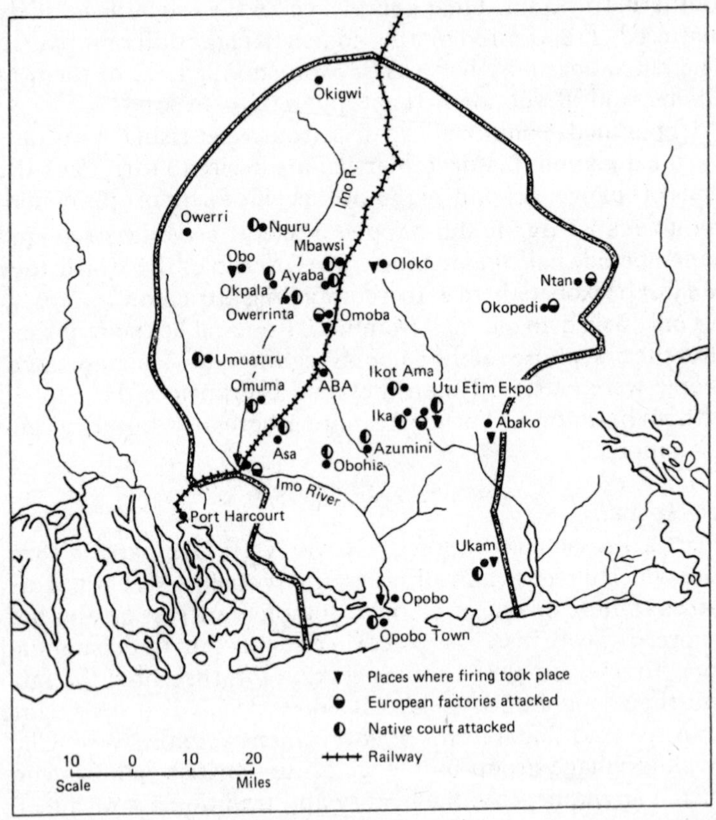

Map 12 The Women's War of 1929–30

of several hundred or even several thousand members. It was impossible ever to meet "the authority". Inevitably some members took more interest than others, and most of the members never attended meetings. The tendency was for a meeting to consist of from forty to eighty members.'[34] In an attempt to prevent the corruption of the Warrant Chief era, the Lockean principle of the separation of powers was introduced – with Native Authorities now separate from Native Courts. A system of Native Treasuries was introduced. The Treasuries were given the task of raising taxes, and were allowed to spend half the amount raised on local projects. The enthusiasm that this might have generated was curbed by the need to give the government a shilling for every shilling spent locally. A proposal made in 1942 to freeze the government quota, and thus encourage the local raising of funds for local projects, was never implemented.[35]

The changes were inspired by excellent intentions, and they created a brief glow of optimism and enthusiasm. But the glow soon died. This is how the Native Courts were described by a neutral observer in 1938–9.

> At the present time not only do the litigants still bribe the judges (now called the 'court members') but they must pay large fees to the native court clerk, which are phrased as 'kola' so that the clerk will record the case as it actually transpired . . . Furthermore fees are paid to the court messengers . . . to have the summons served promptly and efficiently. Bribes are often offered to and sometimes accepted by the white administrators' interpreters who, whenever the case has been appealed, can by skilful interpretation influence the white official in the desired manner. Fees are often paid to Africans who boast of vast legal knowledge and the ability to win cases for them by preparing their arguments and by writing petitions . . . Finally, the court members must pay a fee to the court clerk so that he will allow them to hear a fair number of cases during the monthly period in which they sit.[36]

Where the former Warrant Chiefs were men of strong natural authority, they rapidly re-emerged within the new system.[37] *Plus ça change, plus c'est la même chose.*

The reason for the failure of the new system was basically threefold. First, it was in appearance, but not in reality, a restoration of traditional government. The essence of the old system was that it combined a number of different forms of political authority, many of which, such as secret societies and the role of oracles and divination, were lacking in the new. And as with the Warrant Chiefs they were primarily responsible, not to the community, but to the foreign overlords. Secondly, a political system depends on continuity. It cannot be abandoned for thirty years and then arbitrarily resurrected. An elder of sixty who was called on to play a part in the new system, was expected to carry on a tradition which had been given up when he was thirty and not an elder, and so not yet involved in its operation. Inevitably, they conceptualised their roles in terms of the political system which had been in operation for most of their adult lives. They saw themselves as potential Warrant Chiefs, and were disappointed that their great numbers meant that the prestige and the financial rewards were less.

Most fundamentally, the political reorganisation of the thirties was an attempt to preserve the political forms which had been found appropriate in pre-colonial Igbo society. They were revived at the very time when that society was changing. They gave authority to 'hundreds of somewhat aged and illiterate gentlemen' but 'as things were it seemed there was not and could not be a place in local organisation for educated men and by now these were in appreciable numbers.'[38]

The lack of opportunity for the educated to play a part in local government was the rock upon which the new system foundered. To the educated, it seemed that it was a deliberate ploy to exclude them and hold them back. Nor were these fears without foundation. Among the white officials, only the exceptionally generous could view with equanimity a development – the expansion of the educated classes – which threatened the foundation of their whole careers; '. . . before you know where you are they want to drive you out imagining that they can govern themselves because one or two have been educated . . . it is going on here in the same way as in India. Suppression – not oppression – is the way to treat subject races . . .'[39]

The post-war modification of the system, by which a community could put forward, not necessarily its lineage head, but its member best qualified for the post, did not really meet the situation since practically none of the educated class lived in their own home towns. And by then the whole concept of 'Native Authorities' had become emotionally unacceptable to nationalists.

The thirties saw the swelling of a movement which had begun much earlier – the development of a myriad of Improvement Associations. These grew up, not in the villages, but in the cities, where practically all the educated worked. They attracted the local patriotism which in another context would have found expression in local government. They came to fill many of the functions of local government, taxing themselves heavily to implement local development projects. We shall look at their activities more fully in a later section of this study.

In fairness to the British, it should be recorded that the Unions did not have a monopoly on community development. E. R. Chadwick was District Officer at Udi in the forties, and became deservedly famous for initiating community development projects. One of the most famous was the Owa Road constructed in 1943, which after its completion bore a plaque, *Ike Dimpka*, by the power of man.[40] His achievements are commemorated in the film, *Daybreak in Udi*. And there were others, too, such as D. R. Gibbs, 'whose memories can hardly tarnish at Awgu.'[41]

11 The Growth of Christianity in Igboland

We do not speak of accomplishing great things, for we must expect difficulties; but the work is the Lord's who has graciously promised, 'My work shall not return to me void': therefore we believe, that in the Ibo country also, as in other parts, the Lord has 'much people'.

the Igbo Christians of Sierra Leone to the Church Missionary Society, in 1857[1]

THE PRELUDE

The history of the Christianisation of Igboland begins in 1841, when Simon Jonas, an Igbo who had been sold into slavery and rescued and resettled in Sierra Leone, spent three weeks at Aboh, and preached to the children who flocked around him.[2] The first permanent mission in Igboland was established at Onitsha in 1857, under the leadership of the Reverend John Christopher Taylor, who was born in Sierra Leone of Igbo parentage. For almost thirty years, all the missionaries on the Niger and in the Delta – the two frontiers of Igboland most exposed to mission influence – were Africans from Sierra Leone, often, though not always, of Igbo descent. As time went by, the local people joined in the work of evangelisation. Onitsha Christians first brought the Gospel to nearby Obosi,[3] and the slaves of Bonny began a remarkable evangelical work in the oil markets of southern Igboland.[4]

The slaves of Bonny gave Christianity a whole-hearted welcome, from the first inception of the mission in 1865. Their faith withstood persecution, for many of the chiefs feared the new religion's implication of social equality. Many were imprisoned and beaten in the early seventies. One, Joshua Hart, became Nigeria's first martyr. Refusing to sacrifice to pagan gods in

1875, he was bound with cords, thrown into the water, and beaten with paddles and stabbed with spears until he died.[5] Perhaps, like so many Bonny slaves, he was of Igbo origin. In any case his ethnic origin is immaterial; his life and death belong to the heritage of Nigerian Christianity. The slaves sent to trade in Igboland ignored the protests of their masters, and held evangelistic meetings on Sunday – an activity in which they persevered for many years. For some of them, mission education proved the gateway to higher social status. One of them, David Okparabietoa Pepple, born in Igboland, was ordained a deacon, and ended his life as the pastor at Ohumbele, where he had once been sold as a slave.[6]

In 1885 there was a change in the personnel of the missions. The C.M.S. Niger Mission was taken over by white Evangelicals. The Delta Churches, in protest, became a separate Pastorate, in 1892, remaining within the Anglican communion. Two Catholic congregations came to the Niger: the Society of African Missions, on the west bank, with its headquarters at Asaba, and the Holy Ghost Fathers in the east, with their headquarters at Onitsha. The Presbyterians, who had been at Calabar since 1846, set up their first Igbo station in 1888, at Unwana, notable as the home of Sir Francis Akanu Ibiam, one of the first two Igbo doctors, and one of the outstanding Nigerian Christians of our time. The station was only occupied spasmodically in the nineteenth century, and the real history of Igbo Presbyterianism does not begin until the twentieth.

The evangelicals of the Niger Mission and the Catholic Fathers had much in common. Despite the exquisite charity with which the aged Bishop Crowther gave the Holy Ghost Fathers a plot of C.M.S. land,[7] they tended to be suspicious of, and hostile to, Christian denominations other than their own. Both were even more hostile to Igbo religion; not once, but repeatedly, in their writings and correspondence does one find Igboland described as the kingdom of Satan.[8] The explanation for this attitude can be found partly in the religious attitudes of Europe at the time, and partly in the psychological circumstances of their work. Only the belief that each conversion meant another soul destined for Heaven gave them the courage to labour, suffer and die for the conversion of Igboland. Had they seen Igbo religion as one manifestation of that Light which enlightens every man born into the world, they would never have come to the Niger at all.

Both missions, in the nineteenth century, remained closely confined to the Niger and its tributaries. Both affected only a small number of conversions. But the success of a mission is not measured only in statistics, and the Christianity of the late nineteenth century produced lives of great holiness, both among the missionaries and among their Igbo converts. Of the white C.M.S. missionaries, Archdeacon Dobinson was a man of towering stature, justly beloved by his colleagues and by the people of Onitsha. Of the Catholic missionaries, no single figure emerges beyond the rest. One might mention the singularly attractive figure of Father Piotin, who lived on pieces of yam in order to devote his slender financial resources to the people around him, but his life belongs rather to the as yet unwritten history of the Afenmai. The now forgotten name of Father Ferrieux, another Frenchman, should perhaps be rescued from oblivion. He studied some medicine before coming to Africa, to such good effect that he performed a successful amputation. Stationed at Ibusa, he spent his days in medical work, in house to house visitation, and in prayer. He always dined with local families, and spent the evening with them. The Ibusa people gave him several Igbo names – among them, ones which meant He who does good, and Stay with us (the latter, he wrote, corresponded with his own desire to live and die there). He was accidentally drowned in 1911, when swimming in one of the clear streams of western Igboland. A superior wrote of him, 'Since I have been on the Niger I have never seen a missionary of this calibre. A devout and holy priest, devoted to the point of complete immolation and self-forgetfulness, a joyful and charming Confrère . . .'[9]

The bulk of the first Christian converts were drawn from the poor, the needy, and the rejected: the mothers of twins, women accused of witchcraft, those suffering from diseases such as leprosy which were seen as abominable. Finding little satisfaction in the world around them, they turned to Christianity with a single-minded devotion which astonished all who beheld it. The Christian village at Aguleri, peopled mainly by the poor, maintained for many years a way of life which was almost monastic in its devotion. The whole community thronged to daily mass and communion, and joined in groups in the evenings to recite the rosary.[10]

Not all the converts were poor. Several wealthy and prestigious chiefs sacrificed their standing and their family ties to become Christians. In the words of a missionary who worked for many years in Iboland,

> In most cases . . . such a conversion deserved to be described as a miracle of grace, because it meant dismissing extra wives, thus breaking up normal home life, and surrendering much of one's social standing, thus denying oneself many of the joys of public life, and of course it involved an uproar in the wide and elastic circle that made up an Ibo family. Yet there were men who took the step . . . [11]

One who took the step was Chief Idigo of Aguleri,[12] whom we have had occasion to mention repeatedly in this study – one of the most interesting and best-documented figures of nineteenth-century Igbo history. Born in the early nineteenth century, he was a classic example of the New Men. He was a priest and *dibia*. He became wealthy and married many wives, taking the *ogbuefi* title early in life. He was noted for his courage – on one occasion he fought a duel with a famous warrior of Ifite Oguari. He won the duel, and spared his opponent's life. He 'travelled widely and got wide experience which made him influential and respected at Aguleri resulting later to his being recognised as ruler of Aguleri. When the servants of the National African Company came in 1884, he was the only man who stood firm to receive the strangers.' In the late eighties, he began issuing a series of pressing invitations to the Holy Ghost Fathers at Onitsha. The invitation decided the whole pattern of their expansion strategy, for at the time they were hesitating as to the direction in which to develop. Influenced by Idigo, they set up a chain of stations in the Anambra. Oddly enough, they procured an elderly horse from the Royal Niger Company, so that Idigo could take the *ogbuanyinya* title – an action in curious contrast to the mission's later condemnation of title-taking, which was to cause Igbo Christians so much laceration of heart.

Idigo was baptised in 1890, having dismissed all his wives but one. Why did he embrace Christianity, and why did he seek it out, when it was still unknown to him? If it was to win the favour of the whites he would scarcely have courted imprisonment, a little later, by defying the Royal Niger Company. It seems that he was alienated from traditional religion by a number of misfortunes, especially the successive deaths of his children. It seems too – although such explanations are now unfashionable among historians – that he was a seeker after truth, whom God rewarded with an extraordinary grace. As the priest who instructed him put it, 'I perceived above all, that he was religious, and put his confidence in a Supreme Being, Whom he had doubtless been seeking in his idols.'[13]

After his conversion, the persecution that he suffered forced him to leave the town, and set up a Christian village near the river. Despite the persecution, he remained loyal to his people – a loyalty that earned him, as we have seen, four years' exile in Asaba. In 1896 he was able to return to Aguleri, where he died in 1900.

There were other notable convert chiefs, such as Alexander Ubuechi of Issele-Uku, who devoted himself to the service of God so entirely, in the four years that elapsed between his baptism and his death in 1903, that the missionaries acclaimed him as a saint.[14]

Another category of notable Igbo Christian pioneers were the catechists. Poorly paid, often of humble origins and little education, they did the real work of bringing Christianity to the villages. To take our example this time from the C.M.S., one of the best-documented examples was Joseph Obimgbo Egbola, who became a Christian in 1894, while working as a gardener for the Royal Niger Company, teaching himself to read in the evenings. Despite his sincere protestations of unworthiness, he was sent to take charge of the new mission station at Akwukwu. This is a contemporary description of his work:

> When he began his work at Akwukwu, everything was discouraging. The opposition of the heathen was great and the popular feeling ran high against the message he had to deliver. Very patiently he went about his work, and gradually opposition began to give way . . . He was versed in the knowledge of herbal remedies, and he put his knowledge into good practice for the benefit of the Akwukwu people. Many persons, once victims of repulsive ulcers, were cured by him,

> and some of them are now grateful and humble followers of the Lord Jesus . . .
>
> When speaking once to his people on the importance of studying the Scriptures, he said, 'I did not get much teaching from the C.M.S., all I know I learned from God's word.' . . . On another occasion . . . he said, 'The work presses me, it is God who does the work.'[15]

He died in 1904, apparently of tuberculosis. He preached his last sermon at Akwukwu on a text from Thessalonians, 'In our great longing for you, we desired nothing better than to offer you our own lives, as well as God's gospel, so greatly had we learned to love you.'

In 1893 the greatest of the C.M.S. expatriate missionaries wrote to London: 'Oh for more native Agents! They are 3 times as valuable as any European Agent for their work. We are as fading flowers.'[16]

THE YEARS OF GROWTH

By 1900, the success of the missions was very limited indeed. The Catholic provided annual statistics of their members, but they tend to be misleading, for they exclude on the one hand, many who attended church but could not be baptised, as polygamists, and include on the other, many non-Catholics baptised *in articulo mortis*, who recovered. In 1900, the Society of African Missions had a nominal roll of 446, and the Holy Ghost Fathers, of 1322. But of the S.M.A. figures, all but eighty were baptised *in articulo mortis*. Of the eighty, thirty were Royal Niger Company employees. So the fruits of fifteen years of missionary work were fifty local Catholics.[17] If the Holy Ghost Fathers statistics were similar, they had perhaps 150–200 Catholics. We have no statistics for the C.M.S., whose adherents were more numerous. All their stations were clustered around Asaba and Onitsha, where they reached, according to one estimate, one per cent of the population.[18] At the outside, it would seem that the first half century of Christian mission work had produced about a thousand baptised Christians, of all denominations.

In the years that followed the position of the Christian churches in Igboland underwent an astonishing transformation. The 1921 census claimed that 284,835 out of 3,927,419 Igbo were Christians. The largest single denomination was

Catholicism, which had an estimated 26,499 adherents in Onitsha province and 43,053 in Owerri province, but was outnumbered by all Protestant groups taken together.[19] The 1931 census put the total number of the Igbo at 3,172,789, of whom 253,378 were Protestants and 94,049 Catholics.[20] All these figures were under-estimates.* Catholic records showed that in 1932 there were 110,049 Catholics and 85,049 catechumens under Bishop Shanahan's jurisdiction, which included the non-Igbo communities of Ibibioland and Ogoja, but excluded the Igbo Catholics west of the Niger.[21] In 1937 the Government anthropologist, Meek, estimated that 600,000 out of four million Igbos were Christians.[22] In the 1953 census, 26·5 per cent of the population of Onitsha Province, and 64·7 per cent of that of Owerri Province, described themselves as Christians. The percentage was 5·3 per cent in Abakaliki Division, 13·9 per cent in Afikpo Division and 92·5 per cent in Port Harcourt Division.[23] By 1963, it had risen to 60·4 and 88·3 per cent respectively.[24] Now, in the 1970s, the churches of Igboland have emancipated themselves entirely from expatriate control. At every level – bishops, clergy and teachers in training institutions – the churches have become entirely Igbonised. Bigard Memorial Seminary in Enugu is one of the three largest seminaries in the world.

The seeds of this astonishing transformation were sown between 1900 and 1920 – especially, perhaps, between 1906 and 1914. Bishop Shanahan often said that he gained more and lost more in 1912 and 1913 than in any other years.[25] The full fruits of the harvest were gathered many years afterwards.

Why did the Igbo adopt Christianity with such astonishing enthusiasm after almost half a century of relative indifference? One obvious change after 1900 was the British conquest of Igboland. Previously the missionaries had lived on suffrance in sovereign states on the borders of Igboland. Now the country was 'opened up' – they could travel to the Igbo interior in relative security. All denominations welcomed the Aro expedition, for this reason. The observations of a Presbyterian missionary

* The interpretation of Nigerian census data requires an essay to itself. In 1921 only townships were enumerated – the rest was an informed guess. The 1931 census was overshadowed by the Women's War in Igboland, and again includes many informed guesses.

at Calabar – especially noteworthy as coming from a man who had been active in exploring on the frontiers of his mission – betrayed an almost incredible ignorance of Igboland:

> What is sad about the Aro Expedition is that nearly all the town names in connection with it are unknown to those of us who thought we had a passable knowledge of Old Calabar. I never heard of the Aros, of Bende, or of Arochuku.[26]

In the wake of the expedition, the various Christian denominations made a move to the interior, which we shall look at in more detail when we consider the history of the individual denominations. A far larger number of Igbo communities were exposed to mission influence.

We have still to explain why so many welcomed it. An Igbo historian, Professor Ekechi, lays his primary emphasis on the dangers and impositions of the early colonial era.[27] Igbo groups looked to the missions as allies and defenders both against the violence of conquest and, as individuals, against the extortion of forced and unpaid labour, and the other forms of oppression of the early colonial period. This, certainly, was a factor in the equation. Ozubulu and Ihiala, destined to become two flourishing Catholic centres, showed little responsiveness to mission teachings until after a disastrous conflict with the British, when the local people 'seeing that it was good policy to be on good terms with the whites came from many places to look for the Father to beg him to come to them and set up schools.'[28] There is much other evidence to the same effect. And missionaries tended to intervene on the Christians' side in local disputes, even when, as sometimes happened, they were wrong.[29]

But this is far from being the whole story. Many other areas of Nigeria went through the same experiences, but did not turn to Christianity in the same way.

The key factor, undoubtedly, was the close association between the missions and education. The Igbo communities on the Niger had shown relatively little interest in Western education in the nineteenth century, when it seemed to offer no overwhelming advantages vis-à-vis their own and some clear disadvantages, such as the insubordination of the young. In the twentieth century the picture changed dramatically. On the one hand, Western education offered an escape from the petty tyranny of Court Clerk and Warrant Chief; on the other, colonialism created new opportunities for paid employment. Both the government and the commercial firms needed large numbers of clerks. The missions themselves employed large numbers of catechists and primary-school teachers. At first, clerical posts were held mainly by youths from Onitsha, Bonny or Calabar, or even further afield, from Lagos, Sierra Leone or the Gold Coast. As the products of local mission schools began to compete with them, the commercial advantages of education became universally evident. The same emphasis on competitive achievement which had led the Igbo to struggle to accumulate the wealth to take a title, or to grow sufficiently numerous and excellent yams for a yam title, was easily transposed to education. Bishop Shanahan, in particular, recognised this secular demand for education, and exploited it to the full.

The emphasis on competitive achievement applied not only to individuals, but to towns. Onitsha appeared the paradigm of a town which had prospered through education. 'In the eyes of most Igbo, Onitsha is a model of a town which has gotten up.'[30] Bishop Crowther had described the phenomenon, with almost prophetic insight, in 1859.

> From all I could gather by observation, the Ibos are very emulative: as in other things, so it will be in book-learning. Other towns will not rest satisfied until they have learned the mystery of reading and writing, by which their neighbours may surpass or put them in the shade.[31]

And so it proved. 'When people in one place discovered that a neighbouring town was arranging for a teacher, they immediately called a meeting to discuss the pros and cons.'[32]

Other factors, of course, contributed. Some individuals were converted through mission medical aid. The first man to bring Christianity to Arondizuogu was a certain Akweke. He went to Iyi-enu hospital for treatment for an eye defect in 1910, and returned, cured and a Christian, in 1912, to become the first pioneer of Christianity in Arondizuogu.[33] In the days when leprosy was treated with injections of hydnocarpus oil, many Igbos spent years at the Presbyterian leper colony at Itu, founded in 1928, finally returning to their villages cured, and Christians.[34]

The growth of communications, the increased knowledge of the wider world, the growth of urbanisation, all weakened traditional religion. Traditional religion is essentially local – tied to this local shrine, this village festival, this village taboo. A man who left his village for Lagos was almost bound to cease to practise his inherited religion.

The period from 1885 to about 1950 was the age *par excellence* of the expatriate missionary. The best tribute to their success was the shortness of their stay. Nevertheless, there is a certain imbalance in existing accounts of the missionary enterprise in Igboland.

The only general account of Catholicism in Igboland after 1914 is a life of Bishop Shanahan. We have a full length autobiography by another Irish missionary, Father Mellett, but only a pamphlet about the first Igbo Catholic priest, Father Emecete, and no account at all of the first Igbo Catholic bishop, Bishop Anyogu. McFarlan's history of the Presbyterian church in south-eastern Nigeria lays most of its emphasis on the work of expatriates. If one seeks further published studies of Presbyterian history, one must turn to the various lives of Mary Slessor, and the study of Dr Hitchcock, or the autobiography of Dr MacDonald. Even a study by an Igbo historian, Professor Ekechi, gives more space to Archdeacon Dennis than to any Igbo evangelist.

All the studies I have mentioned stress explicitly the value of the work of local missionary agents. Nevertheless, the main picture one gets is of a faith brought and established mainly by expatriates, whether from Europe or Sierra Leone. But if one studies the history of an individual Igbo community – unless it was a place like Emekuku or Asaba, where a white missionary resided – one finds the chief role is played by the local agent. The expatriate missionary visited the out-stations occasionally. The day-to-day work of running them, of teaching the children, instructing the catechumens, or baptising the dying, was done by a legion of obscure men whose names are now forgotten, except in the villages where they worked. Every year, the village group of Ngwo holds a thanksgiving service in memory of one of them – a C.M.S. agent: '*Chukwu gozie* Isaac Ejindu'.[85] The account of the individual churches which follows, attempts to rescue at least a tiny number of these forgotten servants of God from oblivion.

At least a word should be said about the relationships between the various Christian denominations. Professor Ekechi sees the dominant note of their relationship as rivalry – so much so that missionary rivalry becomes part of the title of his book. There is evidence on both sides. It is difficult to forget the words with which Bishop Crowther gave the Holy Ghost Fathers a plot of C.M.S. land: 'I acquired this for God's cause – take it.'[36] But the C.M.S. Annual Report for Onitsha in 1886 shows an ambivalent attitude to the Catholic Mission – admiration for their 'active charity, devotions and self abasements' and dislike of their 'pernicious' doctrines: 'The heathens have already observed that only a little difference exists between themselves and them as to the modes of worship.'[37]

As time went on, relations deteriorated rather than improved. To evangelical Protestants, the Catholics brought a religion tainted with idolatry. To the Catholics, the Protestant missions were simply converting pagans into heretics. Relations between the various Protestant missions were, for obvious reasons, much better. In the twentieth century they held a series of Boundary Conferences, and agreed on lines of demarcation between them, though not without friction and altercation. The main Protestant missions, too, succeeded in establishing a number of joint ventures, beginning with a joint C.M.S.-Methodist-Presbyterian Womens Training College at Umuahia in 1936 and later including a number of Union secondary schools, a theological training centre and the Queen Elizabeth Hospital also at Umuahia.

Traditions collected in various parts of Igboland make it clear that the Protestant-Catholic rivalry, in particular, often seriously divided Igbo communities. An Igbo Holy Ghost Father from Ihembosi recalls his childhood:

> For all practical purposes the first article of our creed which was our first Commandment was: 'Thou shalt hate "paganism" and all that is connected with it, with thy whole heart, with thy whole mind, with thy whole soul and with thy whole strength.' The second was like the first, 'Thou shalt regard "Protestants" as thy enemies.'[38]

An elder from Edem Nsukka recalls, 'The Fathers' churchmen told us that the C.M.S. churchmen attended a church made by man while the C.M.S. churchmen had been telling people that the Fathers' churchmen worshipped neither the supreme God nor the native gods but medals.'[39]

THE CATHOLICS

In the early twentieth century, the history of the Catholic missions east and west of the Niger became, for a time, sharply different. Until the death of Father Zappa, in 1917, the Society of African Missions kept essentially to its nineteenth-century policies. Zappa was a Milanese; he distrusted reliance on education as a source of mission recruitment, which he felt would attract children primarily for material aims, and fill the church with mediocre Christians. He and his colleagues continued to apply the techniques of individual persuasion. Visitors admired them for their personal austerity and devotion, but their dwindling congregations compared ill with the growth of the Holy Ghost Fathers' missions across the Niger. In his last years, Father Zappa became converted to the value of schools as a means of evangelisation, though the change of policy was not to be implemented until after his death. When he died, a Holy Ghost Father wrote, 'He was a saint and an apostle: the dust in his tomb will preach in his stead.'[40]

The outstanding achievement of this phase of S.M.A. activity was the training of the first indigenous Catholic priest in British West Africa. Father Paul Obodechine Emecete was born in the little western Igbo town of Ezi in 1888, the youngest child of an entire family which adopted Christianity and suffered much persecution in consequence.[41] He was chosen for training as a catechist. After a short period of secular employment, he became the mission's solitary seminarian, choosing celibacy at a time when few Igbo Christians were prepared to commit themselves to monogamy. After ten years of study he was ordained in 1920. Father Paul, as he was always called, was the beloved protégé of the continental priests – Father Zappa died in his arms. Oral traditions suggest that when the Irish took over the mission, he became increasingly isolated, and the recipient of less confidence. His health began to fail in his middle years and he retired, still relatively young, in 1942 and died, after years of illness, in 1948. Oral traditions pay glowing tribute to his outstanding qualities of intellect and heart. He lies buried in a quiet grave in Ezi, under an umbrella tree.

After Father Zappa's death, the Catholic Mission west of the

Niger was transformed. His Irish successor, Bishop Broderick, began a whole-hearted educational programme on the lines of the Holy Ghost Fathers, though some twenty years later; 'depending on ignorance for the advancement of Catholicism is surely against every principle of our faith.'[42]

East of the Niger, Catholic mission policy saw a dramatic transformation, which began under the Norman, Father Lejeune, and was completed under his more famous Irish successor, Bishop Shanahan. Like other denominations, they pushed into the Igbo interior in the wake of the military expeditions. In the years before the First World War a whole chain of missions were established. In 1908, a mission was opened at Ozubulu.[43] After several false starts in the Owerri area, a mission was established at Emekuku.[44] Both were destined to be the focal point of a vast network of out-stations. After the discovery of coal at Enugu, the Catholics joined with other denominations in a race for Udi, and established a station at Eke in 1918, which became, in its turn, a springboard for missions in the Nsukka area.[45]

Bishop Shanahan was a masterly strategist. He recognised and exploited to the full the two salient factors of the early colonial situation – the Igbo people's thirst for education on the one hand, and the colonial government's need for educated African personnel, on the other. The government (and the commercial firms) needed clerks, storekeepers, and so on. It was not prepared to undertake the expense and responsibility of establishing a large network of schools. By subsiding mission schools, it attained the same ends more cheaply. The mission, for its part, was delivered from its utter dependence on small donations from Catholic charitable organisations. Government subsidies came to be one of the chief financial pillars of the missionary enterprise.

The running costs of the schools were paid for by local Igbo communities. The Igbo community built the school, provided the school materials, and paid the teacher. The teacher's salary came partly from the pupils, partly from the community – that is, the Christian community. The pupils often went to extraordinary lengths to raise their contributions, farming 'bad bush', or making mats and keeping chickens for miniscule profits. 'Nothing', wrote a missionary in 1920, 'is given for nothing.'[46] A pupil who did not pay his fees could not advance to the next class. If the community's total was not paid in full, the school was closed.

The results were remarkable. By 1920 the Holy Ghost Fathers had 559 primary schools, with a total of 33,737 pupils. By 1932, there were 1386 schools and churches, though – in depression years – the number of pupils had fallen.[47]

Nevertheless, it is mistaken to consider the history of the mission as a simple success story, for there were losses as well as gains. Devoting themselves to the schools, the Irish Fathers lost their predecessors' close touch with the people. As early as 1907 it was reported, 'Knowledge of the language: little or not at all.'[48] As time progressed, matters worsened. It became generally recognised that missionaries engaged in the schools did not learn the language.[49]

An increasing income led to a higher standard of living, and more frequent home leaves. This in itself was all to the good, but oral traditions mirror both the heavy weight of the church's financial exactions, and a sense of increasing distance between the expatriate missionaries and the people they served. This was true of all the denominations. Each denomination's history includes stories of patients left on the steps of mission hospitals, unable to pay the fees, and of brilliant boys sent away from school for the same reason. The continental missionaries of the nineteenth century lived in destitution and spent their tiny income on condensed milk for abandoned babies. Judged by the terrible and exacting standards of the religion they professed, they were not less successful than those who came after them . . .

The emphasis on fund-raising has left a grim imprint on present-day Nigerian Catholicism. Anyone who has seen a penitent turned away from the confessional because his church-dues card is out of date must be disturbed by a practice which, in another context, one might call simony.[50] An Irish missionary who has devoted his life to Nigeria writes of 'a senior service priesthood based on Church taxation . . . The Irish missionaries set up . . . a money-grinding and anti-intellectual Church . . .'[51]

The attitudes of colonialism affected the Catholics, like the other missionary groups. Oral traditions collected in Nsukka speak with a sad unanimity: 'White men have low opinion of us. I remember when I asked Father G. to carry me in his car when he was going to Enugu, he told me to go to Zik.'[52]

This sense of disdain and distrust led to a severity which no European congregation would have tolerated. The S.M.A. demanded of catechumens the equivalent of a monk's vow of stability. 'As a Christian you cannot be gadding about from town to town . . . 'I promise to make farm for this town, sir.'[53] East of the Niger, Bishop Shanahan expected public penance for certain offences, and opposed the baptism of unmarried girls living in 'corrupt towns' – a policy which led to much inquietude among his colleagues.[54]

Bishop Shanahan was a great servant of God, who, more than any other single individual, laid the foundations for the Christianisation of Igboland. His holiness became ever more apparent in his later years, as he went through a kind of Dark Night of the Soul, compounded of illness, blindness, failing mental powers, and protracted depression. Nevertheless, the missionary work of his time had certain grave limitations, and no good purpose is served by seeing it in terms of a romantic hagiography.

If one were to look for an example of the outstanding Igbo Catholics of the time one should find them, perhaps, in its heroic army of forgotten schoolmasters. Father Jordan paid a warm tribute to

> great men like Patrick Okolo, Charles Ndaguba, Willie Onucukwu and Paul Anekwe . . . They obtained the highest teaching certificates the Government could offer, controlled and organised great schools, trained and guided innumerable younger teachers, and gave in their personal lives a splendid example of Catholicism.[55]

Here, however, I shall concentrate, albeit briefly, on two men whose vocation lay in other directions – Bishop John Anyogu and Father Cyprian Tansi, O.C.S.O.

John Anyogu was born in Onitsha, and sent by his father to secondary school in England, an advantage which might well have led to a successful secular career. When he returned to Nigeria, Bishop Shanahan tested him by sending him to teach in Ogoja – on foot. He survived the test triumphantly, and went on to become in 1930 the first Igbo Catholic priest east of the Niger, and in 1957 the first Igbo Catholic bishop. He died in

1967.[56]

Michael Iwene Tansi was born at Aguleri in 1903. He entered the seminary in 1925, and was ordained after long years of study in 1937. He worked for some years as a devoted parish priest, and in 1950 went to England, to enter the Cistercian monastery of Mount St Bernard. He lived there, as Father Cyprian, O.C.S.O., until his death in 1964, bearing in his voluntary exile a remarkable witness against the materialism of his society and his time.[57] He is generally regarded by those who knew him as a saint.

THE ANGLICANS

From 1892 until their reunion in 1931 there were two Anglican bodies at work in Igboland – the Church Missionary Society, and the Niger Delta Pastorate. The Delta Pastorate endured many difficulties, in lack of trained personnel and finance, and faced a shattering internal crisis during the First World War, at the time of the Prophet Braid, but despite these difficulties, it continued with evangelical work in Igboland, in the tradition of the Bonny trader-evangelists of the nineteenth century. In 1894, Archdeacon Dobinson wrote of the 'excellence and stability' of the Pastorate's work, which was 'wonderfully organised throughout'.[58] After the Aro expedition, the members of the Delta churches made a gallant if short-lived attempt to occupy Arochukwu and Bende. Lacking clergy to spare, they sent relays of lay volunteers.[59]

In the years that followed, the Pastorate established a network of missions in southern Igboland, in the Ndoki and Etche and Ikwerri clans. Its members built churches in Port Harcourt, Aba, Owerrinta and Umuahia, as well as in non-Igbo areas. The Ikwerri stations were pioneered almost entirely by Christians from Okrika, and the Aba area by Christians from Opobo. Other stations were pioneered by Delta Christians who were government employees. By 1925 the Delta Pastorate had established three hundred stations in its 'Interior Mission'.[60]

The Church Missionary Society, like the Catholic missions, broke rapidly away in the early twentieth century from its narrow confinement to the Asaba and Onitsha areas. In 1903 a station was established at Awka. The training institute for teachers and catechists was transferred here, where many notable Igbos were to obtain their post-primary education, among them, Mbonu Ojike. In 1905, a mission was established in the Owerri area. Like the Holy Ghost Fathers, the C.M.S. avoided Owerri town – apparently to avoid identification with an unpopular District Commissioner – and made their headquarters at Egbu. The church in the Owerri area spread with amazing rapidity; by 1930 there were a hundred C.M.S. churches there.[61] It was pioneered by Archdeacon Dennis, by a West Indian, the Reverend Fred G. Payne, and by the future Bishop Onyeabo (to whose life we shall return).

In the nineteenth century, the C.M.S. had had more adherents than the Catholics; in the twentieth, the Catholic mission soon outstripped it. The reason was that, like the S.M.A., the C.M.S. hesitated to throw its resources into the work of secular education. It built fewer schools: by 1911 it had fewer than half the number of pupils in regular attendance which the Holy Ghost Fathers had.[62] In the schools it did run, its insistence on vernacular education made it less acceptable to a people whose primary desire was to become literate in English. As in the S.M.A. the question of educational policy caused a painful crisis within the mission itself. Missionaries such as Basden compared the successes of the Catholic schools with their own Society's 'fatal curbing policy of retrenchment' and lamented a lost opportunity. 'We have already lost so much ground that it is doubtful whether the lee-way can be made up now.'[63] Later, policies changed, but as Basden predicted the opportunity had been lost, and the Catholics retained their dominating role in education east of the Niger.

Because they did not demand celibacy of their clergy, and also because they demanded of them a less rigorous and protracted period of intellectual formation, the C.M.S. indigenised their clergy decades before the Catholics. The C.M.S. pastors and catechists often had large families whom they educated with great care, and who have supplied many of the members of the contemporary Igbo élite.

The outstanding C.M.S. clergyman of the colonial period was undoubtedly Alphonso Chukwuma Onyeabo.[64] He was born in 1879 in Onitsha, and was the nephew of the first Igbo C.M.S. priest, the Reverend George Anyaegbunam, and the son of one of the first Onitsha Christians. After a period in C.M.S. schools, he was sent to St Andrew's College, Oyo, making the long journey on foot. After his training – when he confronted and resisted the temptation to resign and take a more lucrative civil service post – he worked as a pioneer catechist in the Onitsha hinterland, and west of the Niger. In 1912 he began his real life's work in the Owerri area, and was ordained two years later. He established a vast network of schools and churches, and was loved and esteemed by the people he served, who would bypass the corrupt Native Courts and entrust their conflicts to his judgement. In 1937, despite his genuine *nolo episcipari*, he was made a bishop, and was stationed at Aba as Assistant Bishop of the Niger Delta, until his retirement in 1948. 'The Reunion made his appointment possible and acceptable; and, in return, his appointment contributed largely in cementing the Reunion.'[65]

THE PRESBYTERIANS

The Presbyterian church in south-eastern Nigeria has always had its main base of strength in Calabar and the Ibibio area. Its impact in Igboland has been highly localised to a number of centres in Ohafia, Abiriba, Arochukwu and the north-east, but within these areas its impact has been great, both in education and in the sphere of medical missions. The mission in Arochukwu was pioneered by Mary Slessor, the justly celebrated Scotswoman whose literal following of the Gospel gave her a superficial appearance of eccentricity. The next step was to Ohafia, in 1911. 'The desire for education swept the Ohafia towns like a bush fire.'[66]

The special glory of the Presbyterian mission lay in its medical work.[67] In 1915, a hospital was built at the ancient salt centre and trade fair of Uburu. It will always be linked with the name of Dr Hitchcock, who founded it, and who died there of exhaustion during the influenza epidemic of 1919, in his thirty-seventh year. There was another medical mission at Itu, which attracted patients from as far afield as Onitsha, when Dr Hastings (who later went on to spend twenty-five years at Uburu) began treating yaws with neo-salvarsan injections. On one occasion he treated six thousand sufferers, with his own hands blistered and bandaged from the arsenic content of the drug. In 1926, Dr A. B. MacDonald encountered his first leprosy patient at Itu. It was the beginning of the famous leper colony there, which was to treat twenty thousand patients in the next twenty years, many of them from Igboland.

Appropriately enough, the outstanding son of the mission proved to be a medical missionary. Dr (later Sir) Francis Akanu Ibiam* resolved to serve as a missionary when he was studying at the University of St Andrews (whence he returned to Nigeria in 1934). His own account shows the inflexible resolution with which he adhered to his vow in the face of many obstacles – not least from his own church.

> First the Missionary Society in Britain to which I applied was not even courteous to me at the interview. They sent me packing and advised me to present my application to their representatives in Nigeria . . . The job of starting a new hospital [at Abiriba] was to be entirely my own effort. There would be no other relief by other missionary doctors, I was told, nor could I relieve any of them either. My salary was a pittance and even then it was placed on a different scale to that of the European missionaries. There was so much discrimination against me, you would not believe it . . . Although missionaries were provided with transport as soon as they arrived in Nigeria, I was not entitled to any. So I bought a pushbike . . . During my 25th year of service as a missionary doctor I was earning the sum of £540 a year, and I barely had any savings in the bank. . . . And yet, if I had to start all over again, I would choose the same path and react in the same manner all the way . . . to show that the grace of God abounds for both European and the African . . .[68]

So far, in considering the years of growth, we have considered the well educated and the eminent. But among the Presbyterians, as among all the mission churches, there were countless more obscure but equally devoted Christians. One was Agwu Otisi of Abiriba (*c.* 1862–1922). He was a skilled herbalist, who enjoyed much success in his profession. In or after 1912 he was converted to Christianity by the preaching of Onuoha Kalu Onuoha, the town's first schoolmaster. In 1916 he destroyed all his personal gods and was baptised with his whole household. He became the first Elder of the church in Abiriba, a staunch

* He renounced his knighthood – and his first name – during the Nigerian civil war.

advocate of Western education, and the defender of twins and their mothers. 'This is my only sorrow', Agwu used to tell his friends, 'that Christianity came to me in my age of grey hair.'[69]

It was a Catholic missionary who observed that Igbo women were more attached to traditional religion than the men, but that once converted they embraced Christianity more zealously. There are many examples of this – the Catholic mission at Emekuku was established as a result of an initiative from the local women.[70] The local historian of Abiriba preserves the memory of one notable woman Christian, Ikpeghe Oyediya Anya.

> Her family were pagans but she chose to be a christian against the wishes of the family . . . This love of God and humanity grew stronger and stronger when she became a mother in her own house. [Ekeghe goes on to relate how she once befriended a sick old woman being taken to Abiriba hospital, and was later offered gifts by the woman's relatives.] 'When Ikpeghe saw all these, she laughed and refused all. They gave her money; she refused saying that God was her true rewarder . . .
>
> This woman had not long served God and her fellow men when an ill health disarmed her. This ill health was dangerous and one that people fear. Though she grew worse everyday yet her faith never faded. Later on an ulcer added more to her torture and her days became numbered but never was she forsaken. At last this good woman died just in her middle age. Before she died she appealed to her friends and well wishers to follow charity.[71]

THE METHODISTS

The Methodists were the last major Christian denomination – of those which have made a real impact in the area – to enter Igboland. Until 1932, world Methodism was divided into a number of separate churches, each with its own missionary organisation. The Wesleyan Methodists concentrated mainly on Western Nigeria, though they had a flourishing mission at Opobo, with 49 out-stations, by 1925.[72] The Primitive Methodists had their base at Oron, and, like the Presbyterians, have always worked primarily in areas to the south-east of Igboland. They first penetrated Igboland in 1910, establishing a mission at Bende. In 1913, work began on the Port Harcourt-Enugu railway, and the Primitive Methodists made a deliberate decision to set up a chain of missions along the railway, at Uzuakoli, Umuahia, Ihubi and Ovim, and in the Udi area. Each of these stations was the nucleus for scores of outstations. In 1917, they established a mission at Aba, and in 1925 at Port Harcourt.[73] It appears that their expansion was greatly aided by the Prophet Braid's work. 'The movement swept up the railway line and in all the villages on both sides of the line there was an eager desire for the mission.'[74]

In 1923, they established an important training college and secondary school at Uzuakoli, but in the main they stressed evangelisation rather than education, an emphasis inherent in the church's own history and origins.

The Methodists had some outstanding expatriate missionaries – such as Dr Frank Davey of Uzuakoli Leper Colony – but as in the other churches, the bulk of the work of evangelisation in Igboland was done by obscure Igbos such as Solomon Izuegbu, the apostle of Amuda, or Emmanuel Hart, the apostle of Item Okpi. Solomon was frequently imprisoned for his conflicts with a local secret society. The local District Officer liked having him in prison because 'the prison was a much better place when Solomon was there.'[75] Emmanuel Hart was born in Okoko, Item in 1887, and sold into slavery in Azumini in the early twentieth century.[76] There he gained his freedom, and in 1913 returned home. He started a small children's band and choir, which sang hymns all over the town until 'both market women and farmers continued singing as they moved about'. Having attracted a crowd, he geared his preaching to the realities of colonial conquest, preaching 'about one God who could conquer a nation without any matchet, spear, gun or bow and arrow.' The first church services were held in the private home of another Christian pioneer, Ogan Onuoha, of Amokwe, Item. 'By 1916 . . . Christianity swept everywhere.' Hart died in 1923, 'the uncrowned saint', and lies buried before the Methodist church in Okoko. Ogan Onuoha died at an advanced age in 1960, 'a father to all and sundry'.

THE SMALLER CHURCHES

It would be a mistake to write the history of Christian growth in

Igboland purely in terms of the major denominations. As time went by, a great variety of denominational life developed. Even collectively, these churches could not rival the adherences of the C.M.S. or the R.C.M., but they formed, nevertheless, an important strand in Igbo religious life.

One important group of these churches were those of Nigerian origin. The United Native African Church was formed in Lagos, by Christians of different denominations, in 1891, as an attempt to reformulate Christian practice in African terms. It tolerated polygamy among the laity, but not the clergy. By 1925 it had twenty churches in the Aba area, with over four thousand adherents.[77] Garrick Sokari Braid was a remarkable Kalabari fisherman from Bakana who established a powerful Christian movement in 1909.[78] He laid his primary emphasis on faith healing, but also tolerated polygamy. He was a charismatic figure who made many converts from the Delta Pastorate – including the pastor of the Bonny church – and transformed Bakana, for a time, into a place of pilgrimage. He was imprisoned by the British during the First World War, and died in gaol in 1918, but his influence outlived him. Many of his adherents formed the Christ Army Church, which had many followers in southern Igboland. In many other cases, in Igboland, his was the first Christian influence on those who later joined one of the established mission churches.

The attraction of the African churches was obvious. The established churches, by their condemnation of polygamy, placed many polygamists in a cruel dilemma. Either they had to remain perpetual second-class citizens of a congregation, excluded from its sacramental life, or destroy their family life by expelling one or more wives, and bitterly anatagonising their children. Others, who had hoped to remain monogamous, found themselves under an intolerable strain if their marriage proved childless. Others again were alienated from the missions by an experience of white prejudice or injustice, or by the mission boundary agreements. (These last meant that Ohafia, for instance, was a Presbyterian monopoly, so that a Methodist in Ohafia was forced to be a Presbyterian, or nothing.) Many, in these circumstances, joined the African churches. By 1919–21 there were, in Eastern Nigeria, 29,225 Christians attached to the African churches of Lagos, and an almost equal number, 28,435, attached to churches of local origin.[79] Later, the Aladura churches reached Igboland from the west, and have spread very rapidly in quite recent years. They seemed to offer a more fervent congregational life than the more stereotyped worship of the older churches: no sound is now more typical of Enugu late at night than their all-night services.

Other churches of European or American origin came to Igboland, from the twenties on, recreating there the variety of denominational life so characteristic of Christendom in our time. This variety was most striking in a city environment such as Port Harcourt. A visitor in 1935–6 wrote:

> In one street alone, the inquirer finds the Methodists, the Niger Delta branch of the Church Missionary Society, the Roman Catholics, the Faith Tabernacle, the Baptists, the African Church, the Salvation Army, the African Methodist Episcopals (Zion branch), the African Methodist Episcopals (Bethel branch), the New Church (Swedenborg), the Apostolic Mission, the Seventh Day Adventists, the First Century Gospel (an offshoot of the Faith Tabernacle) . . . Other sects come and go, showering badly printed pamphlets as they pass . . .[80]

The individual influence of most of the smaller churches was slight, though in an area of local concentration, it sometimes attained some importance. One outstanding figure who deserves at least a brief mention in any history of Igboland is the Reverend Samuel Wadiei Martin of Issele Uku (born *c.* 1875). He was taken by a missionary to America as a boy. After many years of work and study, he returned as a Baptist pastor to his native town in 1922. After years of solitary struggle and privation, he built up a flourishing church and a far-flung network of schools. He insisted that his mission remain an independent one: 'how could we show our white co-workers that we could stand on our own? It was time to tell them the black man was capable to do these things they had done . . .' Gradually, with American Baptist financial help, the town acquired a fine stone church, a secondary school and vocational school, and a splendid modern hospital. Martin was one of the few Igbo Christians of his generation whose faith was strong enough to withstand the strain of a childless marriage. Now in extreme old age, his memory has begun to fail, but the basic inspiration of his life remains undimmed – 'The Lord's is a gracious name, a gracious name.'[81]

One question which is difficult to answer is the extent to which the Christianisation of Igboland has been completed. Missionary accounts portray missionary history as a triumphal progress. But if one looks at a study like Shelton's monograph on the Nsukka area, which concentrates on traditional religion, one would scarcely know that missionaries had visited the area at all. Statistics give part of the answer, suggesting that many though not all Igbos have become Christians, though there is a staunch rearguard of elderly traditionalists. Occasionally, they speak in the records in their own voice: (from Nsukka) 'The people who go to church say that gods are no longer gods and that we should throw them away. But, *ogene*, do not listen. . . . I have said that I do not go to church and that church men had destroyed the world.'[82] (from Aguinyi, to a student inquirer) 'You have got a new deity because you know more than your fathers, not so? [Ironically] that is why you were able to defeat and capture all your Hausa enemies during the civil war. Please bring another topic. Leave that one aside.'[83]

The extent of the Christianisation of Igboland is a question of depth and sincerity, as well as of numbers. The first generation of Igbo Christians often displayed an apparent contradiction – on the one hand they were enthusiastic and fervent Christians, but on the other, they frequently embraced practices which the churches condemned. Many became polygamists, or defied the churches' embargos on title taking, or consulted diviners or wore charms in time of trouble. To the present writer, this type of eclecticism does not reflect insincerity. On the contrary, it reflected the reality of the supernatural world. The early Christians were suspended between two world views, two sets of religious techniques, promising different but not mutually exclusive benefits. Traditional religion offered techniques for avoiding evils and attaining temporal blessings. Christianity offered blessings in a world to come. Early Christians felt that the churches had deprived them of a set of efficient methods of limiting the role of chance, and controlling or limiting misfortunes, so that 'we seem to go sheepishly in a sea of vicissitudes.'[84] They bitterly resented the strict sanctions which the mission churches applied against eclecticism: 'When a man is driven from one country into another, if the inhabitants of that country would not receive him, is he to live in the air?'[85]

Inconsistency, the dichotomy between Sunday and Monday, is too common in Christian experience to require a special exegesis in Igboland. No Christian society has ever taken the Sermon on the Mount as the norm of its conduct. The New Testament has more to say about unkindness and avarice than about title taking or polygamy, but inconsistency of this type has become so common in the Western world that it is not seen as shocking or scandalous. The inconsistencies of the early Igbo Christians occurred in a context where the churches claimed much control, of a rather legalistic kind, over their members' lives, and where infringements were especially vulnerable to this kind of sanction. Too many of them, having cut themselves off from one world and being imperfectly accepted in another, were forced to live, in the imagery of the Onitsha Christians, in the air.

12 Education and the Growth of Social Differentiation

THE EDUCATION SYSTEM

We have already seen, in our study of the missions, the basic factors which produced the educational system in Igboland. To the missions, the schools were an invaluable way to influence the young in their impressionable years, and government subsidies a precious supplement to their meagre budgets. The government needed a large cadre of Africans who were literate and numerate to staff the railways, postal services, police force, and fill a large number of clerical posts; the expatriate commercial firms, likewise, needed the same type of personnel. It was cheaper to subsidise mission schools than to start their own, or to import educated Africans from further afield.

Neither the government nor the missions were interested in education *per se*. The government started very few schools of its own, and its subsidies to mission schools formed only a miniscule part of its own budget. The amount colonial governments spent on education was always dwarfed by their expenditure on expatriate salaries and pensions. In 1918, the Nigerian government devoted one per cent of its total expenditure to education. By the 1930s, it was between 3 and 4 per cent.[1] (In 1958–9, the self-governing Eastern Region spent over 40 per cent of its income on education.)[2] Government officials were troubled by the low standards of the schools, and repeatedly (in the Education Code of 1903, and the Ordinances of 1916 and 1926) attempted to use their subsidies as a lever to ensure higher standards. But they were not interested in raising levels to a point where they represented a realistic proportion of government income, let alone in creating a body of Nigerians who were sufficiently educated to endanger their own position and careers.

Since the best paid and least laborious jobs were clerical, Nigerians opted for a 'literary' education. Government officials – and certain missions – tended to hymn the virtues of technical education and the dignity of manual labour, but as long as clerks got more pay for less strenuous work than carpenters, and as long as those who praised the dignity of labour showed no inclination to exemplify these virtues in their own lives, their exhortations fell on deaf ears.

The missions, who were concerned to reach as many children as possible, concentrated on quantity rather than quality. At first the schools were staffed by teachers who themselves had only a primary education. The C.M.S. was the first body to provide any form of post-primary education. In the late nineteenth century it established a training school for catechists. This was held first at Lokoja (but all the pupils but one were Igbos), and then moved to Asaba, to Iyienu, and finally, in 1904, to Awka. Here it developed two branches, a teachers' training college, and a theological school for pastors. In 1913, the Catholics followed suit, establishing a combined training college and seminary in the remote rural environment of Igbariam – a site chosen to avoid the supposedly corrupting effect of town life. It was given up in 1918, and refounded as St Charles Training College, Onitsha in 1928. These mission training colleges, together with those the government opened, filled an invaluable role in Igbo education. Before secondary schools were set up in Igboland, they provided the only avenue to post primary education (a tiny handful of individuals, among them Nnamdi Azikiwe, obtained a secondary education in Lagos, or at the Hope Waddell Institute, Calabar). The distinction of opening the first secondary school in Igboland belongs to the Methodists, who founded a school at Uzuakoli in 1923 which soon combined both a secondary and a teachers' training section. Archdeacon Dennis had urged the establishment of a C.M.S. secondary school at the turn of the century. The project was finally realised some years after his death, in 1925, in the school at Onitsha which became his memorial. In the same year Government College, Umuahia was founded. The Catholics followed suit with Christ the King College, Onitsha (1932), Queen of the Rosary, for girls, Enugu (1942) and St Patrick's, Asaba (1944).

Until a real expansion of secondary education began in the 1950s, its provision was appallingly inadequate. Pupils were admitted after a tough entrance examination. The schools charged fees, so tended to be monopolised by the children of those already enjoying a regular cash income, such as teachers and pastors. It was the beginning of the creation of a self-perpetuating élite, which is such a troubling feature of our own times. Because the training colleges charged little or nothing, they provided an invaluable opportunity for boys from poor homes.

> There were a few Secondary Schools in those early days. The few who had the urge to go beyond the envied Standard 6 refused to have a go at entrance examinations to those few Secondary Schools since the money was not there to begin with. The result was to resort to Teachers' Training Colleges . . .[3]

Many of the alumni of the training colleges went far beyond primary-school teaching in their ambitions and achievements. Some went on to become doctors, lawyers, politicians and top administrators. An astonishingly large number of Igboland's modern élite never attended a secondary school at all. In the seventies the number of training colleges has expanded vastly, but since they now charge fees comparable with those of secondary schools, this avenue of social mobility has been lost.

It was extremely difficult to expand the narrow circle of mission secondary schools by private initiatives. It was a vicious circle – one could not run a secondary school without more education, and it was difficult to obtain further education when there were so few secondary schools. Very few, moreover, could command the necessary capital. Nevertheless a few pioneers managed to overcome these obstacles, and deserve to be remembered in any history of the Igbo people. In 1933, Alvan Ikoku founded the Aggrey Memorial College at Arochukwu, one of the first half dozen colleges in Igboland, after teaching for many years at the C.M.S. training college, Awka. The Sierra Leonian, the Reverend Potts-Johnson, who died in 1947, established Enitona College in Port Harcourt.[4] In 1935, it taught 90 boys and 16 girls. P. E. Chukwurah started a series of evening classes in Onitsha which developed in 1940 into the Africa College.[5] Other Onitsha entrepreneurs pioneered commercial education, in the Etukokwu Commercial College and the Prince Commercial Institute.[6] The private colleges charged lower fees, and accepted larger numbers, without the maximum age limits of the mission schools. Their standards, inevitably, were lower but they gave a secondary education to many who would not have obtained it otherwise, and number some very distinguished men among their alumni.

Not all Igbo children, of course, attended schools in Igboland. As Igbo families spread throughout Nigeria in search of employment, their children attended local schools. Many Igbo children received a good education in the west. Igbo communities in the north, concerned at the lack of educational facilities, provided them themselves – and not only for their own children. The Igbo secondary school at Kano was 'a centre of enlightenment for the children of all Nigerian groups in that education-starved northern city.'[7]

One of the key grievances of the colonial era was the lack of opportunities for higher education. The education policy of thus far and no further engendered enormous frustration, and made it impossible for aspiring Nigerians to man the higher echelons of government, and overthrow colonialism. Until the 1930s, there were no Igbo graduates. The tiny handful of Nigerian doctors and lawyers were men of Sierra Leonian descent, or Yorubas. In the 1930s, two avenues of higher education opened.

Yaba Higher College began as a medical school in 1930, and opened fully four years later. About 150 applied for admittance each year, of whom the highest number accepted in any one year, in its first ten years of existence, was thirty-six. Preference was given to the products of government colleges, and Igbos admitted tended to come from Umuahia Government College. After a course of study lasting longer than the equivalent overseas, the students were awarded not degrees but diplomas, and became medical assistants, engineering assistants, and so on. Each year some of the initially highly selective intake were ruthlessly discarded. It is difficult to better the words of Otonti Nduka:

> Of all the waste of the colonial regime in Nigeria, probably none was more pathetic than the spectacle of the erstwhile brilliant pupil, discarded after four or five years of gruelling toil at the Higher College, Yaba. Four or five years' work had gone down the drain, and a personality virtually wrecked: some committed suicide. That was part of the glory that was Yaba, the colonial institution *par excellence*.[8]

Yaba was designed to perpetuate subordination to the colonial regime. One could only discover Archimedes' platform, and overthrow it, by going outside it. In the 1930s a few pioneers began to do so. The epic struggle of Nnamdi Azikiwe anticipates that of many less famous men who came after him. His father, like many later Igbo fathers, sacrificed part of his retirement gratuity to send him to America in 1925. He arrived at a time of worsening Depression. His life became an unremitting struggle for existence – he worked as a furnace stoker, a dish washer, and even as a coal miner, and was once driven by his hardships to the brink of suicide. He obtained two Masters degrees and most of the credits for a Doctorate, and then deliberately sacrificed the comfort and stimulus of American college life to return to Africa, in 1934. His achievements were a convincing demonstration of the words he later addressed to Mbonu Ojike:

> There is no achievement which
> Is possible to human beings which
> Is not possible to Africans.[9]

Partly inspired by his example, a trickle of Igbos went abroad in the thirties and early forties. In the late forties and early fifties, the trickle rose to a flood. In 1947, Ibadan was opened, and many Igbos obtained a university education there. Others went overseas, mainly to English speaking countries, but often to non-English speaking ones. The intellectual difficulty of mastering French, German, Polish or Russian as an adult and then studying engineering or medicine in it is more readily imagined than described, but many of the Igbo élite have emerged successful from the experience. Not all, of course, succeed. Some who fail, and fear to return empty handed, stay abroad, in perpetual unhappy exile. Many have died abroad, often the victims of an unfamiliar climate, or of poverty, overwork and strain. One tragic case was Nnodu Okongwu, who died after obtaining a Ph.D. from the University of New York, in 1946, for a pioneering history of education in Nigeria.

The educational system which developed in the colonial era had certain built-in tendencies and biases. Inevitably, those seeking education sought it mainly as a passport to employment, as an escape from a life of grinding toil and poverty. A certain measure of utilitarianism is necessary in a developing country and a philosophy of learning for learning's sake is probably a luxury it cannot afford. (One of the points made by radicals in late nineteenth-century Russia was that to the poor, poems are less valuable than boots.) Insensibly, however, this natural bias developed into an obsessive concern with gaining qualifications and preparing for examinations which has blighted the whole educational system. Primary-school children copy the parts of a plant into their 'Note', without observing any actual plant, or learning the names of the plants in their vicinity. At a higher level, students of literature practically memorise a set-book – or, worse still, a commentary on a set-book – without showing the slightest interest in other works by the same author, or other authors who happen not to be set. And ironically the process is self-defeating, for it is precisely that wider reading which would provide a basis for comparison, and an enriched understanding, which would reflect itself in an enriched examination answer.

There are many reasons for this situation, among them the difficulties of study in a second language and consequent slow reading speeds. But the basic factor which robs learners at all levels of the joy and excitement of intellectual discovery and exploration is obvious. 'For, behind the disposition of students to pay attention to "only those things that are examinable" . . . lies a heartless monster – insecurity.'[10]

THE ÉLITE

The élite which emerged in Igboland in the colonial period was in no sense a uniform or homogeneous body. It included men of different occupations and education, it was not equally representative of all parts of Igboland, and it changed very considerably as time went on.

For many years the Igbo élite included a disproportionately large number of natives of Onitsha. Her early access to mission schools, her later concentration of secondary schools and a training college, gave her unique advantages which no other Igbo community could equal. It is no accident that the first Igbo C.M.S. bishop, the first Igbo Catholic bishop, and the great nationalist leader Azikiwe were all Onitsha men. Hair, writing in the early 1950s, observed that 'The people of Onitsha consider themselves the aristocracy of Iboland.'[11] They were followed by those from the area round Onitsha – towns such as Nnewi, which had shared many of their advantages – and from Asaba, across the Niger, from Awka and from the Owerri area. With a handful of notable exceptions, Udi division remained poor and educationally backward. In 1948, the financial returns of the Onitsha union in Enugu showed that 47 per cent of its members earned over £100 per annum, 90 per cent were in government employ, and 49 per cent were clerks. In the union of a village group from Udi the percentages were, respectively, 1 per cent, 48 per cent, and none at all.[12]

Frequently, Igbo communities which had been especially prosperous and successful in pre-colonial times were slow to espouse education. Nike, a wealthy slave-owning group with ample land, sent no children to school for many years,[13] despite the proximity of Enugu. The wealthy craftsmen and traders of Nkwerre thought similarly. 'Nkwerre did not embrace education in time. She concentrated on gun-making and trading'. Her hesitations were confirmed for a decade when the first Nkwerre child sent to Dennis Memorial Grammar School died there.[14] Other communities with fertile and abundant land were slow to embrace change; in the words of an Oratta local historian, 'The lands in Oratta Clan are very productive . . . This question of easy feeding makes our people not to be as interprising [sic] as they should.[15]

The Ezza made a conscious decision to stick to farming and warfare, the spheres in which they had always excelled. In 1911, in an interview which later Ezza saw as a symbolic – and tragic – turning point, the oldest Ezza man, Uche Mbele, rejected a British proposal to adopt schools and Native Courts. 'On the establishment of school and courts, wearing of trousers, and most obnoxious of all, the change of religion, all Ezzas were one in oposing the suggestion.'[16]

The confrontration of traditional Igbo society with Western culture meant that every Igbo was in some sense suspended between two worlds, and that every Igbo, whether consciously or unconsciously, had to evolve his own synthesis between them. The dilemma presented itself most acutely to the educated, who were most exposed to the forces of change. It was felt most intensely by the first generation of the educated, who had no precedents to guide them. In our own time, such syntheses are evolved almost effortlessly, in a mould shaped by scores and hundreds of examples.

The confrontation was made more painful than it need have been by the Eurocentricity of the missions and the educational system. Primary-school pupils wrote essays on windmills, Beowulf, snowflakes and walks in London, and memorised, among other verse of equally dubious value, the following effusion by Bulwer-Lytton:

> Where is the Briton's home?
> Where the free step can roam,
> Where the sun can glow,
> Where a free air can blow,
> Where a free ship can bear
> Hope and strength . . . everywhere
> Wave upon wave can roll
> East and west, pole to pole,
> Where a free step can roam . . .
> There is the Briton's home.[17]

An educational commission which visited Nigeria in 1920–1 reported that if an African class was asked to sing a song of its own choice it was likely to be the British Grenadiers'.[18] Bishop Shanahan stated in public that 'Europe has been the chosen Continent, the chosen nation of God . . .'[19]

Dilim Okafor Omali's moving memoir of his father gives an interesting example of the kind of ambiguity which often resulted. His father named him Sigismund, after a long search for an English name which was as meaningful as an Igbo one. A postal employee in Port Harcourt, he spoke only English to his children. When Sigismund was taken at the age of five to his village group, Enugwu Ukwu, he was frightened and alienated, and asked to leave – but in pidgin, because he had not mastered English either[20] . . . Later, as an adult, he changed to an Igbo name, and, like his father, devoted himself to the development of the town in which he had once refused to live.

The first generation élite were nearly always Christians and often, though not always, polygamists. They had two uncomplicated ambitions – to educate their large families to the highest possible standard, and to erect the largest possible house in their home villages. They spent their working lives elsewhere (to rise above the standard of living of the village it was almost always necessary to leave it) but always retired there. The large unarchitected 'storey buildings', erected (in the case of schoolmasters) on a monthly income of £18 6s 8d, began to appear from the thirties on, when the retrenchment caused by the Depression produced a widespread sense of insecurity. In a sense, that insecurity has never left the Igbo élite, who still try to eliminate it with cement. Most consulted herbalists and diviners, and took titles in their old age.

Their children evince a stronger attachment to Igbo culture – manifested in the widespread, though not universal, use of Igbo given names – but understand it much less, since they have normally grown up far from their home towns. They buy titles, if not for themselves then for their older relations, and give their parents elaborate second burials. More self-assured and sophisticated, they do not consider that this implies a breach with the church – to which, in any case, many are less profoundly attached. They still build houses in their villages, but do not live there. They are not often attracted by polygamy, nor do they consult diviners.

Probably, this synthesis has been attained too effortlessly. A respect for tradition involves us, nevertheless, in rethinking its implications in each generation. It is doubtful, for instance, if second burials should be retained when the religious belief which first inspired them is gone. They waste the meagre resources of the poor, and in the case of the rich become a form of that wasteful competitive conspicuous consumption which is already too prominent in southern Nigerian society. They would do better to honour the dead by establishing scholarships in their name.

Some of the first generation élite were railway and post and telegraph employees, like Christopher Nweke Okafor of Enugwu-Ukwu (1898–1944) mentioned above. The first Standard VI boy from his town, he became a postmaster, serving in Port Harcourt, Enugu and Bansara. He fought against denominational strife in his community, and established its first improvement union.[21] Some of them were government clerks, like Chukwuemeka Azikiwe of Onitsha (1879–1958). He received a primary education in the teeth of his father's opposition. After a short period as a teacher, he was appointed a clerk in the Northern Nigeria Brigade, serving in Lokoja, Zungeru, Kaduna and later Calabar. As a senior clerk, at the age of 46, he was insulted by a European half his age, and resigned. 'Recollecting his twenty-three years of service, which had been chequered with insults of various kinds, he concluded that an African servant was merely a cog in the wheel of the machinery used to put the African in his place' – and gave his savings to his son, to pursue Archimedes' platform . . .[22]

Many of the first generation élite were primary-school teachers. They were more than schoolmasters, they were leaders and models for the communities in which they lived. 'The first bringers of "civilisation" to the town [Nsu, in Okigwi] were teachers . . . Most of these early teachers lived by what they taught. Teachers therefore became objects of hero-worship. Parents who sent their children to school had no other job in mind for them than teaching.'[23]

Francis Okoafo Isichei of Asaba (1900–73) may stand for their number. He too received his primary education despite his father's opposition, and went on to the teachers' training college at Warri. He rose to the rank of headmaster, and wrote a prize-winning monograph on Igbo dialects. He was an activist in the Nigerian Union of Teachers, and the colonial government, to restrain him, demoted him from his headship and exiled him to the distant island of Bonny. Undaunted, he continued to teach with all his heart, and studied Latin, French and mathematics in his leisure hours, to such good effect that he taught them at secondary-school level after he retired. He longed to study law, but devoted his resources instead to the education of his children (not all men in his position made the same choice). He kept in his household over the years many children who were not from his family, or even from his town, and sent them to school. In his old age he still grieved over the lost promise of one of them, a gifted mathematician, who ran away from school some forty years earlier . . . In his late sixties, with failing eyesight, he tackled the examinations for the Intermediate LL.B. In his seventies, old and ill and near death, he retained an intellectual curiosity and openness of mind which would have been remarkable in a man half his age. He was not a famous Nigerian. I knew him only because he was my father-in-law.

UNEMPLOYMENT AND THE URBAN POOR

The education revolution which created a new élite also created social inequality – or, more precisely, enormously magnified those incipient social inequalities which we observed in our study of the nineteenth century. Colonialism created what has been called a revolution of rising expectations. Nothing has caused more suffering during the colonial period and beyond than the constantly rising threshold of educational qualifications, and the constant shrinking of employment opportunities relative to the demand. In the first thirty years of this century, a primary-school graduate was sure of secure, respectable white-collar employment. In the Depression years, when direct taxation was imposed, we hear the first whispers of their employment problems; in words which might well stand as an epigraph to the social history of Igboland in the last forty years: 'At present I have about five boys who have passed Standard VI, and they have nothing to do, will you kindly assist me to get them something to do? this is our main trouble.'[24] Thirty years later, the tide of unemployment began to touch the secondary school leavers as well.

A young man from Ihembosi, writing in the early sixties, gave poignant expression to the dilemma of his age-group and his time.

> We may do well to recall the large number of our boys who having entered various institutions, later came out without completing the required number of years due to financial stringencies . . . It must be admitted that we are still held firmly in the grip of chronic poverty. The highest educational standard for some of our boys and girls is now standard six. After this achievement, according to our poor parents, the next step is to switch over to 'Ntengwo' [palm wine tapping] or 'Ika-Rubber' [rubber tapping] business which does not normally need much money to set it up. The parents assume that training a boy or girl to a standard six pass means cutting the Gordian knot. Even to help them do simple typing and shorthand in small institutions is not considered possible because they may be asked to pay about £5 a year for the

> course. Again to do trading is not easy because there is no capital to begin with.[25]

He went on to point out that farming offered no viable alternative:

> . . . without certain big production units, the small scale farming of our individual poor farmer will continue to impede the development of the farmers who already wallow in abject poverty. Is it not tragic that some people will continue to work at home and 'Olu' [work] with their families throughout the farming season, but during the harvest they pick up baskets, and trek to Nkwo Okija to purchase yams. It is not even wrong to say they are unable to provide for themselves and their families.[26]

Since an education had been sought as an escape from the grinding monotony and poverty of rural life, it was inevitable that its products should leave the villages. In the towns there was at least a possibility of employment, there was an environment of greater stimulus and variety, there was always at least the chance of a sudden change of fortunes.

In 1965–6, Mr Uwa Kanu conducted an interesting survey of employment in Arochukwu. In 1964, 152 pupils read Elementary VI; only 31 of them were able to go on with their secondary education. By the end of 1965, 82 of the rest had gone to the towns in search of employment. He interviewed 35 boys and 18 girls in Aba, Enugu and Nsukka, suggesting that they should return to farming if they could not obtain jobs by the end of the year. All rejected the idea. 'One of the boys said, "Farmers are very poor . . . They work and work, but never grow rich." One girl said, "I cannot think of going to Bianko or Isiajirija [Aro farmlands] every morning while my school mates are coming to town to enjoy life. If I do not secure the type of job I want, I should do whatever other girls do to keep body and soul together here. I like Aba."'[27]

The influx of primary school leavers into the towns produced numberless other social evils. In the end, unemployment often drove the boys to crime, the girls to prostitution. They lived for long periods with 'brothers' in overcrowded tenements, depressing their already precarious living standards. The pool of unemployed depressed the wages and security of the unskilled employed, and added to the already formidable problems of labour organisation. Many in the end joined the underpaid and underemployed, the domestic servants and the apprentices (among them apprentice lorry drivers!) or became absorbed in the retail distribution network which employs such an astonishing proportion of Igboland's population, often at the humblest level – the pathetic adolescent retailers of bread, groundnuts or peeled oranges.

A Government Blue Book observed in 1935 'A ration of cooked native food consisting of gari, palm oil, greens and condiments is sold in the markets for a penny. Two such rations daily are fair sustenance for an African of the labouring class.' Protein, it would appear, was superfluous for an African of the labouring class.[28]

RURAL LIFE: ON CHANGE AND CONTINUITY

Historians inevitably tend to concentrate on manifestations of change, rather than on continuities. So far we have been considering the questions, how did the colonial era change life in Igboland, and how did the Igbo respond to its new challenges, problems and opportunities? But an equally important question is: how far was Igbo society changed at all? To understand Igbo history in the colonial era it is essential to understand that for many, perhaps most Igbo, life was not changed very fundamentally.

In the middle thirties, an anthropologist studied the village group of Umueke Agbaja, south of Okigwi. It was an exceptionally poor area, little touched by Western influences – and she chose it for study for that reason. But her survey showed that after a third of a century of colonialism, the quality of life had scarcely changed at all. A mission school had started in the mid-thirties, but mission influence was still in a 'very embryonic state' and only one couple had married in church. No villager owned a bicycle, or a sewing machine, and the only piece of machinery there was a single-hand press for palm oil, introduced in 1937. All the houses were of mud and thatch; there were none of the 'zinc houses' and 'storey buildings' erected by successful sons abroad. The people lived from subsistence agriculture and petty local trade. Their diet was extremely deficient in protein: they did not eat eggs or drink milk, and meat and stockfish were rare luxuries. They grew yams but were too poor to eat them. They sold them, and ate cassava. They were unable to grow enough food for their needs, and purchased extra food with part of their palm oil profits. There was little margin left for imported goods, school fees, or medical care.[29]

In 1938–9, another scholar analysed the finances of sixteen individuals from Ozuitem. The picture which resulted confirmed that from Umueke Agbaja – the low level of cash incomes, the continuing importance of tradition, the limited scope of change. The man with the highest cash income, 'one of the richest men in the community' earned an *annual* income of just over £19 from trade and contracting. The man with the lowest earned £4 13s 0d a year. The most important sources of income were the sale of yams, the sale of palm products and petty trade in European goods, though there were many other small supplements, such as the sale of wild products gathered in the bush, of locally caught fish, and so on. Food purchases accounted for 8.8 per cent of men's expenditure and 23.7 per cent of women's. Traditional obligations (bride price payments, contributions to funeral costs, etc.) came to 14.9 per cent of men's expenditure and 23.7 per cent of women's. The next two most important items on the list were clothing and (for men) court fees, fines and bribes. Native medicine came high on the list; European medicine scarcely figured at all. Contributions for traditional sacrifices absorbed more money than church fees (0.60 per cent of the men's total), school tax (0.29 per cent) or school fees (2.3 of men's and 1.6 per cent of women's expenditure).[30]

It was a society not wholly immune from change. It had trader sons abroad, and an improvement union; the secret society was declining, because the young preferred to join the church. But it was a society where continuity was vastly more important than change, and where government exactions were bitterly resented precisely because they bore such little tangible fruit.

Even in the sphere of government, traditional institutions sometimes seemed more real and terrifying than the whole elaborate mechanism of colonial rule. In the 1920s, two chiefs from Nsukka division wrote, 'In our Town there is one Ju ju called Odo, which rules all the area; and this ju ju has power of life and death over our people. Up to the present it can kill people just as it likes.' Fifty years have passed, and colonialism has gone, but the Odo cult still flourishes.[31]

In the 1953 census, an analysis was made of the proportion of the population over seven years of age which was literate. In Onitsha province it was 13.9 per cent, in Owerri province, 20.3 per cent, in Abakaliki division, 2.2 per cent, in Afikpo division, 4.6 per cent.[32] Some parts of Nigeria had higher proportions of the literate, and others had lower. The important thing to the historian of Igboland is the sobering reflection that after half a century of colonial rule and mission education, over 80 per cent of the population was illiterate.

13 Some Patterns of Social and Economic Change

COAL, AND TWO CITIES

In 1907, Governor Egerton wrote to the Colonial Office advocating the construction of a railway from Oguta to Itu. The permanent officials at the Colonial Office replied with one voice that the project was too expensive, and that there was no hurry about it.[1] Two years later, coal was discovered at Udi.

The British regarded this discovery – the only coal found in West Africa – as of the greatest importance. Hitherto railways and steamer refuelling stations had depended on coal shipped from England, and keen though the British were to find a market for their exports in their colonies, their enthusiasm did not extend to products as bulky and as uneconomic to transport as coal. Moreover, the coal was of strategic importance, as soon became apparent in the conflict which Europeans, with typical ethnocentricity, call the First World War.

The first coal samples were carried to the Niger in fifty-six pound bags, on the heads of weary carriers,[2] but the effective exploitation of the coal fields required more efficient transport. It was decided to build a railway to the Delta, and after extensive inquiries the terminus was provisionally located at Okrika. While the area was being surveyed, the surveying party discovered, by accident, the area of high cliffs near deep water which later became Port Harcourt. The area was the main farmland for several kindred of the Diobu clan, a branch of the southern, Ikwerri Igbo; part was also used by Okrika as a fishing camp. Its name, *obumotu*, meaning *abukotu*, or we are one, reflects a pattern of inter-community relations which later inhabitants of Port Harcourt might have done well to follow.[3] The Diobu were understandably reluctant to sell their land, but their reluctance was overcome by coercion.

The whitemen then wanted to buy the land and pay money

for it. Our people told them that land was not sold . . . They got in people at first from Okirika; and they started to destroy our agricultural products such as yams, cassava, and coco-yams. The Chiefs . . . were made to enter warships, with guns of different sizes pointed at them. There was the threat to send them to England and imprison them there if they continued in their refusal to grant the request of government . . .

When we saw that we could do nothing to let the whitemen go, we determined to invite a Surveyor to survey our land and ascertain its value. For this reason I was sent to Lagos to invite one Herbert Macaulay to come and survey the land for us. We paid him the sum of £73. But he failed to come. We never knew the reason for his failure to come. And the £73 was not refunded. We continued to suffer the hardship of starvation and precarious conditions at the hands of our uninvited visitors . . . But by various threats and intimidation, they succeeded in getting our people to agree with their requests to give out more land to the whitemen.[4]

The Diobu ceded their land 'in considerations of benefits which will accrue to us', but in protest, refused to cash the payment voucher. In the 1920s, 'The Colonial Office announced that the Government's title to the land at Port Harcourt was not sound . . . as there had been no "real consideration" in law.' The then Resident of Owerri Province persuaded them to accept an annual rental, overcoming their hesitations by bringing the first payment in shillings![5] But the Diobu continued to be unhappy about the agreement, and finally took the government to court. The case went as high as the Privy Council, where, in 1955, it was finally decided against them.

The construction of the new township began in 1913. The first labourers were obtained by coercion, and suffered great hardships – a doctor said their high mortality rate was 'due as much from malnutrition as diseases'.[6] The expatriate firms immediately recognised the significance of the site, and established offices there – it was the building of Port Harcourt, rather than the earlier British occupation of the interior, which finally sealed the doom of the old Delta ports such as Bonny and Opobo.

As time went on, immigrants flooded into Port Harcourt, mainly from Owerri and Bende divisions, with a number from Onitsha and Orlu divisions. Many of them lived crowded into the slum area of Diobu Mile Two.[7] They came to Port Harcourt to make money, but their affections remained in their towns of origin. As in other new urban communities, the men outnumbered the women. Mrs Leith-Ross described it in 1935–6: 'No one takes root in Port Harcourt, no one visualizes his future in Port Harcourt, no one hopes to die in Port Harcourt. Men come to make money and have no thought of settling there for good.'[8] It was not surprising when one compares her account of the township (not the slums of Diobu) with almost any tree-shaded Igbo town.

> The township is even more depressing . . . Roads are broad but unshaded, houses are according to official specifications but have not one single feature of comfort or beauty . . . The streets are thronged with men in ragged singlets, dirty shorts and shapeless felt hats, going to their work among the freight wagons or the cargo boats, the lorries or the casks of palm oil.[9]

But immigrants continued to be coerced by the need to earn a cash income, and the city continued to expand rapidly during and after the Second World War, with a population of 71,634 by 1953. Between 1953 and 1963 it increased by 151 per cent, bringing the population to an official total of 179,563 – but unofficial estimates put it as high as half a million. In 1957 it was chosen as the headquarters of Shell B.P., which led to a further period of expansion as an oil boom town.

There is some evidence that in the middle sixties some of the Igbo migrants were coming to regard Port Harcourt as their home. Some built their first homes there, rather than in their villages,[10] and I have spoken to an Igbo lawyer who was born there, and still nostalgically regards it as his 'home' although he no longer lives there. Events which followed, and especially the long scandal of 'Abandoned Property', have confirmed the élite, for another generation, in practices which were becoming obsolescent. Again, they build their houses in their villages of origin. Again they devote themselves to the improvement of their village of origin, rather than to the cities where their children attend school, and they themselves live. The construction of the railway proceeded as rapidly as the construction of the township. The route chosen passed through Aba and Umuahia, and laid the foundation of their future growth. In 1916, it reached the mining area.

The area where the coal was produced underwent, like Port Harcourt, a shattering experience of rapid social change. At first it was called Udi, though Udi is fifteen miles away. Later it came to be called Enugu, after the adjacent community of Enugu-Ngwo. In 1915, a group of men from Ngwo and Ogui ceded 'without charge, freely and voluntarily unto the Government of Nigeria all such lands as may be required . . . for the purposes of a station and colliery . . .' Two later agreements, in 1917 and 1924, expanded the area to ten square miles, for a compensation of two hundred pounds.[11] Like the Diobu, the local people soon came to regret it.

The actual work of mining was unpleasant and dangerous, like mining everywhere. A party of prospective miners from Bende went back home, when they saw what the work entailed. The first miners came from Onitsha; the name of their leader is perpetuated in Alfred's Camp. In 1915, seven thousand tons of coal were produced, with the simplest equipment – picks, shovels and locally made baskets. In 1916, it was 24,000 tons, and rose steadily thereafter, with the occasional fluctuation, until nearly 364,000 tons were produced in 1929.[12] The first mine, Udi mine, was opened in 1916 and closed, worked out, in 1936. Iva and Ogbete mines were opened in 1917–18. The coal field was a small one, and the coal was expected to run out by the end of the century.[13] In the event, technological changes have meant that the coal industry has declined through a shortage of demand, rather than a shortage of supply. Each year, like mines everywhere, they exacted their casualties – in one year, taken at random (1935), two were killed and 252 injured . . .[14] In the early days of the mines, there was no treatment or compensation for injury. I know of an old man from Udi, now in his eighties, whose foot was seriously injured as he worked in the pit. It never healed, he could not afford treatment, and he limped throughout the colonial period and beyond, with a dirty bandage round the open ulcer. In the 1970s, in the evening of his life, an Udi man (who recalled seeing the injury as a small boy) returned from Europe a surgeon, and treated it.

For a time, after the First World War, when the labour supply was depleted by the twin disasters of smallpox and influenza, labour had to be coerced by force. It was a fertile source of oppression and corruption when peasants paid to be exempted from mine labour, or, alternatively, for the privilege of retaining their earnings.[15] Through the 1920s, the British paid local chiefs annual retainers of between £400 and £500 to keep the mines supplied. During the 1920s, with the shortage of paid jobs, the position changed, and by 1930 there were more vacancies than openings. It was not the end of exploitation, which simply took a different form. As a British official minuted:

> There is no doubt that more men are engaged by the Boss-boys and given work than are necessary for the needs of the colliery and that regular hands, who are anxious to work five days a week, do not get their desire unless they pay for it or, for some other reason have curried favour with the Boss-boys and Headmen.[16]

Worse still, the Boss-boys exploited the practice of monthly payment, by dismissing workers shortly before the end of the month, and taking their pay.[17] To the white officials of the mine, the miners were faceless and nameless, and many injustices were committed in their name.

It was in the 1930s that the management began a deliberate policy of recruiting illiterates from Udi, rather than relatively well-educated workers from Onitsha and Owerri, who might be expected to understand their grievances and take steps to remedy them.[18] In 1949, decades of injustice and bad labour relations reached a bloody finale in what is euphemistically called the Enugu Colliery Shooting Incident, when twenty-one miners were killed, and fifty-one were wounded.

Enugu developed as a coal town pure and simple. The first colliery manager was a Mr Leck. His address was 1 Leck Avenue, and his telephone number was Enugu One.[19] Until 1929 the colliery and the railway were the only large employers of labour. As in Port Harcourt, men vastly outnumbered women, and prostitution flourished in consequence.[20] In 1929 Enugu became the administrative headquarters of the southern provinces. Later (until 1966) it was the capital of the Eastern Region and later still of East Central State. The Second World War, as in many Nigerian cities, was a period of rapid expansion. In 1945, the town had a population of 35,000, of whom 87 per cent were Igbo.[21] By 1953 it had risen to 62,764, and by 1963, to 138,457. Like other Nigerian cities, Enugu developed great extremes of wealth and poverty. There are those who live in the Government Residential Area, with its spacious houses, and ample shaded gardens; others live crowded in insanitary slums, where the roads are scarcely motorable, and where uncollected rubbish festers in piles on the street corners.

URBAN DEVELOPMENT AND DECLINE

Enugu and Port Harcourt were probably the most dramatic examples of urban growth, but Onitsha, Aba, Umuahia, and to a lesser extent, Owerri, also underwent rapid expansion.

The twentieth-century history of Onitsha[22] has two main themes: the diaspora of her educated sons to which we have already referred, and the remarkable expansion of her market. The expansion of the Waterside town, at the expense of the Inland Town, which had begun in the nineteenth century, continued. By the 1930s, the waterside town had a population of 14,000, the original settlement, 1300.[23] In the years that followed it attracted large numbers of Igbo immigrants, who came to outnumber the original inhabitants: by 1953, 73 per cent of the population were non-Onitsha Igbos. The Onitsha market Otu Nkwo expanded enormously, developing from a periodic to a daily market, and becoming part of a complex nationwide commercial network (to which we shall return). By the late fifties it was generally accepted as the largest market in Nigeria.

Like the Diobu in Port Harcourt, and the Agbaja and Ngwo in Enugu, the local people had a history of tension and conflict with the immigrants. Professor Henderson has made an interesting analysis of the Inland Town in recent times; nearly all the élite lived elsewhere, and the town was inhabited by the elderly and by those who had failed in the race for advancement – 'a welfare home for the underprivileged and the retired.'[24]

Aba, in pre-colonial colonial times, was a market – Eke Oha, near the head of canoe navigation on the Aba (Aza) River – but not a settlement. It was not the most important Ngwa market, being overshadowed by Obegu, twelve miles further south.[25] (If one compares the present importance of the two towns, one has an interesting example of the way in which colonialism rewrote economic geography.) After the Aro expedition, it was chosen, like Owerri, as an administrative centre and garrison town. Later, its location on the railway and nodal situation on the road network aided its growth as a market centre. It attracted 'settlers from Arochuku, Awka, Nnewi, Bende, Nkwerre and the coastal town of Opobo'[26] and developed, for a time, a complex system of economic specialities, organised by traders' towns of origin.[27] The key period of expansion was the fifties. An interesting account of the early fifties recalls that

> Aba was still a fairly small town in those days, although it was growing at a rapid pace. This was the period of the massive immigration of traders from Bende and Abriba areas. Trade was booming everywhere in Aba, and Aba market was beginning to acquire its reputation as one of the largest in the country. One thing about Aba at the time was that most of her inhabitants had not yet acquired what one might call an urban mentality.[28]

The researches of Mr Ananti have shed some interesting light on its growth, and on the changing attitudes of the surrounding Ngwa clans towards it. He points out that many migrants come to Aba originally as children (this is also true of other Igbo cities). 'A great number of them are brought as small children to serve elderly persons. They grow up in their masters house and are set free with a sum of money to start their own trade.'[29]

Ninety-two per cent of the population was Igbo in 1952, but many of these, as we have seen, were Igbo migrants from elsewhere. At first the Ngwa despised the new town in their midst, and the immigrants. 'Their earliest attitude was that of shunning and looking down on the town dwellers whom they called such derogatory names as "Umu Ohuhu" or "Those brought by vehicle" or "Those who go home facing backwards".' Later, attitudes changed. A few pioneers worked in Aba, and came home prosperous. 'This set off the trigger of migration to Aba town which became such a craze that at a point they began a dream of driving away the "Ohuhu" people.'[30] The Aba settlers in time developed a sense of local patriotism, and of Aba identity, comparable to the development we have noted in Port Harcourt. This was mirrored in the growth of an 'Aba dialect'.[31]

If one turns from these particular examples to the history of urban growth in Igboland as a whole, certain broad patterns emerge. Until the 1930s the area was lacking in big urban centres, in striking contrast to the cities of Yorubaland. In 1921 the largest urban centre in Igboland was Onitsha, with a population of under 11,000 (Ibadan, at the same time, had over a quarter of a million). As late as 1931 no city in Igboland had a population of over 20,000. In the twenty years that followed, Igboland had the highest urban growth rate in Nigeria, and by 1953 there were four cities with a population of over 60,000. Onitsha retained her traditional lead with 76,921, followed by Port Harcourt with 71,634, Enugu with 62,764 and Aba with 57,787. By 1963 the population had sky-rocketed further. Port Harcourt had a population of 179,563, Onitsha 163,032, Enugu 138,457, and Aba 131,003.[32] This was, of course, a year of inflated and controversial census returns, but many people returned to their villages to be counted, and some observers considered these urban figures as under-rather than over-estimates.

The rapid pace of growth exacted a high cost in social dislocation, in shortage of accommodation and pressure on amenities of every type. Municipal governments in the 1950s underwent a great deal of basically well-directed criticism, but the problems which confronted them were perhaps beyond the power of any local government to solve. They were not, of course, peculiar to Igboland, and no city in Nigeria has experienced them as acutely as Lagos.

Just as in the colonial context, some individuals prospered, and others, like the *dibia*, declined, so urban communities were differentially affected. Some reached undreamed of wealth, size and importance, and others experienced a sad decline from their pre-colonial greatness. This was true of the great fair-towns of Bende and Uzuakoli. Uzuakoli had certain advantages – a secondary school, and proximity to the railway – and for a time it flourished as a palm oil depot. But gradually, like Bende, it was eclipsed by Umuahia. The expatriate trading firms departed, and its former prosperity gave way to 'signs of decay, ruin and desolation'.[33]

Arochukwu underwent a similar experience. As an Aro grandmother told her grandson:

> You weren't born when Aro was teeming with slaves and full of life and festivity. Only the women, and the young boys like you stay here now. The others are lured away to distant places by the promise of wealth. And what do they call wealth now? Just a few seeds in the palm of your hand.[34]

Today, most Aro people live abroad, many of her houses stand in ruins, part of her farmlands stay uncultivated, and weeds and grass grow in the public squares . . .

Often its selection as an administrative centre helped a town's development, but not always. There was a popular song current in the fifties which ran '*Obodo nile emeghesige ofudu Okigwi na Orlu*' (All towns have developed except Okigwi and Orlu).[35]

Perhaps the most dramatic example of urban decline, however, was Ossomari. Last century, as we have seen, she was a major naval and mercantile power. Today, the very name cannot be found even on detailed maps. It is almost inaccessible in the dry season, and totally so in the rainy season. There are a number of reasons for the town's decline, among them a catastrophic migration by her slave population in 1928, and the periodic flooding which made the town unattractive to missionaries, administrators and traders. The historian of Ossomari, however, finds the key reason in an attitude of mind, which is summed up in a local proverb, 'No living person can vie to sleep long with a corpse.'[36] In other words, the great power that they had enjoyed was impossible under the British. They could not compete with the British, and therefore preferred not to compete at all.

DIASPORA

Not all Igbo who left their villages in search of employment, of course, settled in cities in Igboland. We have seen how in the nineteenth century population pressures forced some Igbo groups to fight a series of boundary wars. Colonialism put an end to this type of adjustment, but it made possible a much more fundamental one – the solution of Diaspora, which is one of the most striking features of Igbo twentieth-century history.

One might call this phase of their history, indeed, the second Igbo Diaspora, the first being that of the trans-Atlantic slave trade.

The decision to live outside one's place of origin, the process of living with the consequences of this decision – what sociologists call an interlocal orientation – is a revolutionary change of the greatest social importance. Igbos came into this situation in various ways. For government employees, there was no choice; they had to accept whatever posting they were given, which was almost never in their place of origin. This is how Nnamdi Azikiwe was born and brought up in the north – 'To all intents and purposes I was a Hausa boy then.'[37]

Many Igbos left their homes for the first time when conscripted to work on the railways. (A document in the National Archives, Enugu, an annual report from the Nsukka area – dated 1921, sheds a graphic light on the process of recruitment. It describes the great difficulty found in obtaining labourers for railway construction. Another hand – apparently the Resident editing the document for inclusion in his annual report – has changed it, to state that there was no trouble!)[38] Some labourers died on the railways; others returned home, repelled by the conditions, and indignities of the life. Others persevered, and followed the railway in its progress north. An interesting account from Idomaland describes the process.

> When the railway was under construction from the North to the East, the Ibos settled along the route, wherever there was a camp. The camps were built to help the workers on the roads and these camps were mainly inhabited by Ibos who came to work on the Railway line. They came first of all singly. After sometime, they brought their wives, 'small brothers' and sisters, usually to help them in domestic work. Along the railway route where there were camps in the North, the Ibos settled down with their families and began to farm the land around the camp.[39]

Gradually they diversified into trade and produce buyers. Increasingly, they appeared to their new neighbours as a privileged group, and aroused resentments accordingly.

> The Ibos brought European goods into the market. They had

> the lorries and maintained trade links between the other parts of the country and Idoma Division. They were the middle-men.
>
> The Ibo man was the headmaster of the primary school. He was the teacher, he was the railway station master, he was the post master, etc. . . . The feelings of a lot of people about the Ibos in Idoma before the civil war were that they were the controllers of trade, administration, the school systems – and 'our women'. . .
>
> Before the crisis, some of the Ibo traders in Idoma were buying their farm products from the farmers directly in their farms. Some of them would buy a whole plantation of corn or yams when the crop was still growing. They would pay the farmers very little for that . . .[40]

In 1911 there were 291 Igbos in Lagos; in 1921, there were 1609, most of them men.[41] Thirty years later, there were 31,887. They formed 44·6 per cent of the non-Igbo inhabitants of Lagos; many of them lived in Yaba, or along the Ikorodu and Agege roads. They formed 53·5 per cent of the non-Edo inhabitants of Benin, 38 per cent of the non Hausa-Fulani inhabitants of Kano and 40·7 per cent of the non-northern inhabitants of Kaduna.[42] There were nearly 167,000 in the northern region: about 40,000 of them were border minorities, and the rest lived in the strangers' quarters of the cities of the north. Apart from the cities just mentioned there were substantial Igbo communities in Ibadan, Zaria, Lafia, Maidugari, Gusau, Minna, Kafanchan and Makurdi.[43] Most of the miners at Jos were Igbos; according to one observer, 'the Ibos developed Jos almost by themselves.'[44]

It was perhaps inevitable that intercommunal tensions should develop where they settled (a little later, we shall look briefly at some of the factors which caused them). The Igbo traders 'incarnated all the characteristics of clannish and hard-working migrants.'[45] They came to be regarded as taking opportunities which rightly belonged to the local people, or even as exploiting them – as the passage from Idoma, quoted above, implies.

The resentment seems to have been particularly acute against those Igbo traders who were themselves struggling on the margin of subsistence. Two American anthropologists, who lived in Tivland in the 1950s, gave an interesting example of this:

> An Iyon elder said that Ibo 'journey *kpenga kpenga*'. He explained that the term came from the word for a carrying tray, (*kpen ga*), and that the Ibo leave their compounds with only a carrying tray; they buy in one market and sell in another and live on the profit. 'This', he said, 'was a very bad thing'.

When Tsar market was developing at this time, the Tiv welcomed Hausa traders, but insisted on the exclusion of the Igbo. But the Hausas themselves came to demand the admission of Igbo traders:

> Now they remembered that no large Nigerian market could (at that time) be fully effective without an Ibo contingent. Ibo had access to certain types of trade goods – especially European cloth and hardware – which were available only at much greater expense from other peoples. Ibo were also good carpenters and blacksmiths. Finally, there was the vast kinship-like network of Ibo between the trading outposts (such as Obudu), and the large market-centres (such as Onitsha). If a market is to be fully successful the Hausa said, it must have Ibo. The Tiv, however, stood adamant: no Ibo . . . The Tiv finally did allow Ibo to come to market.[46]

In a time of rapid social change, or of economic hardship, they easily became scapegoats, identified with a host of problems for which they were not in fact responsible. In 1953 communal jealousies – exacerbated by the actions of southern politicians – erupted in the Kano riots. Thirty-six people were killed and 277 were wounded, according to the official figures, but most commentators thought the real figures were much higher. But during the later fifties and early sixties, the flood of Igbos to other parts of Nigeria increased. By the middle sixties there were about a million – perhaps more – in the north.

The pattern of Diaspora spread beyond the boundaries of Nigeria. Some went as traders or craftsmen to other West African countries. Some were driven by poverty to Gabon and Fernando Po, as migrant labourers: a long sad story of oppression and exploitation which awaits its own historian.

The migration was not, of course, all one way. There were parties of Hausa elephant hunters living in Igboland before the British came.[47] In the early period of colonial rule – partly as a result of the employment of Hausa soldiers in the colonial forces – Hausa traders and craftsmen came to settle, especially in garrison towns. Later, they came to dominate the cattle trade. The numbers involved were much less than the numbers of Igbos in the north; northerners formed two per cent of the population of Enugu in 1950–1.[48]

TRADE, TRANSPORT, AND ENTREPRENEURS

The colonial period saw a tremendous increase in the volume of trade, both within Igboland and *vis-à-vis* the rest of Nigeria. There were many reasons for this – the growth of urban communities which needed to buy food, the need for cash incomes which gave a strong motivation for trading, the improvement of internal communications, were all important. The gradual substitution of traditional currencies doubtless helped; traditional currencies were regional, and their bulk made them unsuitable for major transactions. The decline of internal warfare made it safe to travel to other areas. The Ohafia, whose warlike exploits had made peaceful travel impossible, now were able to work abroad. 'By 1913–1920 most of Ohafia sons were now firm in trading at Itu and Calabar.'[49] Mr Oji's researches suggest that the very name Ohafia has been changed this century from *oha-ofia*, people living in the bush, to *oha-afia*, people who trade.

The scale of trade, and the extent of individual's participation in it, varies greatly. At the humblest level, one has the petty trading, often part-time, which is typical of housewives. They include the forestaller, who waylays women coming to market with little bundles of assorted produce, and sorts, bulks and resells them. Those engaged in full-time trade vary greatly in the extent of their enterprises and of their capital. In the 1930s a more prosperous class appeared – the transport owners, to whom we shall return. Since the Second World War, there has been an increasing number of produce buyers, most of whom started out as agents of the expatriate firms. Until the Second World War, the import-export business was almost, though not entirely, a monopoly of the expatriate firms (though much of what they imported was distributed by indigenous retailers). Since 1945 the expatriate firms have greatly reduced their own retail networks, and since 1960 an increasing number of Igbos have entered branches of the import trade, dealing in commodities such as stockfish and textiles.[50]

Typically, though not always, the market trader begins with a period of apprenticeship which lasts, on average, five years. We have an interesting account of the system at work in the 1930s, in the story of a man from Item, who later became a successful entrepreneur.

> 'My father wanted me to become a wealthy trader [rather than complete his primary education] for trade is a more popular occupation for our youths' he said. In 1930, he left Item for Aba and became apprenticed to Okoji Amadi. 'We were twelve articled-traders under the same master . . . 'In 1935, he left his master and decided to trade on his own with a capital of £150.[51]

The apprentice gained experience, and was usually given a gift or loan from his master when he started trading on his own account.

Because youths tended to be apprenticed to relatives or fellow-townsmen, a system of specialisation by place of origin grew up. Ananti gives an interesting description of the process at Aba, while adding that in the middle sixties, when he wrote, it was on the wane because youths were preferring to choose for themselves.

> People from Udi area are mainly butchers at Aba town, Nnewi people specialise in transport and selling of miscellaneous articles; Unubi and Amichi people on cotton and woollen cloths; Item people specialise in sewing and selling of singlets and in later years in second hand clothes; Akokwa, Osina and Akpele people specialise in plate and stockfish and so on.[52]

Very often those communities which had been prosperous and successful traders in pre-colonial times, continued to be so in an era of rapid change. This was true of Oguta, Nkwerre, Abiriba and Nnewi, and of other towns as well.

This is how a sympathetic observer described the traders of

Onitsha in the late fifties:

> Where the cheap Japanese enamelware or the trade goods from the Coast appear, it will be a sign that an Ibo trader from Onitsha . . . [has] been there . . . Two main kinds of trader work in Onitsha – those selling locally and the big wholesalers buying to sell to distant markets in the North. These Ibo traders will have agents to whom the lorries go in Jos, in Maiduguri, sometimes in Kano. Many of them work extraordinarily hard. If you notice a man half-asleep in the back of his stall, while a boy is serving, it is quite probably because two days ago he set off in a crowded lorry to cross the Niger Ferry in the evening, sat all day in the jolting lorry for 400 miles to Lagos, traded there all day, and was back in the lorry in the evening for the return journey . . . Many of these Ibo men will work like this (sometimes making two journeys in a week) for little reward . . . No one could fail to admire the energy and vitality of these traders, the range of their contacts and interests, their sharp eye for the slightest chance of trade, their hard work for small results.[53]

The research of Dr Onyemelukwe, conducted in Onitsha market in the early sixties, adds more details. He describes the mutual trust and cooperation existing between the Igbos of the Diaspora and those at home. They would often avoid a tiring dangerous journey by consigning unaccompanied goods to each other – which were safely delivered by Igbo lorry drivers, or sent large sums of money by the same drivers. Often their consignments were only partially prepaid. The traders of Onitsha would sometimes make interest-free unsecured loans to each other – a remarkable index of honesty and generosity.[54]

This Nigeria-wide trade network depended, of course, on adequate transport facilities. We have noted the devotion of early colonial governments to road-making, largely through unpaid local labour. Navigable creeks and waterways were cleared, usually with dynamite, though the frequency with which the clearing of the same waterway is noted in colonial records casts some doubts of the efficacy of the process! We have noted that in 1916 the railway reached Enugu. Thereafter it moved north steadily, reaching Kaduna in 1926.

But the contribution which the roads made to the growth of

internal trade depended, of course, on the kind of transport which was available to run on them. Until the 1920s, apart from the odd car owned by a white official or wealthy Warrant Chief, the only transport available was head porterage or cycle. Both, of course, are still in use today, and carrier cyclists still perform prodigies of balance and endurance. But the real transport revolution began in the 1920s and expanded in the thirties and forties, with the introduction of lorry transport.

Lorry transport proved one of the triumphs of Nigerian enterprise, competing successfully with the railways despite the government's support of the latter. Some transport entrepreneurs made great fortunes; others succumbed to cut-throat competition and a deficient system of accounting which often made too little allowance for depreciation. The early history of lorry transport in Nigeria, with self-taught mechanics, over bad roads, is an epic in its own right. Even today, to drive an overloaded and under-maintained lorry over Nigerian roads demands courage and mechanical skill. Their painted mottoes fill every highway in Nigeria with a constant series of affirmations of the goodness and providence of God: '*Chi bu Uzo*', 'The Lord is my Shepherd', '*Ekene dili Chukwu*', 'Psalm 121'.

We have been examining trade and transport but, especially from the fifties on, many Igbo came to specialise in various types of workshops and small-scale industry (the latter on a very low technological level). A survey of small industry in fourteen eastern Nigeria towns in 1961 reflected large numbers of repairers of cars, bicycles and radios, battery chargers, welders, blacksmiths, bakers, tailors, shoe repairers, sandal makers (both from leather and from tyres), printers and bus body builders. Sixty per cent were housed 'in raffia sheds, corrugated metal huts or market stalls'. Only 9 per cent possessed power-driven machinery. The average number of workers per workshop was 2·7.[55]

These small-scale Igbo entrepreneurs often sought opportunities outside Igboland. Many of them took their technical ingenuity and skill to the north.

> In these areas [i.e. in the north] they controlled to a large extent, most of the urban economic activities, trading, carpentry, smithing, mechanics of all types, building contracts,

as well as providing the largest numbers of non-local people in commercial and merchantile [sic] houses, and in government and local government establishments.[56]

In this world of cut-throat competition and small profit margins, it seems almost incredible that some individuals managed to rise to great wealth. But in fact a number of Igbo entrepreneurs attained a success which deserves mention in any narrative of Igbo history. The following are just a couple of outstanding examples and not, of course, a complete list.

Especially in the interwar years, a number of women from Niger communities such as Oguta, Onitsha and Ossomari enjoyed remarkable success as merchants. One of the most famous was Madame Okwei of Ossomari (1872–1943). She started in a small way at Onitsha, and like many indigenous entrepreneurs obtained her 'economic takeoff' as an agent of one of the big expatriate firms, acting as a palm produce buyer and retail distributor. She accumulated capital rapidly. Like many other merchants of the colonial period she lent money at high interest rates, and she cemented good relations with both African and European trading partners by providing them with mistresses! She kept careful records, despite her lack of formal education. During the depression, when the palm oil trade slumped, she turned to the specialist distribution of luxury products, which she imported direct from Britain. She invested her wealth in land, houses and a fleet of lorries and trade canoes, and in 1935 was made the *omu* (queen) of Ossomari.[57] She was one of many Nigerians who profited by an era of rapid change, transforming its difficulties into opportunities.

The transport magnates of Nnewi were another notable group of pioneering entrepreneurs. In the 1930s, a number of them became wealthy and well known, among them C. Egwuatu, operating in the Nsukka area, and D. D. Onyemelukwe and J. C. Ulasi, in the Aba area. The most outstanding member of the group, Louis Philip Ojukwu,* entered the field later, buying his first second-hand lorry in 1937. He had begun as a produce inspector, resigning in 1934 to become a John Holt sub-agent in Lagos (another example of an entrepreneur accumulating capital and experience in the service of an expa-

* When he was knighted, he took his Igbo name, as Sir Odumegwu.

triate firm). His attention was attracted towards transport by the needs of his textiles customers from the East.

In the forties, with amazing rapidity, he built up a large transport fleet. He succeeded partly through circumstances – it was a time of economic expansion, with a great demand for transport – and partly through iron diligence and meticulous attention to detail. At its height, his fleet consisted of fifty or sixty lorries, plus other forms of transport. In the early fifties, by which time he employed a dozen highly paid expatriates, competition was reducing the profits of the transport business. With characteristic acumen and decision he pulled out of it, transferring his vast resources to company shares and landed property. In the last decade of his life (he died in 1966) he was the chairman of a large number of public corporations and major businesses, among them the African Continental Bank, the Nigerian National Shipping Line, the Coal Corporation and the Eastern Region marketing board, retaining to the end the same relentless industry. (His son remembers him reading business documents until three in the morning, and attending three or four meetings a day.) He died during a visit to one of the companies he headed, the cement works at Nkalagu.[58]

RESPONSES TO URBAN LIFE: THE IMPROVEMENT UNIONS

The workers in early nineteenth-century England, who left their villages for the first time during the Industrial Revolution and went to live in big industrial cities, very often joined together in clubs, friendly societies or masonic-type secret societies. They did so in an attempt to find friends, and a sense of identity, in 'a desert of individuals', and in an attempt to guard against at least some of the dangers and insecurities of their new life by providing a small measure of social security and mutual aid. The Igbo who left their villages for the first time responded in exactly the same way. They too formed associations, bound by strict rules, meeting regularly and providing a network of benefits and obligations. The main difference was that in Igboland these societies were organised according to a man's town of origin, and had as one of their main purposes the provision of amenities for it.

The first reference I have seen to one of these improvement associations was a Young Men's Association at Onitsha in

1905.[59] An Owerri (Division) Union was established in Enugu in 1917 and retained a continuous existence thereafter, the doyen of the Enugu ethnic unions.[60] In Port Harcourt, a very active Owerri Union developed. It had twenty-three sub-secretaries, representing its twenty-three component towns. It collected regular subscriptions, repatriated the dead for burial, assisted members involved in law cases, made loans to members, and settled disputes among them. An expatriate observer in the mid thirties attributed to the work of this Union the absence of destitution in Port Harcourt, despite the depression and widespread unemployment.[61]

Especially in the early years, the unions often exercised great authority over their members' lives, even to the point of repatriating delinquents. Like the friendly societies of Victorian England, the first benefit they paid was always a funeral benefit – in disregard of middle-class criteria of rationality and prudence.

Although many were founded earlier, the key period for the foundation of these unions was the 1930s and early forties. The Ozuitem Young Men's Welfare Society was formed in 1937, mainly by mission-educated young men. An observer described it in 1939:

> Most of these men are traders or others who work outside Ozuitem and form small branches in the trading centres of Aba, Port Harcourt, Calabar and Enugu where they are employed . . . The mother group . . . meets every Christmas in Ozuitem. Its function, and that of the branch, is primarily social. The minutes are given over to lengthy discussions of the internal organisational affairs of the society. As yet there have been only a few attempts to deal with the larger community problems, but the tendency is in that direction.[62]

The aims of the unions were threefold: to provide companionship and a measure of social security for villagers in the town, to preserve town unity and culture, and to raise money to introduce amenities in the town. The second goal is sometimes encouraged by periodic compulsory General Returns Home. The success of the third depended largely, though not entirely, on the economic resources of the community concerned. Usually, though not always, the first branches were formed in the cities, and a home union followed later.

The first Uratta Union was formed in Port Harcourt in 1939. A home branch was formed in 1941 to fight a land case. It later played a valuable role combatting 'injustice and bribery' in the Native Courts, and sent one of its members on a loan scholarship to England to study engineering. The union split in two in 1950, but the sections later reunited.[63]

The Enugwu-Ukwu Patriotic Union was formed in Enugu in 1942, primarily to combat corruption and injustice in the Native Court. Its founder stated in his inaugural speech, that 'This union has two main objectives – to seek the interest of its members, and to seek the welfare of our town. . . . One thing has brought us to this meeting – love for our town, which is called patriotism.'[64]

The unions of Nkwerre and Abiriba, composed in the main of wealthy traders, were especially successful in providing amenities for their home communities. The Nkwerre Aborigines Union was formed in 1939, followed by a women's section in 1943. The men's section built St Augustine's College, Nkwerre, a postal agency and were responsible for a water scheme. The women's section contributed to the water scheme, and built St Catherine's College.[65]

The first improvement association in Abiriba was the Abiriba Youngmen Christian Association, founded in 1919. After several changes of name in the thirties, it finally became the Abiriba Communal Improvement Union in 1944. It took as its motto, 'Self-help is the sure path to success'. Partly through utilising the traditional structure of mutually competitive age-grades, the union built two secondary schools, a town hall, a post office, a 78-bed hospital, a rubber plantation (to provide local employment) and awarded five overseas scholarships. Up to November 1956, the union had spent nearly £12,000 on its scholarships. The girls' secondary school cost £40,000, the hospital £20,000, the postal agency £5000, and the union borrowed £10,000 for the rubber plantation. In 1965, there were a thousand dues-paying members. The union and the age-grades contributed far more in these voluntary levies than they did in taxation.[66] Its achievements represent a quarter of a century of patriotism and self-sacrifice for which there can be few parallels.

It would be wrong to depict the history of the unions as a simple success story. Some unions have a history of sectional conflict, others have suffered through peculation, or – not always the same thing – suspicions of peculation. The goals have not always been well chosen. Often members have made great sacrifices – virtually compulsory levies – to build empty prestige projects. Post offices (often in an area already served by a postal agency) town halls and village sports stadia are frequently erected, where a more rational selection of priorities would have built a cottage hospital, an electrification scheme, or an improved water supply. The energy and resources of urban dwellers tend to be deflected too exclusively into the development of their village of origin, rather than to the cities where they spend their lives. At least some of the money and time would be better devoted to the overcrowded and under-equipped city schools their children attend.

As successive generations become more adapted to urban life, there are signs that the unions may be coming to be resented as a burden. They invariably meet on Sunday afternoons, eating into their members' leisure time. The burden is made worse by the fact that each individual is supposed to attend not one but a whole pyramid of meetings – corresponding to the lineage, the village, the town and sometimes the division – though it is only the 'family meetings' (the maximal lineage) and the town meetings which are obligatory. As early as the 1940s, the sophisticated and urbanised Onitsha sons abroad began to resist union demands.

> In contrast to the unified and active Ibo 'town' and divisional unions the O[nitsha] I[improvement] U[nion] never established any approximation to compulsory universal membership . . . Even after World War II when a concerted effort was made everywhere to woo maximum membership . . . OIU branches frequently reported widespread lack of interest and outright refusal to join. The basis for this refusal lies in the fact that Onitsha men 'broad' are more thoroughly urbanised and more individualistic in their social orientations than are their Ibo counterparts, because their education, manifold urban experience, and general occupational security . . . have given them greater independence from the collective

constraints of Union demands.[67]

The unions, of course, replace the horizontal bonds of class loyalty with the vertical bonds of locality. As the gulf between rich and poor widens, an increasing minority of the working class are coming to see them as reactionary, as concealing the realities of the class struggle, and deflecting their members' energy from more profitable channels, such as trade unionism.[68] At the other end of the social spectrum, there were signs that class identification was coming to replace identification by town of origin among the Igbo élite. The Okaa Society, founded at Aba in 1963, was 'an exclusive association of wealthy men' – businessmen, professional men and civil servants. It spread rapidly through Nigeria, though most of its members were Igbos. It was banned by the Ironsi regime in 1966.[69]

The Ibo State Union had only its name in common with the local unions. It was founded in 1947 (though prototypes existed from the mid thirties) and ceased to exist when banned in 1966. In theory, it consisted of representatives of all the local unions, but in practice only a small minority played any part in it, and it was dominated by businessmen, mainly of little education, from Port Harcourt and Aba. For all but five years, its president was Z. C. Obi, a Port Harcourt businessman, who personalised the union to such an extent that he kept all the records in his own home. For a time – from 1948 to 1952 – some leading NCNC members held office in the union (Azikiwe was President from 1948 to 1952), but they came to find their membership of it an embarrassment, and resigned.

It suited the leaders of the Ibo State Union to represent it as a powerful monolithic organisation speaking for all Igbo people. Frequently, it suited the opponents of the NCNC to portray it in the same light, and identify it closely with the NCNC. In fact it was a paper tiger:[70] its only concrete achievements were the building of a secondary school in Aba, and the promotion of Ibo Day, an annual holiday in honour of Igbo accomplishments – this last a measure of doubtful wisdom and utility.

Two other types of organisation which evolved in the colonial period, which were similar in many respects to the improvement unions, were the church meetings and the credit associations. We have noted how denominational rivalries often disrupted the unity of the village. Within the village, especially, church meetings came to fill many of the functions filled by the improvement unions in the towns. In the 1930s they were especially characteristic of Protestant women.

> These [Church meetings] are . . . called by a woman leader and are held regularly either in the church or at members' houses in rotation. After prayers and the singing of a hymn, Church matters are discussed and a collection taken towards the women's share of the local teacher or catechist's salary, repairs to the church, the entertainment of travelling members, gifts to a visiting pastor, etc. These meetings will certainly become more numerous and influential as time goes on.[71]

Today, a great proliferation of organisations characterises all the churches, Catholic and Protestant. Depending on the individual's interests and circumstances, he gives more or less of his time to the improvement unions, more or less to church organisations. (One mildly startling feature of Igbo Catholicism is the extent of devotion to St Jude, who is honoured in a large number of St Jude societies.) Many men find a similar satisfaction in Freemasonry, or in its Nigerian equivalent, the Reformed Ogboni.

The contribution club, like the improvement association, is a body which combines social and utilitarian ends.[72] The contribution clubs developed in the colonial period, as an answer to a widespread difficulty in Igboland – the problem of accumulating capital on small incomes. Money lenders charged preposterous rates of interest, and commercial banks required a collateral which was beyond the dreams of most Igbo. (Their reluctance to lend money to Nigerians, in the colonial period, was rooted not in racial prejudice, but in the well-known proclivity of banks for lending money to those who do not actually need it . . .) The contribution club collected regular payments from its members, who took it in turns to draw the total. Some were large and highly formalised, some were informal agreements among a few friends. In some, the social functions outweighed the utilitarian, and the beneficiary was expected to spend most of the proceeds on entertaining the others. All, of course, presumed a high degree of honesty and self-discipline among their members.

HEALTH

In Igboland, as in other parts of the world, the history of disease and its treatment, and of epidemics, is an important and neglected variable of social history. The real achievements of pre-colonial African societies in the sphere of medicine are now generally recognised. Even today, traditional *dibia* include some superbly successful bone-setters, and pharmacologists in Nigeria (and elsewhere in West and East Africa) are conducting a scientific analysis of traditional herbal remedies.

In this connection we might well remember a certain Chive of Igbariam. Chive was a former *dibia* who had become a Christian, and suggested to the local missionary in 1921 that a 'University of Medicine' should be established, where *dibia* could hand on their medical knowledge, in isolation from the corpus of traditional religious beliefs. The missionary snubbed the proposal, telling Chive 'how organised society regarded quacks'.[73] Chive was obviously fifty years before his time.

Nevertheless, the treatment of disease was clearly a sphere where colonialism brought an unequivocal betterment. In pre-colonial Igboland, for all the skill of the herbalists and bone-setters, many diseases remained untreatable, susceptible only to religio-magical explanations and remedies.

In both the nineteenth and twentieth centuries, Igboland has been repeatedly plagued by epidemic disease. There was a smallpox epidemic in Onitsha in 1873 'which carried off many of the inhabitants', among them the Obi,[74] and there were other epidemics, earlier and later in the century. There was a major smallpox epidemic in north-eastern Igboland in the 1890s, which goes far to explain its failure to resist colonial conquest effectively. In the early twentieth century there were repeated smallpox epidemics among the Cross River Igbos; one of them killed about two thousand people in Asaga Ohafia.[75] A local smallpox epidemic after the First World War was one of the main factors making it difficult to obtain labour for the Enugu mines.

In 1920 Igboland was swept by a deadly influenza epidemic which was, of course, world wide. In the north-east a mission doctor estimated that 80 per cent of the population was affected.[76] It was especially severe, too, in the towns behind Onitsha. 'In the town of Abaja nine out of ten people seemed to be down. The roads were deserted. Here and there across them could be seen clumps of feathers and ashes – the sacrifices of *dibias* to keep away the spirits that bring the disease.[77]

In some areas the epidemic, 'driving men to despair and madness', even led to a recurrence of human sacrifice.[78] In the oral traditions of many Igbo communities, the influenza epidemic is remembered as the greatest disaster of their history, and events are dated as so many years before or after influenza. In the late sixties, Igboland was again involved in a world-wide epidemic, this time of cholera, which caused great ravages, especially among the poor. Like the influenza, it caused unnumbered obscure tragedies: the writer knows of one villager who in a week lost his entire family (two wives and six children) and died, soon afterwards, of grief.

Several diseases were almost eliminated during the colonial era. Yaws, painful and disfiguring, though not fatal, was once regarded as a normal accompaniment of childhood: now it has practically disappeared. Leprosy was once very widespread throughout Igboland. Mission and other records give us many moving vignettes of the physical and mental sufferings of its victims, who often had to live in separate villages. Now, thanks to treatment with Dapsone, it has been almost eradicated from Igboland. Again, pre-colonial Igboland had only religio-magical remedies for abnormal and difficult births. These caused an incalculable amount of suffering, and usually resulted in the death of both mother and child. It was one of the areas where Western medicine was most rapidly appreciated, and most extensively used.

The colonial era brought a wider appreciation of the basic facts of nutrition. In pre-colonial times yams were regarded as the optimum food. Eggs were seldom eaten, and a fondness for meat was thought to reflect an extravagant and wasteful disposition (which was especially to be discouraged among the young!) and fruits and vegetables tended to be despised as the food of the poor.[79] The colonial era brought many new fruits, and eradicated these taboos, but poverty still restricts the protein in the average Igbo diet. Children are still admitted to hospitals suffering from no disease but malnutrition, and the diet of the poor in both the cities and the villages consists primarily of gari. Gari is filling, and palatable, and pure carbohydrate . . .

The twentieth century eliminated some diseases, and introduced others, such as venereal disease and measles, the latter being a serious illness in Igboland, with a 25 per cent mortality rate. It also saw an astonishingly high incidence of high blood pressure, both among the Igbo middle class and in the trader community. This incidence is also found among other Nigerian groups, so much so that it has been made the subject of special studies.[80] It may be physiological in origin, but it seems likely that it mirrors the great stress and tension of their lives.

Not all traditional diseases were susceptible to Western medical treatment. Sickle cell anaemia remains one of the scourges of Igboland, a scourge for which Western medicine offers an explanation, and palliatives, but not a cure.

The availability of Western medicine is, of course, quite a different matter from its use. Many Igbo still consult herbalists, and faith healers, and patent medicine vendors, not because these are thought to be more efficacious, but because they cannot afford hospital fees. In the words of two informants from the Nsukka area, 'Although many people still prefer to adopt traditional medical ways of treatment, a greater percentage do so because of their inability to meet hospital demands rather than because of ignorance.' 'Many rich people go to hospitals today when they are ill. But most of us have no money to meet the heavy charge given there.'[81] Some hospital doctors estimate that two per cent of the people who would benefit by hospitalisation in Igboland receive it.

14 The End of Colonialism: 1945–1960

'We lived many lives in those swirling campaigns, never sparing ourselves any good or evil; yet when we had achieved, and the new world dawned, the old men came out again and took from us our victory, and remade it in the likeness of the former world they knew . . . We stammered that we had worked for a new heaven and a new earth, and they thanked us very kindly and made their peace.'

T. E. Lawrence, quoted in a letter to the editor in The Renaissance, *22 Jan 1974*

The exercise of the historian's profession demands three preconditions: plenitude of information, tranquility of judgement, and candour of expression. The closer one approaches to the present, the more difficult these conditions are to fulfil. Many of the relevant sources are not yet open to scholars. Most of the participants are still alive, which inevitably acts as a constraint, especially for those who, like the present writer, choose to write the history of the society in which they actually live. For these reasons the last two chapters of this book have been the most difficult to write. Nevertheless, the attempt must be made; it would be absurd to write a history of the Igbo people and exclude from it the turbulent and eventful years between the Second World War and the present.

In the earlier chapters of this book, I concentrated on the theme of Igbo history in isolation, in the main, from the general history of Nigeria. After 1945 this narrow focus becomes impossible. The history of the Igbo becomes inextricably entwined with that of other Nigerian peoples, and everything of real importance that happens has implications that are Nigeria-wide.

The Second World War was a climacteric in the decline of colonialism, for many reasons. Its follies and crimes, and the many reverses suffered by the British, destroyed forever the myth of white invincibility. Many Nigerians served overseas, and came home with a clearer knowledge of the limitations of the whites, and with greater self-assurance and sophistication. (A minor but not unimportant theme in social history, was that the bride price was pushed up to a level from which subsequent legislation has been unable to dislodge it, and which has produced many social evils.) And it was difficult to see why the principles of the Atlantic Charter should not apply to Africans. There was a change in the climate of opinion in Europe itself – its collective self-confidence undermined at last by a depression and two world wars in thirty years. The Labour Party came to power in Britain, committed to the support of the underprivileged, both within its own boundaries and internationally. Most fundamentally, the Nigerian nationalist struggle was won in India. Having given independence to a sub-continent, there was no logical reason why the British should not extend the process to Africans as well.

After the war, Nigerian nationalists and British politicians and administrators did not disagree about the ultimate goal. They differed only in their estimates of how rapidly the goal should be attained, the form independence should take (a federal or unitary constitution) and the role to be played by traditional rulers.

The political structure of the future independent Nigeria was determined by three successive constitutions – the Richards constitution of 1947, the Macpherson constitution of 1952, and the Lyttelton constitution of 1954. Later on many Nigerians, with the advantage of hindsight, were to accuse the British of a policy of divide and rule, by introducing a federal constitution without the essential proviso (the equal size of the component parts) which makes such a constitution workable. These criticisms were given point by the fact that various Nigerian nationalist leaders, at different times, advocated the division of Nigeria into smaller units. But in fact the last two constitutions were finalised after prolonged discussions with Nigerians and the three (later four) Regions which resulted were the result of historical accident. More precisely, they date from Lugard's retention of the administrative division between the northern and southern provinces in 1914, and the division of the southern provinces into east and west on the eve of the Second World War.

With the advantage of hindsight, the creation of three regions, each dominated by a majority ethnic group and each dominated by a regionally based party, is the first act of a tragedy which moves to its conclusion with the grim inevitability of a Greek drama.

The first of the three major parties which dominated the era of civilian politics in Nigeria was the NCNC, which was founded in 1944, and ceased to exist twenty-two years later, at the end of the First Republic. Its first president was the veteran Lagos nationalist Herbert Macaulay. When he died two years later, at the age of eighty-two, his last words were 'Tell Oged [his son] to keep the flag flying.'

To what extent, after his death, did the NCNC become an Igbo – or Eastern – party? Certainly the NCNC, and the whole nationalist movement in the forties, was dominated by the personality of Nnamdi Azikiwe. After three years in the Gold Coast, he returned to Nigeria in 1937, and started a newspaper, the *West African Pilot*, which warmed Nigerian hearts with its outspoken criticisms of the colonial regime (though his basic caution always kept him on the right side of the law). His charm, attractive presence, eloquence and learning attracted a degree of adulation which is difficult to understand in an age more disillusioned with politics. The radical wing of the nationalist movement called themselves Zikists. He even had a church established in his honour.

Azikiwe's alliance with Macaulay meant that he inherited the enmities which the old man had acquired over decades of political life. To many, his prominence was sinister and alarming. Chief Awolowo, a Yoruba from Ijebu, was a politician of commanding talents whose life, like Azikiwe's, was a desperate triumphant struggle with adversity. He blamed Azikiwe for dividing the earlier Nigerian Youth Movement. As early as 1940, he wrote in later years, 'It seemed clear to me that [Azikiwe's] policy was to corrode the self-respect of the Yoruba people as a group; to build up the Ibos as a master race.'[1] He found many examples of pro-Igbo reporting in the *Pilot*, even in accounts of school football matches. And it was not difficult to find examples of Igbo chauvinism in Zik's voluminous writings and speeches, as in his presidential address to the Ibo State Union in 1949: 'It would appear that the God of Africa has specially created the Ibo nation to lead the children of Africa from the bondage of the ages.'[2] In 1945, with others, Awolowo formed a Yoruba cultural association, the Egbe Omo Oduduwa. In 1951, he launched the Action Group. In 1949 a group of northern leaders had already formed the Northern Peoples Congress.

How true is it that Zik introduced ethnic divisiveness into national politics? Just as there was no contradiction between his role as a Nigerian nationalist and his undoubted attachment to pan-Africanism, so he was both a genuine Nigerian patriot, and deeply attached to the Igbo subgroup. The two were not necessarily incompatible. Today, in his old age, his past as a national and international figure does not prevent him from being deeply absorbed in the small world of Onitsha local government.

It was the great British political philosopher Edmund Burke who wrote, 'No cold relation makes a zealous citizen', and again, 'To be attracted to the subdivision, to be attached to the little platoon we belong to in society is the first principle, the germ as it were, of public affections.'

'The NCNC was always more than an Ibo party'.[3] Azikiwe contested the 1951 election from a seat in Lagos. In the federal election of 1954, the NCNC won a majority of the seats in the Western Region. In 1958, less than half the officials in the NCNC party apparatus were Igbo. In 1960, three out of ten NCNC federal ministers were Igbo.[4] The NCNC leadership were deeply concerned to maintain a national, rather than an ethnic image, and the Igbos themselves were deeply committed to a national unity from which they had everything to gain. In 1956, a Fulani cattle dealer from Sokoto, Mallam Umaru Altine, was elected as the first mayor of Enugu. In the late fifties and early sixties Igbos studying abroad would sometimes refuse to state their ethnic identity, proclaiming that they were simply Nigerians. The typical decor of an Igbo student's room in London comprised a map of Africa, a map of Nigeria, a Nigerian calendar and a picture of the University of Ibadan.

The evolution of three major parties, each identified more or less with an ethnic group, and each with a primarily regional base, had two main implications. One was that none could govern alone, and that the federal government must consist of an alliance of two of them, against the third. Since patronage was of key importance in Nigerian politics, no political party could contemplate with equanimity an indefinite sojourn in the wilderness. After the 1959 federal election, Azikiwe made the momentous decision to ally with the NPC, rather than the Action Group. Several reasons have been suggested for this – the fear of northern secession, which had been mooted repeatedly in the fifties, the bitter competition between the Igbo and Yoruba élites, and the pressure of western supporters of the NCNC who feared that an alliance with the Action Group would deprive them of their *raison d'être*.

The second major consequence was that in each region the minority groups began to agitate for their place in the sun, reinforcing their demands by allying with a major party from elsewhere. In the Eastern Region, fear of Igbo domination led to the COR (Calabar-Ogoja-Rivers) movement, founded at a meeting at Uyo in 1954, and allied with the Action Group. In 1958, the British appointed the Willink Commission to look into the fears of minorities. Predictably, in accordance with its terms of reference, it recommended against the creation of new regions, but at the same time it described, *vis-à-vis* the Igbo, 'a feeling of apprehension and resentment of whose reality no one who was in Calabar when we were there could have any doubt.'[5] It mentioned an incident when the Igbo community in Calabar boycotted an Efik restauranteur, and added, 'Such incidents obviously invite retaliation, which takes forms steadily more violent; feeling thus becomes progressively embittered. This process is already taking place, and we saw examples of violent propaganda against Ibos.'[6]

Fundamentally, what the COR groups feared was perpetual Igbo political domination on the one hand, and the ascendancy of individual Igbos in local economic life, on the other. There was no doubt as to the reality of both. Okpara told the people of Enyong on one occasion, 'I will give you all the amenities you require but you must first vote for me.'[7] An Idoma writer records,

> An Ibibio told me that the people of Calabar, and the Ijaws, and Ogojas in the former Eastern Region did not like the Ibos because of many reasons . . . He said that Calabar town, which should be an Efik town, is an Ibo township; the same thing happened to Port Harcourt which should be joint land of the Ijaws and the Ibos . . . He said that the Ibos took these towns and by a gradual manoeuvre they dominated them before the January coup. He said that a lot of Calabarians and Ijaws believe that the Ibos like to control and dominate where they can and where they can't they will have the place destroyed.[8]

The evidence suggests, however, that they were not in fact deprived of amenities. The Willink commission found little substance in most of the specific charges made against the Igbos, and an official document of 1963 claimed that the COR areas had 35 per cent of the population, 47 per cent of Ministry of Agriculture expenditure, and 42 per cent of money loaned for industrial and agricultural projects.[9]

In 1950, the system of local government in the East was changed to one on the British model – a network of elected County and Urban Councils. In the dry season of 1951–2 Nigeria's first general elections were held, returning the NCNC with a large majority in the East. In 1956, one election later, the East was granted internal self-government. In 1960, Nigeria became independent.

If one analyses the use made in the East of this ever-increasing autonomy, one finds that it anticipates the experiences of the First Republic in a number of striking respects. As throughout Nigeria, there were real achievements in the sphere of development. This was partly because there were more funds available. In England, the crisis of conscience which heralded the end of colonialism also inspired the 1945 Colonial Development and Welfare Act, in which Britain committed herself to devoting part of her own resources to the colonies which had done so much to enrich her in the past. At the same time there was a phenomenal increase in the demand for Nigeria's primary products, and hence in the value of her exports.

Partly through government sponsorship, partly through private investment, Igboland's industrial capacity increased greatly in the late fifties and early sixties. The Eastern Region

Development Corporation made a loan of over half a million pounds for the cement works at Nkalagu thirty miles from Enugu, which started production in 1957. Aba became the centre of a growing industrial complex. Nigerian Breweries opened a branch there in 1957. It acquired a soap factory, and a pharmaceutical factory, and in 1964 an American firm, Indian Head, opened a textile factory there. In 1961 Umuahia, the home of the Eastern Region premier, also acquired a brewery. It was also the location of 'a novel all-Nigerian enterprise, the manufacture of drilling clays and paints.' In 1963 a British firm, Turner and Newall, opened an asbestos factory in Enugu, to prevent a continental rival from cornering the Nigerian market. A government-sponsored furniture factory in Enugu became an important centre for the diffusion of skills, leading to a number of small workshops, producing furniture of excellent quality. In 1965 a subsidiary of UAC opened a textile factory at Onitsha, and in the following year, work started on a textile factory across the Niger, at Asaba.[10]

An industry which dwarfed all these in importance, however, was the production of petroleum. In 1937 Shell began prospecting for oil; in 1956 the first producible well was drilled. A number of other oil fields were developed in rapid succession – some of them, like Igrita and Imo River, in southern Igboland, and others further south – and the first shipment of Nigerian oil left Port Harcourt in 1958. The headquarters of Shell B.P. was located at Owerri for a time, and then shifted to Port Harcourt.

The implications of the oil discoveries belong to Nigerian rather than to Igbo history. They offer a superb opportunity to finance rapid development, and combat the poverty which darkens the lives of most Nigerian citizens. But experience elsewhere in the world suggests that wealth from oil revenues does not necessarily contribute much to the betterment of the average man. It remains to be seen what use Nigeria will make of this challenge and opportunity.

At a humbler level, the same period saw the mushroom growth of the small bakeries, car repair workshops, welders, sandal makers and so on to which we have already had occasion to refer. A survey published in 1963 recorded no less than 10,728 firms in fourteen towns in Eastern Nigeria.[11]

The Eastern Region Development Corporation aided other forms of economic development. It operated a number of Pioneer Oil Mills, and financed a number of smaller projects such as poultry farms. It made a loan of half a million pounds to rebuild Onitsha market (the results were destroyed in the war). The Eastern Region government spent three million pounds in roads and bridges, and later, in the sixties, the Federal government gave a massive boost to east-west communications by building the Niger bridge.

It would be wrong, however, to depict the history of industrial growth in those years as a simple success story. The Pioneer mills were badly designed, as an Igbo engineer pointed out, and ran at a loss.[12] Political considerations sometimes led to a wasteful duplication of facilities: the siting of two rival breweries at Aba and Umuahia, thirty miles apart, is an obvious example. Sometimes the new industries failed to make a profit – a particularly bad case was the glass factory at Port Harcourt which ran at a loss partly as a result of overstaffing and technical difficulties, and partly because of lack of adequate prior consideration of the nature and extent of the demand for its products. It imported all its raw materials but sand.[13] Often the expatriate investor enriched himself at Nigeria's expense. In the words of a brilliant Federal Permanent Secretary:

> There are known cases where the foreign investor is the consultant who prepared the feasibility study for the project, the financial adviser and the banker who finalised the credit arrangements, the manufacturer who supplied the equipment, the technical partner and management agent who runs the factory under a management agency agreement, with fees and commissions. The economic 'Mikado' then gets a government guarantee that if the project fails, the government would from its budgetary resources service the loan for the equipment.[14]

Since the factories were concentrated, in the main, in a handful of urban centres they greatly exacerbated the problem of overcrowding, lack of accommodation and excessive pressure on amenities, to which we have referred. This was equally true of the small-scale enterprises; 75 per cent of the 10,728 firms referred to above were in the four big urban centres.[15]

Most Nigerians saw the steps made towards industrialisation as a great advance, enhancing Nigeria's economic independence, increasing the pool of skills and employment opportunities in the society, and improving her balance of trade. Nevertheless, a glance at the experience of Italy, on the one hand, and of New Zealand and Denmark on the other, shows that industrialisation cannot necessarily be equated with prosperity, nor agriculture with poverty.[16]

The fifties were also a period of rapid expansion in education. In 1948 there were 38 secondary schools in the Eastern Region; by 1958 there were 84.[17] A number of them were built by local community initiative. If one limits the analysis to schools to Igbo-speaking areas, east of the Niger, there were 67 secondary schools in 1960, and 160 in 1964. There was a similar expansion in primary education, though much dislocation was caused in 1958 when the East Region government was forced by financial stringency to return to a system of fee paying, which it had abolished the previous year. By 1960, in Igbo areas east of the Niger, there were 845,287 primary-school pupils in 4178 schools.[18] Both in the fifties and in the sixties, rapid growth was accompanied, inevitably, by falling standards, and the choice between quality and quantity is still a pressing issue in Nigerian education.

1960 saw the foundation of the University of Nigeria at a pleasant rural site, forty-seven miles from Enugu. In its early years it went through a number of difficulties, and then it was dealt a crippling blow by the Nigerian civil war, from which it has made a gallant recovery. But the site, for all its beauty, was badly chosen. The corporate life of the university is weakened by its division into two widely separated campuses, and the major campus is situated far from the large city which the talents of its members might well serve. Since most of the buildings are temporary, since a number of alternative uses have been suggested for the Nsukka campus, and since Nigerian universities are becoming increasingly aware of their responsibilities towards the community, the mistake may not be, even now, beyond remedy.

Again presaging the experience of the First Republic, the shadow of corruption crept across the texture of political life. 'At one time or another all the major urban councils were found guilty of corruption.'[19] Perkins, in his report on Enugu, stated 'I am fully satisfied that there have been maladministration and corruption so grave as to warrant my recommending immediate and urgent action.'[20] The Grant inquiry at Aba declared, 'In this bleak, dark tale of corruption, greed and irresponsibility, it is difficult to find much light.'[21] The Floyer report on Port Harcourt observed grimly that the city had the government it deserved . . .[22]

Professor Ottenberg, in a paper based on fieldwork in Igboland in 1952–3 and 1959–60, stated:

> Soon it became clear that many [of the councils] were in trouble. There was ineffectiveness and inefficiency and mismanagement of funds, projects and contracts, and the councils have come to be viewed with cynicism by the local public as organisations where individuals can feather their nests with relative ease . . . The most characteristic feature of corruption in the local government councils in Southern Nigeria is that it occurs throughout almost all levels of council activity and is found a good deal of the time.[23]

The same shadow of corruption reached regional and national politics, though the *cause célèbre*, in the East in the middle fifties, was perhaps not an example of corruption at all.

In 1955 the NCNC set up a commission to look into corruption. Mbonu Ojike, the regional Minister of Finance, was accused of making a profit in connection with the contract for reconstructing Onitsha market.[24] Ojike had been an outstanding nationalist since his return from America in 1947. His eloquence, his charm, his advocacy of Nigerian dress, his slogan of 'Boycott the boycottables' had left a notable mark on Nigerian public life and the evidence was far from conclusive. Now Azikiwe requested his resignation.

Soon afterwards, it was Azikiwe's turn to come under attack. The Chief Whip of the Eastern Region government, in April 1956, accused him of abusing his office by allowing two million pounds of public money to be invested in the African Continental Bank, in which he was a large shareholder, and which was then running at a loss. The Foster-Sutton tribunal looked into the case, and decided that his conduct had 'fallen short of the expectations of honest reasonable people', though with extenuating circumstances. Azikiwe promptly held a regional election, and was returned with an overwhelming majority.

Ojike refused to testify against Azikiwe, sacrificing the possibility of revenge to a memory of past loyalties, or an attachment to the nationalist cause, or attachment to the NCNC, or a sense of Igbo solidarity. Two weeks after the tribunal finished sitting he was dead, the victim of hypertension induced by strain.

The ACB inquiry well demonstrates the inextricably complex nature of Nigerian political realities. Azikiwe started the bank as a patriotic enterprise, to assist Nigerian businessmen starved of credit by the expatriate banks. He undoubtedly believed that in rescuing it from disaster he was protecting the interests of the investors, who had trusted him, and that this was a more pressing obligation than an – alien – notion of political propriety. And it is difficult to better the verdict of Professor Sklar, an American scholar with an unrivalled knowledge of Nigerian politics in the fifties:

> It seems basically false to this writer to say that Azikiwe's political activities were intended in any important or meaningful sense to increase his private wealth. It seems, on the contrary, that he could have become much wealthier than he is, if the accumulation of wealth had been his major object.[25]

In the case of the ACB, cries of corruption may have been wide of the mark. But corruption became more and more characteristic of Igbo – and Nigerian – public life.

Like the Warrant Chiefs before them, and the politicians of the First Republic after them, the men of the fifties were corrupt for reasons which are easy to understand. The hardships which most of them experienced in early life gave them a compulsive psychological need for financial security. (And in a country like Nigeria, lacking free education or social security, men with large families cannot afford to be indifferent to financial security.) Often they were corrupt in order to be generous. Many sacrificed their domestic comfort by keeping large numbers of hangers-on in their own houses. They assisted numerous relatives, and were expected to donate handsomely to community projects. The nepotism which gave a job to a needy fellow townsman was seen by the donor as an act of charity. To reject the clamorous demands of the needy in the name of an abstract ideal of honesty or patriotism demands the evolution of a tradition of public life where corruption is seen as unthinkable. In Nigeria, this tradition has never had a chance to develop.

But to understand corruption is not to extenuate it. It wasted scarce resources which should have been devoted to the betterment of the poor, who are nearly all Nigerians. (In 1948, the average per capita income in Eastern Nigeria was £21 *a year.*)[26] What Nigeria needed most urgently was an austere and self-sacrificing leadership which would lessen, not increase, the élite-masses division which was the legacy of colonialism, and which would lead, by its example, the élite to a steady renunciation of its privileges. That this is not too much to ask of human nature is seen in the post-independence history of Tanzania, under the leadership of President Julius Nyerere, who is always known in his own country as Mwalimu, the Teacher. Nigeria was governed by rich men who used their tenure of office to become richer. Their example corrupted the whole quality of Nigerian public life. An official document of 1970 – the First Report of the Adebo Commission – stated:

> . . . it is clear not only that there is intolerable suffering at the bottom of the income scale, because of the rise in the cost of living, but also that the *suffering is made even more intolerable by manifestations of affluence and wasteful expenditure which cannot be explained on the basis of visible and legitimate means of income.* (italics in the original)

In another respect, the experience of the fifties anticipated the dilemmas of the First Republic. Nigerians naturally expected a great deal of their freedom. No government could have satisfied the expectations that freedom aroused, in particular the hunger for universal free education and for adequate employment opportunities for the educated. Every village group anxiously awaited its amenities: a good access road, an improved water supply, electrification, schools, a hospital. These demands were not in themselves unreasonable – water is not a luxury – but no government could have commanded the resources to satisfy them. One of the most striking leitmotivs running through the local histories written in the early sixties is their progressive disillusionment with the fruits of freedom. 'Government – Eastern or Federal – had never done ANY GOOD

THING in Item but never failed to collect rates and taxes even from the poorest church-rat. Most of the roads and bridges were built by community development. The Eastern Government remembers that there are people living in this area ONLY when an election comes.'[27] The riots which resulted in 1958, when the Eastern Region government was forced to give up its short-lived scheme of universal free primary education, were an index of the intensity of the expectations, and the intensity of the disappointment.

V The Uses of Autonomy

15 Epilogue: Thirteen Years, 1960–1973

Now pay we forfeit on old abdications
The child dares flames his fathers lit
And in the briefness of too bright flares
Shrivels a heritage of blighted futures

There has been such a crop in time of growing
Such tuneless noises when we longed for sighs
Alone of petals, for muted swell of wine-buds
In August rains, and singing in green spaces.

Wole Soyinka

THE FIRST REPUBLIC, THE CRISIS AND BEYOND[1]

Nigeria attained her independence in what has been called a conspiracy of optimism.[2] Azikiwe, doubtless reluctantly, accepted the 'gilded cage' of Governor-General (after 1963, President). Dr Michael Okpara, a doctor from Umuahia, who had entered politics in 1949 at the time of the Colliery Shootings, became the Eastern Region Premier. In 1964 the Mid-West, with NCNC backing, became a separate Region, under a western Igbo premier, Dennis Osedebay. The region, in its ethnic diversity, was a microcosm of Nigeria itself, a diversity which could either enrich the society, or divide it.

As time went on, clouds gathered above the conspiracy of optimism. The first disturbing strand was corruption, about which sufficient has already been said. The second was the rapid collapse of parliamentary democracy of the Westminister type. In the Regions, most members of the opposition crossed the floor. Chief Awolowo, the leader of the opposition party, was imprisoned. The Tiv area was in a state of open revolt for years on end; after 1964, under a blatantly unpopular minority government, so was the West.

The third disturbing element was the growth of regional and

ethnic antagonisms. Tribalism existed at different social levels. At one level, it meant competition for market stalls, or a struggle among applicants for scarce employment opportunities. At another level, in the civil service and universities, it meant a struggle between the members of a highly gifted and ambitious élite, who readily employed the stereotypes of tribalism as weapons in their mutual relations. Bitterness between different groups was exacerbated by the famous and controversial census exercises of 1962 and 1963, which did much to destroy the NCNC-NPC alliance. 'The rift became less of a party and more of a regional one. Ibos rather than the NCNC as such were attacked. There were wild speeches on both sides.'[3]

The fourth disquieting element was that of class antagonisms. The social orientation of the pioneer nationalists was basically ambiguous. Azikiwe supported the General Strike of 1945, but was a wealthy entrepreneur and banker. He sometimes used the language of socialism, but defended the right of the individual to acquire wealth.[4] (The same ambiguity was characteristic of Awolowo.) Only briefly had the nationalist movement acquired overtones of working-class radicalism, under the leadership of a young Asaba Igbo, Nduka Eze, then in his twenties. A UAC clerk, he succeeded in uniting the UAC workers in a successful strike in August 1950. For a variety of reasons he later fell from prominence, and working-class radicalism did not become an issue in Nigerian politics again until the 1960s.

The urban clerks and workers, who had idolised Azikiwe, were disappointed at the failure of independence to yield more tangible fruit in their lives. In 1964 the signs of division along class lines became clearer. Michael Imoudou, another Mid-Westerner (not an Igbo) led a large group of unions in a successful General Strike. The disturbances which shattered the West through 1965 were partly economic in origin, and had some of the overtones of a peasant *jacquerie*.

By the end of 1965, the malaise of Nigerian political life was universally recognised. In the West, all political authority appeared to be breaking down. The discontent and disillusion with the use the politicians had made of their autonomy were universal. This was the background of the coup of 15 January 1966.

The coup was planned by army officers, a number of whom

were Igbo.[5] In its strange mixture of brutality and idealism it recalls the self-sacrificing populist assassins of the twilight of Tsarist Russia. The plotters were more concerned to overthrow the First Republic than to rebuild in its stead. There were assassinations in Kaduna, Ibadan, and Lagos. There was no coup in Benin, and the coup in Enugu was abortive. After a short period of confusion, Major General Johnson Aguiyi-Ironsi took over authority. He appointed Lieutenant-Colonel Emeka Ojukwu as Military Governor in the Eastern Region.

The coup in Kaduna had been led by Major Chukuma Nzeogwu, an Igbo from Okpanam who had been brought up in the north. He was a teetotaller, a non-smoker, and an exceptionally devout Catholic (a daily communicant),[6] and prepared to kill in a cause he believed right. In a radio speech on the afternoon of 15 January, he announced an assortment of goals. Some were naive and incongruous, but the basic point was clear.

> Our enemies are the political profiteers, swindlers, the men in high and low places that seek bribes and demand ten per cents, those that seek to keep the country permanently divided so that they can remain in office as Ministers and VIPs of waste, the tribalists, the nepotists.[7]

He was killed in combat, in the early days of the civil war, fighting for Biafra on the Nsukka front and was buried in Kaduna with full military honours. The coup in Lagos was led by Major Emmanuel Ifeajuna, from Onitsha, an international athlete who had held the Commonwealth record in high-jumping. A unitary nationalist to the end, he was shot in Enugu in the early days of the war, for plotting against Ojukwu.

If the sincerity of the coup was patent, so was its brutality. The plotters shot the Sardauna of Sokoto, and the wife who tried to shield him with her body, and the faithful messenger who came to defend him with bow and arrows. Akintola was killed in Ibadan after battling for twenty-five minutes for his life. In Lagos they killed Sir Abubakar Tafewa Balewa, one of the very few men who emerged with enhanced stature from the First Republic. He asked for, and was granted, time to say his prayers.

The mixture of good intentions and dreadful consequences hung like a curse over Nigeria for three years.

Public opinion welcomed the coup with jubilation. The *Morning Post* resorted to pidgin to express its enthusiasm. 'Bribe? E Done Die. Chop-Chop – E No Dey.'[8] An expatriate working in the North recalled:

> It was a good time to be alive. There was an enormous sense of relief, even of elation, and an air of expectancy for a week or two in which everyone worked hard at his own job, anxious to prove his allegiance to the spirit of the revolution.[9]

The coup was not an attempt at an Igbo takeover, but inevitably bore the appearance of one. No Igbo politician was killed; Okpara may have been saved by the fact that Archbishop Makarios was his guest at the time. There was no coup in the Mid-West, with its Igbo premier.

But meanwhile, Ironsi was left with a unique opportunity, not of his making, which his background and temperament rendered him unable to grasp. The key need was that his regime should be clearly seen not to be one of Igbo domination. He himself saw this, and with great courage surrounded himself with northern soldiers. But perhaps scarcely realising it, he came to rely more and more on Igbo advisers. These tended to see the Regions as a source of most of Nigeria's ills, and strongly advocated a unitary government. Other things, minor in themselves, seemed straws in the wind. There were army promotions, and since most officers were Igbo most of those promoted were also Igbo. There was a singularly tactless article in the popular magazine *Drum*, about the Sardauna. Finally, in a decree of 24 May, Ironsi announced the abolition of the Regions and of political parties, and the unification of the civil service. It seemed to northerners to herald precisely that domination by southerners which they had tried so hard to avoid.

Peaceful demonstrations by students and civil servants escalated into mob violence in the Hausa areas of the north. As with all mob violence everywhere, it was caused by a complex variety of factors, many having little apparent connection with the object of that violence. In the north, in May 1966, it was compounded of the career anxieties of élite groups, delayed revenge for the killings of January, rising food prices, a trade recession, and the tensions created by an era of rapid social change. The Igbo traders, postal clerks and railwaymen were blamed for and identified with a host of social grievances which they did not, in fact, cause.[10] Perhaps 500 were killed, and 1500 injured.

A few of the survivors left the north, but most chose to remain in cities where some of them had been born, and many had spent the best years of their adult lives. Perhaps, to many, unemployment seemed a more probable and terrifying fate than another pogrom.

On 29 July there was another army coup, in which Ironsi and a number of other senior officers were killed, many of them Igbo. It was apparently inspired by rumours of a further Igbo coup. So many of the tragedies of that tragic year were caused by fear, by rumours and counter-rumours. Colonel Yakubu Gowon, a Christian from a northern minority group, emerged as head of state. It seems that he had not been personally involved in the coup.

Apparently, the original planners of the July coup were advocates of northern secession, but were dissuaded by northerners working in Lagos. For over a month, Nigerians debated various forms of constitution – federal, confederal, unitary. But in the closing days of September, there occurred the most traumatic experience in Igbo history, a history, which as we have seen, has not been lacking in traumatic experiences.

The background of the September-October massacres, when thousands of Igbos were killed, remains obscure. Walter Schwarz writes:

> The idea behind the organisers of the killings was to drive the Easterners out of the North – perhaps out of Nigeria. As in May, ex-politicians, civil servants, local government officials and former party stalwarts stage-managed the pogroms. The main difference was that this time the army joined in.[11]

The immediate occasion was apparently a broadcast from Radio Cotonou reporting attacks on Northerners in the East. A much larger area of the North was involved than in May. The results were unquestionably appalling. Colin Legum – who later opposed secession – wrote in the *Observer* of 16 October 1966:

> Only the Ibos know the whole terrible story from the 600,000 or so refugees who have fled to the safety of the Eastern Region – hacked, slashed, mangled, stripped naked and robbed

> of all their possessions: the orphans, the widows, the traumatized. A woman, mute and dazed, arrived back in her village after travelling for five days with only a bowl in her lap. She held her child's head, which was severed before her eyes.
>
> Men, women and children arrived with arms and legs broken, hands hacked off, mouths split open. Pregnant women were cut open and the unborn children killed. The total casualties are unknown.[12]

Probably between six and eight thousand were killed – though some estimates were higher. It is only just to record that many Northerners – and expatriates – risked their lives to rescue their Igbo neighbours. One of the worst massacres occurred at Kano on 1 October, six years to the day after Nigeria celebrated her independence, with splendour, and extravagence, and a conspiracy of optimism . . .

From all over Nigeria, a million or more Igbo poured back to their crowded homeland, abandoning jobs and property it had taken them a lifetime of struggle to acquire. That they were so readily absorbed was thanks to the generosity of those who had stayed there. Before September, only a small minority had advocated secession. After September, it was probably the wish of the majority. Ojukwu himself was apparently not a hawk but a moderate, advocating a loose form of confederation. For some months affairs drifted, with the East in undeclared separation. In January 1967, Gowon and Ojukwu met at Aburi in Ghana, but little was achieved. On May 27 Gowon announced the creation of twelve states, in a sincere – and in the long run successful – attempt to prevent the tragedy of warring ethnicities. To the Igbos, the new boundaries which cut them off from Port Harcourt – and some southern Igbo clans such as Etche and Ikwerri – were unacceptable. Three days later, Ojukwu made a fateful pronouncement:

Fellow countrymen and women, you, the people of Eastern Nigeria:

Conscious of the supreme authority of Almighty God over all Mankind; of your duty to yourselves and posterity;

Aware that you can no longer be protected in your lives and in your property by any government based outside Eastern Nigeria;

Believing that you are born free and have certain inalienable rights which can best be preserved by yourselves . . .
I . . . do hereby solemnly proclaim that the territory and region known as and called Eastern Nigeria, together with her continental shelf and territorial waters shall henceforth be an independent sovereign state of the name and title of 'the Republic of Biafra'.[13]

To the Igbo, the justification of their action was self-evident – they were leaving a state in which they had not been permitted to live. They claimed that there was nothing especially sacrosanct about the boundaries of Nigeria, which had been imposed by an alien power in quite recent times. They appealed to the principles of self-determination. Their case won sympathisers all over the world.

On the Federal side, it was pointed out that the principles of self-determination must logically extend to the minorities of the former Eastern Region, most of whom supported the Federal side, especially after the creation of the new states for which they had hoped and waited so many years – though individuals from the COR areas played a distinguished part on both sides. Many feared that if secession was successful it would set off a chain reaction of conflicts all over Nigeria, which would dwarf the tragedies of 1966 in their horror. Many who sincerely loved Africa lamented the possible Balkanisation of a state with such obvious potential for greatness. But the foreign powers, who almost unanimously supported Nigeria, were probably moved less by these considerations than by a complex set of economic calculations, and a realistic assessment of who was likely to win.

It was at first thought that the war would soon be over – a 'police action'. It lasted two years, seven and a half months.

Only once did the Biafrans have a chance of victory. In August, soon after the war began, a force of a thousand men, travelling in cattle and vegetable trucks and elderly Peugeot 404s, mounted a successful invasion of the Mid-West.[14] They took Benin and got as far as Ore, a small town a hundred miles from Lagos, better known in times of peace as a lorry stopover, and an excellent place to buy snails. All commentators agree that had the push continued with the same dash and *élan* they might have reached Lagos, and changed the course of the war.

But the movement faltered, the opportunity was lost, and the Federal forces defeated the invaders at Ore, in the decisive battle of the war. Most accounts attribute the delays to the changes of policy of the force's leader, Major Banjo, a Yoruba who obviously lacked conviction in the rightness of his cause. Ojukwu probably gave him the command in an attempt to win support in the West. It was an expensive miscalculation. Banjo himself was later shot in Enugu.

The Biafrans retreated through the Mid-West, blowing two spans of the Niger bridge behind them. The rest of the history of the war was one of progressive retreat into a smaller and smaller enclave, of two and a half years of 'anguished but heroic existence'.[15] The disparity in size and resources between the contestants became increasingly obvious. The Biafrans lacked food; by 1968 they were starving to death in numbers that shook the conscience of the world. Their soldiers fought, often enough, in bare feet, with repeating rifles soldered so that they could fire only one shot at a time . . .

It became evident to everyone that Biafra had no hope of winning a military victory. Ojukwu hoped to hang on long enough for world opinion to rally to his side. Four African countries – Tanzania, Zambia, Gabon and Ivory Coast – recognised his regime (no one took the later recognition by Duvalier's Haiti seriously). France gave some support and material help, which 'decisively prolonged the war, and – equally decisively – fell short of enabling them to win it.'[16]

The secessionists fought with great devotion and self-sacrifice. A British journalist, who was an eye witness, wrote afterwards:

> When half-starved, bare-footed, ragged soldiers, numb with fear, speak glowingly of their 'Biafra'; when poor peasant boys march singing to the front-line with five rounds of ammunition apiece, proudly toting rifles they have never fired before; and when an illiterate peasant woman who has just watched her second child die of starvation dedicates its spirit to the success of Biafra it is impossible not to accept that the masses – the Ibo masses at least – were behind the war.[17]

Many made great financial sacrifices, among them Ojukwu

himself, whose father's vast fortune was mainly in Lagos property. Many relatively poor men made similar sacrifices: an Igbo working in England sold his house, and gave the proceeds to Biafra, and many working or studying abroad contributed a sacrificially large proportion of their income. The war brought to the fore a remarkable technical ingenuity, which produced the deadly *Ogbunigwe* (landmines cased in milk churns) and the do-it-yourself oil refineries.

To many, perhaps, the key attraction of Biafra lay in what one might call the fallacy of the fresh start – the same illusion which had produced the euphoria of early 1966. Many were disillusioned with the post-independence record of Nigeria, and Africa in general. Biafra seemed to represent a break with the errors of the past. Some, probably a small minority, hoped that secession would be a first step to establishing a more just society. This kind of aspiration found expression in Ojukwu's Ahiara Declaration of June 1969.

> Our revolution is a historic opportunity given to us to establish a just society; to revive the dignity of our people at home and the dignity of the black man in the world. We realise that in order to achieve those ends we must remove those weaknesses in our institutions and organisations . . . which have tended to degrade this dignity.[18]

The Ahiara Declaration is a much-criticised document. Critics point out its internal inconsistencies (which mirrored divisions within the Biafran élite) and the unreality of its confidently drafted future, which did not, in fact, exist – 'cloudcuckooland'.[19]

Nevertheless, not many states have found time and inclination, amid the desperation of a losing war, to debate the nature of the just society, and ways in which it might be attained.

But as the war progressed, opposition and disillusion grew. The suffering and starvation in the secessionist enclave mounted. Thousands died of marasma and kwashiorkor – two polite names for starvation, a singularly painful and lingering way to die. Pictures of emaciated children became part of the standard décor on European television programmes and in European newspapers. Ojukwu was accused of prolonging their desperate misery for propaganda purposes. Within Biafra, many thought that he should negotiate, rather than press on to what ultimatelv happened, an unconditional surrender. Sir Louis Mbanefo was a distinguished dove. An increasing number of high-level representatives favoured seeking a confederal solution, a policy apparently blocked by the personal decision of Okukwu himself.[20] The singing volunteers of the early days of the war faded away, and youths ran into the bush to avoid conscription.[21]

Most disillusioning of all were the whispers both within Biafra and on some Biafran missions abroad of precisely that same corruption and misuse of funds which had brought down the First Republic in the first place.[22]

The Ahiara Declaration contained an indictment, as well as an aspiration.

> We say that Nigerians are corrupt and take bribes but here in our country we have among us some members of the Police and the Judiciary who are corrupt and who 'eat' bribes. We accuse Nigerians of inordinate love of money, ostentatious living and irresponsibility; but here, even while we are engaged in a war of national survival . . . we have some public servants who throw huge parties to entertain their friends . . . We have members of the armed forces who carry on 'attack' trade instead of fighting the enemy. We have traders who hoard essential goods and inflate prices, thereby increasing the people's hardship.[23]

These evils were, of course, infinitely more shocking in a state of barefoot soldiers and starving citizens.

When the war finally ended, foreign observers noted, with scarcely veiled disapproval, how very few of the élite had died. This is, in fact, not quite true. To many élite families the war meant mainly the death of a soldier son or brother, the loss of an ageing parent, or a young child. And not all the celebrities survived.

The poet Christopher Okigbo died fighting on the Nsukka front in the early days of the war. He had written a series of slim volumes of poems, *Heavensgate, Limits, Labyrinths*. Some were obscure, some derivative, but in others he was moving towards that discovery of his own authentic voice, which he was not given time to find. These are the last lines of the last poem in

Heavensgate:

> under the lamp into stream of
> song, streamsong
> in flight into the infinite –
> a blinded heron
> thrown against the infinite –
> where solitude
> weaves her interminable mystery
> under the lamp.
>
> The moon has now gone under the sea.
> The song has now gone under the shade.

On 15 January 1970, the Biafrans made an unconditional surrender. Ojukwu himself fled to the Ivory Coast a few hours before the end. This disappointed many of his admirers, especially those who had come no closer to the war than their television screens, and who would have found a Last Stand more aesthetically satisfying. But his flight left no martyr's shadow to darken the reconciliation. (And the writer recalls an elderly and distinguished Biafran emissary in Europe, who as the war news worsened was in a fever to return, lest the war should end, and a massacre ensue, and he should be found in safety outside.)

No one knew what to expect, and for many months Biafran resistance had been stiffened by the fear that defeat would be followed by dreadful consequences. Biafran sympathisers outside published verse expressing their bitterness and apprehension.

> It's over. Let us offer thanks
> To British planes and Russian tanks.
> The oil so precious to the health
> Of Britain and the Commonwealth,
> Is safe again with British Shell.
> The Ibos may not fare so well . . .[24]

But in the event, just as the Igbos had won the admiration of Nigeria, and the world, by their gallantry in war, so Nigeria won the admiration of the Igbos, and the world, by her magnanimity in victory. It is scarcely possible to better the verdict of

John de St Jorre:

> When one considers the brutality, the proscription, the carefully maintained immensely durable hatred that have so often followed wars in the 'civilised' West . . . it may be that when history takes a longer view of Nigeria's war it will be shown that while the black man has little to teach us about making war he has a real contribution to offer in making peace.[25]

The Igbos for their part accepted the realities of their position, and that of the twelve states, with the same wholeheartedness that they had shown in war. The Igbo are not of the stuff of which Jacobites are made. There was no thought of sabotage, or of guerrilla warfare. The villagers, with thankfulness, planted their crops and rebuilt their humble homes. The élite tried to pick up the threads of their shattered careers, repaired their war-torn houses, and gradually reacquired a car, and some furniture. Many Igbo scholars suffered the irreparable loss of their personal libraries and research materials. With indomitable courage, they started all over again.

From an early stage in the war, General Gowon had maintained an Igbo government-in-exile for East Central State, headed by an Onitsha Igbo, Mr Ukpabi Asika, a university teacher. It is as yet much too soon for the historian to attempt to evaluate his government.

All observers were astonished by the speed of reconstruction. It was as if a magic hand had passed over the state, transforming the grass-covered echoing shells of buildings, open to the sky. Paradoxically the war removed much of the bitterness of tribalism, like a festering wound which is painfully lanced and cauterised. The war taught the combattants an enhanced mutual esteem and gave them an unforgettable lesson in the evils of ethnic rivalries. Pockets of bitterness remain, notably in border communities, and in the question of 'abandoned property' in Port Harcourt.

Four years later, it is often as if the war had never been. It is almost never mentioned in conversation. But its victims are still with us: those who lost their livelihood, the youths who permanently lost their chance of education, the orphaned and the widows; the war-blind, the amputees, the children whom malnutrition has permanently harmed.

Sensitive observers sometimes detect a change in the calibre of Igbo life – a greater materialism, a greater cynicism, a greater hedonism.

RENAISSANCE IN IGBOLAND

It would be a mistake to write the history of the last thirteen years purely in terms of politics and war. They were also years of outstanding cultural and intellectual achievement. (It is not, of course, intended to imply that this was peculiar to Igboland; they were dazzling years in Yorubaland, for instance, as well.)

The story of Igbo intellectual and cultural achievements begins well before independence – we have already noted Horton and Equiano. In 1933 Pita Nwana published his prize-winning novel in Igbo, *Omenuko*, which is still 'from a literary point of view, one of the greatest achievements in the language.'[26] In 1954 Cyprian Ekwensi became the first Nigerian to publish a novel in London; like all his work, it dealt with the quality of Lagos life, and the dilemmas it created. In the late fifties, Chinua Achebe began to publish a remarkable series of novels, two dealing with historical themes, and two with the problems of contemporary Nigeria. His *A Man of the People* showed an extraordinary, almost prophetic, insight and his historical novels are notable, not only for their literary qualities, but for their historical accuracy and perception. Flora Nwapa, in *Efuru*, wrote a detailed imaginative study of a woman's sensibility and the pain of childlessness, themes to which she returned in a later novel, *Idu*. Elechi Amadi, in *The Concubine*, wrote a moving, beautifully structured tragedy, which has received less critical acclaim than it deserves. In an entirely different vein, the Onitsha market novels, written for local audiences, have attracted some critical attention and have now been anthologised in America. In poetry, we have already noted the work of Christopher Okigbo.

In painting and sculpture, Ben Enwonwu was the first truly international figure. Two younger men, Demas Nwoko and Uche Okeke, were products of the Art School at Zaria. Okeke produced a series of surrealistic drawings based on themes in Igbo mythology, and, in an entirely different vein, a set of mosaic Stations of the Cross. Nwoko is best known for his heavy sombre satirical canvasses, and for his terracottas, which one critic called 'hardly inferior . . . to the masterpieces of Ife.'[27] Uzo Egonu is another brilliantly gifted painter; one of his works is reproduced in Plate 8.

In history, the outstanding pioneer was Professor K. O. Dike, whose history of the Delta taught a generation of historians to see the Nigerian past with new eyes. He was one of the architects of the greatness of the University of Ibadan, where he was Vice-Chancellor until 1966. He reorganised the National Archives and set up the Benin History Scheme, which bore fruits in several works of outstanding scholarship.

Until 1971, no Igbo historian took Igboland as his unit of study.[28] The late Professor Anene studied Southern (in practice, south-eastern) Nigeria, in a work which included the Delta states and Benin. Dr Ifemesia wrote an as yet unpublished study of European enterprise on the Niger in the nineteenth century. A younger historian, Professor A. E. Afigbo, collected oral traditions throughout the length and breadth of south-eastern Nigeria – and only those who have attempted it appreciate the difficulties of the task. He has now turned primarily to Igbo studies. His most important work is probably still to come. Many Igbo historians have concentrated on areas outside Nigeria. One even presented a successful doctorate on seventeenth-century English Puritanism. In anthropology, Victor Uchendu carried out research in East Africa, and among the American Indians, and wrote a perceptive monograph on his own people.

The late Professor Kalu Ezera, who met a tragic death by violence in 1970, wrote a pioneering study of constitutional changes in Nigeria. Professor Eni Njoku, a botanist, paralleled Dike's double career as a scholar and university administrator – he was a highly successful Vice-Chancellor at Lagos until he became, in 1965, the victim of tribalism and politics. Professor Herbert Kodilinye, an ophthalmologist, became the first post-war Vice-Chancellor at Nsukka. Professor Chike Obi is a notably brilliant mathematician, who briefly entered politics as the leader of a small opposition party. Professor Joseph Edozien built up an international reputation for his work in clinical biochemistry. Professor Njoku-Obi, a microbiologist, won the attention of the world when he developed a cholera vaccine.

Igboland produced chemists, physicists, mathematicians and economists, surveyors, engineers and specialists in every branch of medicine. Many of these latter deliberately sacrificed the research which would have furthered their careers to concentrate on care of the sick and hospital administration, which seemed to them, quite rightly, the more pressing priority.

Many Igbo professional men work abroad. There are many Igbo university teachers among them, especially in North American universities. Igbo doctors work in Canada, America, and most countries in Europe, so rapidly has the tide of 'technical aid' reversed itself.

TWO NATIONS

When Disraeli looked at Victorian England, he saw Two Nations, distinguished by their sharply contrasting modes of life. They were the rich and the poor. (When Saint Augustine looked at society, he saw Two Cities, but he defined their inhabitants differently.)

The present dilemma of the Igbos is the present dilemma of Nigeria, the great and growing gulf between rich and poor. This appears to be hardening into hereditary privilege. The beautifully dressed children of the prosperous invite scores of guests to their birthday parties, are taken to school by car – sometimes a chauffeur-driven car – are coached by tutors, waited on by servants. Something has been done to shrink privilege, especially in the sphere of education. But the gulf between rich and poor remains, made more painful by the constant allegations of the corruption of the rich, and the iron pressure of inflation on the small earnings of the poor.

In a book published in 1516, Saint Thomas More had the courage to pinpoint the key evils of his society:

> . . . when I consider and way in my mind all thies commen wealthes which now a dayes any where do florish, so god helpe me, I can perceaue nothing but a certein conspiracy of riche men, procuringe theire own commodities vnder the name and title of the commen wealth.[29]

To apply it to our own place and time, perhaps only the

spelling need be changed. On 23 July 1973, a writer in *The Renaissance* published an article called 'The Rotten Society', an eloquent appeal for social justice:

> The beggars along the streets in Nigeria are catered for, not by the rich who live for months in the most exquisite hotels, but by the poor and low section of society who move on foot . . . The rich grows richer and the poor has no hope, not because of any natural law, for none like that exists, but because 'The world is too much with us . . .' . . . These Mercedes Benz owners ride unconcerned over rough pot-hole ridden streets . . . They pass the night-soil loads in public places and wind up their car glasses.

His theme was so much a commonplace that only one reader troubled to comment. He did so, most movingly, in the words of an Igbo proverb. 'Like the baby chick which was captured by a kite, "My cry is for the world to know that I am finished, not that I should be released from captivity".'

In the late 1850s, the Reverend J. C. Taylor recorded some proverbs in Onitsha. It was the first occasion on which the inherited distilled wisdom of an Igbo community had been put on permanent record. Here are a few of them (I have left his translations, and his orthography, unchanged).[30]

> *Ošúi ešúi ememe, obeyan ka ya ma.* He that has, and does not give, the poor is better than he.
> *Madu nawo na ba izu, Tsuku se, Ya me atọ.* When two persons talk in secret, God says, I make a third.
> *Akpa ešúu onu.* The bag [of the covetous] is never full.
> *Ri šúi afọ datze uzọ.* Eat greedily and you shut up the way [for all that come after].
> *Para-kuku se, Ya wọ eze, ya šúi ọhan ma ọhan wenya.* The wild-pigeon says, I rule over the country, and the country rules over me . . .

Notes

CHAPTER 1

1. Onuoha Duru of Nguru, aged *c.* 90, transcribed in L.O. Nwahiri, 'Nguru Mbaise before the Coming of the British', B.A. history special project (Nsukka, 1973) p. 55.
2. Cf. for instance Abdullahi Smith, 'Some Considerations Relating to the Formation of States in Hausaland', *J. Hist. Soc. Nigeria* (Dec 1970) 329ff.
3. R. E. Bradbury, 'The Historical Uses of Comparative Ethnography with Special Reference to Benin and the Yoruba', in Jan Vansina, Raymond Mauny and L. V. Thomas (eds), *The Historian in Tropical Africa* (London, 1964) p. 150.
4. Donald D. Hartle, 'Archaeology in Eastern Nigeria', *Nigeria Magazine*, 93 (June 1967) 136–7. This date, and those given subsequently in this chapter, were obtained by radio-carbon dating. All living things contain radio-carbon. When they die, they cease to accumulate it, and the radio-carbon they already contain gradually reverts to nitrogen, radiating the excess energy released in the process. This occurs over a fixed time: half of any collection of radio-carbon atoms (known as carbon 14) will be transformed in 5730 years, so a piece of wood 5730 years old has half the radio-carbon content of modern wood. Wood and charcoal are the organic materials usually used for testing. There are two main disadvantages in the method. There is a certain margin of error (expressed in terms of a plus and minus after the date), and it is hard to be absolutely sure that the sample dates from the same period as other objects excavated with it. Here we rely entirely on the professional skill of the excavating archaeologist.
5. Ibid., pp. 136–7, 139; Donald D. Hartle, 'The Prehistory of Nigeria', mimeo (Nsukka, 1973) pp. 64–6.
6. L. Frobenius, *The Voice of Africa*, I (1913) pp. 274–5, quoted in M. D. W. Jeffries, 'The Divine Umundri Kings of Igboland', Ph. D. thesis (London, 1934) ch. 2, n.p.
7. G. I. Jones, *The Trading States of the Oil Rivers*, repr. (London, 1964) p. 30.
8. M. D. W. Jeffries, 'The Umundri Tradition of Origin', *African Studies*, XV (1956) 121.
9. Barry Floyd, *Eastern Nigeria, A Geographical Review* (London, 1969) pp. 52–3.
10. Information re Illah collected in the author's fieldwork.
11. Donald M. McFarlan, *Calabar, The Church of Scotland Mission Founded 1846*, rev. ed. (London, 1957) pp. 100–1.
12. James Aniekwe of Adazi-enu, Aguinyi, aged *c.*87, transcribed in J. I. Ejiofor, 'A Precolonial History of the Aguinyi Clan', B.A. history special project (Nsukka, 1973) p. 131.
13. A. E. Afigbo, 'Igbo Historians and Igbo History', mimeo (Nsukka, 1972) pp. 9–10.
14. G. T. Basen, *Niger Ibos*, repr. (London, 1966) p. 249.
15. Jones, p. 30.

16. *Journal of the African Society*, x (1910–11) 130.
17. Northcote W. Thomas, *Anthropological Report on the Ibo-Speaking Peoples of Nigeria, Part I Law and Custom of the Ibo of the Awka Neighbourhood* (London, 1913) p. 50. For another version, cf. Jeffries, 'The Umundri Tradition of Origin', pp. 122–3.
18. Informant, Mr James Afoke. *Eze nwawho, abalayi, fzazia* and *okpura* still grow wild in Ezzaland and are gathered by the poor; *nvulu emaa* was domesticated in the 1950s. It is impossible for a non-botanist like myself to correlate this type of locally obtained data with that in articles on historical botany, because of the difference in nomenclature.
19. This paragraph is based on J. Alexander and D. G. Coursey, 'The Origins of Yam Cultivation', in Peter J. Ucko and G. W. Dimbleby (eds), *The Domestication and Exploitation of Plants and Animals* (London, 1969) pp. 405–25.
20. John Barbot, *A Description of the Coasts of North and South Guinea*, in Churchill's *Voyages and Travels*, vol. v (London, 1746) p. 377.
21. *The Gospel on the Banks of the Niger III, Journals and Notices of the Native Missionaries on the River Niger, 1863* (London, 1864) pp. 42–3, 67.
22. Hartle, 'The Prehistory of Nigeria', p. 65.
23. Bernard Fagg: 'The Nok Culture: Excavations at Taruga', *West African Archaeological Newsletter*, x (1968); also information from Professor Hartle.
24. A. G. Leonard, *The Lower Niger and its Tribes* (London, 1906) pp. 36–7.
25. Thomas, *Awka Neighbourhood*, p. 48.
26. M. D. W. Jeffries, 'The Divine Umundri King', *Africa*, VIII (1935) 346 ff.; Anon, 'Nri Traditions', *Nigeria Magazine*, 54 (1957) 273 ff.
27. M. A. Onwuejeogwu and B. M. Akunne, in *Odinani*, Journal of Odinani Museum, Nri, I (Mar 1972) 10.
28. My account of the Igbo-Ukwu excavations is based on Thurstan Shaw, *Igbo-Ukwu: An Account of Archaeological Discoveries in Eastern Nigeria*, 2 vols (London, 1970).
29. Onwuejeogwu, in *Odinani*, I (1972) 6–7.
30. Alan Ryder, *Benin and the Europeans 1485–1897* (London, 1969) p. 259, n. 3.
31. Hartle, 'Archaeology in Eastern Nigeria', p. 138.
32. Ibid., pp. 137–8; Hartle, 'The Prehistory of Nigeria', p. 67.
33. James Barbot, *An Abstract of a Voyage to New Calabar River . . . in the Year 1699*, in Churchill's *Voyages and Travels*, v, plate 26; cf. also p. 462.
34. William Balfour Baikie, *Narrative of an Exploring Voyage of the Rivers Kwora and Binue . . . in 1854* (London, 1856) pp. 310–11.
35. A. G. Leonard, 'Notes of a Journey to Bende', *Journal of the Manchester Geographical Society*, XIV (1898) 196–7.
36. F. Ekejiuba, 'Preliminary Notes on Brasswork of Eastern Nigeria', *African Notes*, IV, 2 (1967) 11 ff.
37. NAI CSO 26/11 (File 28903), P. V. Main, 'Report on Aboh-Sobo Village Groups' (1933) p. 9.

CHAPTER 2

1. Igwe Njoku of Ekka, Ezza, aged 83, interviewed by James Afoke, 1 Sep-

tember 1973.

2. A. U. Njemanze, 'The Precolonial Political and Social Organisation of Owerri Town', B.A. history special project (Nsukka, 1973) p. 14.
3. M. M. Ugwu, 'The Agulu-Umana Village Community: Its Origin and Development to the Coming of the British', B.A. history special project (Nsukka, 1973) p. 53.
4. Cf. for a discussion of this point, Jeffries, 'The Divine Umundri Kings of Igboland', ch. 2, n.p.
5. It is possible that the sense of the word Igbo narrowed during the period of the slave trade. M. A. Onwuejeogwu points out that the word occurs widely in place and personal names in eastern and western Igboland, with the sense, 'community'. At Agbor, deep in western Igboland, palm oil is called *ofi-igbo*, oil for the community. Onwuejeogwu, in *Odinani*, I (1972) 39–40.
6. Richard N. Henderson, *The King in Every Man, Evolutionary Trends in Onitsha Society and Culture* (New Haven and London, 1972) p. 41.
7. M. M. Green, *Igbo Village Affairs, Chiefly with Reference to the Village of Umueke Agbaja*, 2nd ed. (London, 1964) p. 7.
8. Ibid.
9. Baikie, p. 307.
10. Henry Johnson, 'The Mission on the Upper Niger', in *Church Missionary Intelligencer* (Sep 1882) 547 (re Asaba).
11. Ferrier to Poirier, 26 November 1906, in *L'Echo des Missions Africaines de Lyon* (1907) p. 18.
12. *The Interesting Narrative of the Life of Olaudah Equiano*, abridged and ed. Paul Edwards (London, 1967) p. 1.
13. Austin J. Shelton, *The Igbo-Igala Borderland* (Albany, 1971) p. 200.
14. This point is made in CMS G3/A3/1892/194, Julius H. Spencer, 'The Mo'.
15. Cf. Leonard, 'A Journey to Bende', p. 198.
16. Ikenna Nzimiro, *Studies in Ibo Political Systems: Chieftaincy and Politics in Four Niger States* (London, 1972) p. 233.
17. M. C. M. Idigo, *The History of Aguleri* (Yaba, 1955) p. 12.
18. *Journals of the Rev. James Frederick Schön and Mr Samuel Crowther . . . in 1841* (London, 1842) pp. 50–1.
19. The account which follows is based on a wide variety of sources, but is especially indebted to the brilliant account in Chapter 4 of Henderson, *The King in Every Man.*
20. Equiano, p. 7.
21. This is elaborated in Nwahiri, pp. 5, 38.
22. Rev. R. C. Arazu C.S.Sp., Interview with Ezenwadeyi of Ihembosi, September 1966 (transcript in possession of Fr Arazu).
23. Jeffries, 'The Divine Umundri Kings', ch. 15, n.p. and my own fieldwork.
24. NAI CSO 26/51 (File 29017), Shankland, 'Report on the Aro Clan' (1933) p. 12.
25. R. O. Igwegbe, *The Original History of Arondizuogu from 1635–1960* (Aba, 1962) pp. 49–51.
26. Nwozo Onwukeme of Adazi-Nnuburu, aged 85, and Ogbuamazia Ekesili of Obeledu, aged 73, in Ejiofor, pp. 99, 148.

27. W. A. Ikpo, *A Short History of Nkwerre Town* (Aba, 1966) pp. 11, 30.
28. Mr Ugwu's special project, cited above, is a valuable case study of this iron-working centre.
29. My knowledge of iron-working in Ohuhu is based on data in N. E. Esobe, 'A Pre-colonial History of Ohuhu Clan', B.A. history special project (Nsukka, 1973) pp. 67–8.
30. A. E. Afigbo, 'Trade and Trade Routes in Nineteenth Century Nsukka', paper presented to 18th Annual Congress of the Historical Society of Nigeria (1972) p. 6.
31. G. T. Basden, 'On the Borders of Iboland', *Niger and Yoruba Notes* (1901) p. 87 (re Idumuje Ugboku). There is no clue as to whether this was a local or itinerant smith.
32. Equiano, p. 4.
33. Baikie, pp. 287–8.
34. Afigbo, 'Nsukka Trade', p. 5.
35. F. M. Dennis, 'The "Wild West"', *Niger and Yoruba Notes* (1903) p. 23 (re Idumuje Ugboku).
36. Duarte Pacheco Pereira, *Esmeraldo de Situ Orbis*, trans. and ed. George H. T. Kimble, Hakluyt Society, 2nd ser., LXXIX (1937) 132.
37. NAI CSO 26/202 (File 29281), C. T. C. Ennals, 'Report on the Ndoki Clan' (1933) p. 12.
38. Jeffries, 'The Umundri Tradition of Origin', 125.
39. Ryder, p. 60.
40. John Barbot, p. 380; also O. Dapper, *Description de l'Afrique*, French trans. (Amsterdam, 1786) p. 315.
41. Basden, 339. Cf. also Equiano, pp. 6–7.
42. Equiano, p. 6.
43. CO 520/31, 'Political Report on the Ezza Patrol', encl. in Egerton to Lyttelton, 16 July 1905.
44. Mrs T. J. Dennis, 'A Week's Itineration in the Ibo Country', *The Church Missionary Intelligencer* (Sep 1899) 780.
45. Leonard, 'A Journey to Bende', p. 201.
46. Equiano, pp. 7–8.
47. Ibid., p. 10.
48. Rev. J. K. Macgregor, 'Some Notes on Nsibidi', *Journal of the Royal Anthropological Institute of Great Britain and Ireland*, XXXIX (1909) 209 ff.
49. Ibid., p. 212.
50. The account which follows is based on two articles by K. Hau, 'Oberi Okaime Script, Texts and Counting System', *Bulletin de l'IFAN*, series B, XXIII (1961) 291 ff. and 'The ancient writing of southern Nigeria', ibid., (1962) 150 ff.
51. CSO 26/202 (File 29281), Ennals, 'Ndoki Clan', p. 13. Floyd, p. 88.
52. A. E. Afigbo, 'Igbo Historians and Igbo History', paper presented to a Workshop on the Peoples of Southern Nigeria (Dec 1972) p. 7 (pp. 6–7 for the general theory).
53. CSO 26/202 (File 29281), Ennals, 'Ndoki Clan', p. 8.
54. The three rival etymologies are given in Esobe, pp. 3 ff.; cf. also CSO 26/112 (File 27937), E. H. C. Dickinson, 'Intelligence Report on the Ezeni-

hitte Clan' [an alternative name for Ohuhu], p. 6.

55. Shelton, pp. 30–1, 34.

CHAPTER 3

1. Pereira, p. 132.
2. John Barbot, p. 381.
3. Captain John Adams, *Remarks on the Country Extending from Cape Palmas to the River Congo* (London, 1823) p. 129.
4. FO 84/1030, Hutchinson to Clarendon, 20 February 1857.
5. *Report of the Lords of the Committee of Council Concerning the Present State of the Trade to Africa, and Particularly the Trade in Slaves (1789)* Part I, Falconbridge's evidence.
6. Ibid., Part II, Arnold's evidence. For the dreadful punishment visited on mutineers, cf. Elizabeth Donnan, *Documents Illustrative of the History of the Slave Trade to America*, 4 vols (Washington, 1930–5) II, 266.
7. *Memoirs of Captain Hugh Crow* (London, 1830) p. 200.
8. Bryan Edwards, *The History, Civil and Commercial, of the British Colonies in the West Indies*, 3 vols, 3rd ed. (London, 1801) pp. 89–90.
9. M. J. Herskovits, *Life in a Haitian Valley* (New York, 1931) pp. 20–1, quoted in Victor C. Uchendu, *The Igbo of Southeast Nigeria* (New York, 1965) p. 37.
10. C. N. de Cardi, 'A Short Description of the Natives of the Niger Coast Protectorate', in Mary Kingsley, *West African Studies* (London, 1899) p. 48.
11. S. W. Koelle, *Polyglotta Africana* (London, 1854) V, Niger-Delta Languages, First Group, Ibo Dialects.
12. 'Autobiography of David Okparabietoa Pepple', *Niger and Yoruba Notes* (1898) p. 13.
13. Equiano, pp. 7, 15 ff.
14. Igwegbe, pp. 36, 67–70; Esama Kaine, *Ossomari, A Historical Sketch* (privately printed in England, 1963) pp. 62–3.
15. William Allen and T. R. H. Thomson, *A Narrative of the Expedition . . . to the River Niger* (London, 1848) I, 218.
16. There is a great deal of evidence of this, both in archival sources, and in the fieldnotes transcribed in Nsukka history students' special projects, from a wide variety of areas. Cf. also Igwegbe, pp. 75, 133.
17. Baikie, p. 315.
18. Afigbo, 'Nsukka Trade', p. 4.
19. Extract in Thomas Hodgkin, *Nigerian Perspectives, An Historical Anthology* (London, 1960) p. 104.
20. Ifeoma Ekejiuba, 'The Aro System of Trade in the Nineteenth Century', *Ikenga Journal of African Studies*, I, 1 (Jan 1972) p. 21.
21. Mazi Nwagbara Ohaeri of Umudiawa, Ohuhu, *c.*102, in Esobe, p. 100.
22. Basden, p. 249.
23. Henderson, pp. 273–4.
24. Mazi Mbagwu Ogbete, aged *c.*80, in C. B. N. Okoli, 'Akokwa from the Earliest Time to 1917', B.A. history special project (Nsukka, 1973) p. 91.
25. Schön and Crowther, p. 68.

CHAPTER 4

1. James Barbot, (supplement to John Barbot, pp. 455 ff.) p. 459.
2. Ibid., p. 460.
3. John Barbot, p. 383; cf. also p. 361.
4. Adams, pp. 260–1.
5. Esobe, pp. 67–8.
6. Many versions of Onitsha tradition have been recorded, over a period of about seventy-five years. There is a recent good summary in Henderson, p. 78 ff.
7. Northcote W. Thomas, *Anthropological Report, Part IV, Law and Custom of the Asaba District* (London, 1914) p. 8. For a slightly different version, cf. B. N. Azikiwe, 'Fragments of Onitsha History', *Journal of Negro History*, xv (1930) 474–5.
8. Jacob Egharevba, *A Short History of Benin*, 4th ed. (Ibadan, 1968) p. 28.
9. Ryder, p. 14.
10. J. W. Hubbard, *The Sobo of the Niger Delta* (Zaria, 1948) contains much valuable material on Aboh traditions (and those of neighbouring towns) collected from well-placed local informants from 1929 on. It may be compared with the shorter account in Nzimiro, pp. 11 ff, and with NAI CSO 26/10 (File 26769), Williams and Miller, Aboh-Benin Clans (1930–1).
11. S. B. C. Obiora, in *Report of the Inquiry into Oguta Chieftaincy Dispute* (Official Document no. 19 of 1961) p. 78; see the whole of this document for various versions of Oguta tradition.
12. The universally accepted version is that they came from Ibeku, but some versions mention a prior movement from the mid-west. Informant, Mr Oji Kalu Oji, who collected a number of traditions about it. Other Ohafia informants confirm it.
13. Sidney R. Smith, 'The Ibo People', Ph.D. thesis (Cambridge, 1929) p. 14.
14. Based on fieldwork by the author.
15. Bishop Crowther, in *The Church Missionary Intelligencer* (Sep 1876) 536.
16. CMS CA 3/04, John to Crowther, 22 March 1879 and Spencer to Crowther, 14 January 1879; also Baikie, p. 291. My knowledge of present-day Igbokeyni comes from Mr B. C. Agadah.
17. Julius Spencer, 'The History of Asaba and its Kings', *Niger and Yoruba Notes* (1901) pp. 320–1.
18. NAI CSO 26/48 (File 29576), B. G. Stone, 'Anam Villages' (1934) p. 5.
19. CMS CA 3/04, John to Crowther, 22 March 1879.
20. Baikie, p. 297. It is difficult to identify all the towns in lists of this type – spellings vary, and there are many places in Igboland called 'Agbaja', 'Enugu' and so on.
21. Based on fieldwork by the author.
22. Dapper, p. 313. The identification of 'Aboh' and 'Gaboe' may, of course, be mistaken. On Dapper's sources, cf. *The Journal of African History*, vi (1965) p. 41.
23. Kaine, 60.
24. Henderson, pp. 69–70 and Nzimiro, p. 18 (both are based on information

from Mr R. Olisa of Ossomari).

25. Kaine, p. 24. Most accounts of lower Niger trade – including earlier ones by the present writer – overemphasise the role of Aboh and neglect the role of Ossomari, because they are based on the accounts of European explorers who always came to the lower Niger via Aboh, and spent much time at Aboh and little at Ossomari.
26. Samuel Crowther and John Christopher Taylor, *The Gospel on the Banks of the Niger . . . 1857–1859*, repr. (London, 1968) p. 385.
27. MacGregor Laird and R. A. K. Oldfield, *Narrative of an Expedition into the Interior of Africa*, 2 vols (London, 1837) II, pp. 180–1.
28. In my earlier writings I dated the foundation of Arochukwu to the late seventeenth century, on the basis of genealogies collected by Mathews in 1928 and preserved in Rhodes House. But Ekejiuba, 'The Aro System of Trade', p. 13, n. 8, claims that the ten families he studied are all of 'relatively recent origin' and puts the date in the *early* seventeenth century.
29. The best version of Aro traditions (based on fieldwork in 1963–6) is to be found in Ekejiuba, 'The Aro System of Trade', pp. 13–15; see also RH MSS Afr.s. 783, Box 3/4 ff., H. F. Mathews, 'Discussion of Aro Origins' (based on fieldwork in *c.* 1928) and NAI CSO 26/51 (File 29017), Shankland, 'Aro Clan' (1933).
30. G. I. Jones, 'Who are the Aro?' *The Nigerian Field* (1939) p. 102; RH MSS Afr. s. 783, Box 3/65 ff., Mathews, 'Supplementary Report on the Aro', f. 69. On Ukwa, cf. J. E. N. Nwaguru, *Aba and British Rule* (Enugu, 1973) pp. 149–50.
31. Ekejiuba, 'The Aro System of Trade', p. 14. Dried shrimps (known now as 'crayfish') are ground to powder and used to thicken sauces ('soup') – they form probably the main source of calcium in the Igbo diet.
32. Ibid.
33. Shankland, p. 13; anon, 'Inside Arochuku', *Nigeria Magazine*, 53 (1957) 107.
34. CO 520/14, Moor, Memorandum concerning the Aro Expedition, f. 355.
35. Leonard, 'A Journey to Bende', p. 191.
36. I base this date on a study of Ndizuogu and Ndikelionwu genealogies preserved in Igwegbe and Nwankwo.
37. Jonathan Nwene, aged *c.*60, of Ndikelionwu, in J. C. Nwankwo, 'The Early Settlement of Ndikelionwu and its Neighbourhood', B.A. history special project (Nsukka, 1973).
38. Igwegbe, pp. 58, 77.
39. Ibid., p. 75.
40. Informant cited in Ekejiuba, 'The Aro System of Trade', p. 18.
41. Koelle, *Polyglotta Africana*, 'Ibo Dialects'.
42. McFarlan, p. 143.
43. Shankland, p. 12.
44. Ekejiuba, 'The Aro System of Trade', p. 17, n. 19.
45. Ibid., p. 19.
46. Mazi Mbagwu Ogbete, aged *c.*80, in Okoli, p. 90. For the various commodities, pp. 43–4.
47. This paragraph is based on traditions transcribed in Esobe, 'History of

Uhuhu Clan'.

48. Transcribed in Ejiofor, p. 103.
49. Igwegbe, p. 77.
50. Leonard, 'A Journey to Bende', p. 191.
51. Okoli, p. 66.
52. Leonard, 'A Journey to Bende,' p. 191.
53. Ibid., p. 194.
54. Green, p. 38.
55. W. E. Carew in *The Church Missionary Record* (July 1866) 210.
56. For examples of this 'macrocosmic' view of Igbo economic life, cf. Ekejiuba, 'The Aro System of Trade'; Simon Ottenberg, 'Ibo Oracles and Intergroup Relations', *Southwestern Journal of Anthropology*, XIV (1958) 295 ff.; Ukwu I. Ukwu, 'The Development of Trade and Marketing in Iboland', *J. Hist. Soc. of Nigeria*, III, 4 (1967) 647 ff.; David Northrup, 'The Growth of Trade among the Igbo before 1800', *Journal of African History*, XIII, 2 (1972) 217 ff.
57. C. C. Iheagwam, 'Naze Political System from Earliest Times to 1901', B.A. history special project (Nsukka, 1973) p. 26.

CHAPTER 5

1. The account which follows is based on Equiano's autobiography. This is essential reading for anyone interested in the Igbo past, and is readily available in an abridged edition (ed. Paul Edwards, London, 1967). The preface to this edition contains additional information, as does G. I. Jones' introduction to the section on Equiano in Philip D. Curtin (ed.), *Africa Remembered. Narratives by West Africans from the Era of the Slave Trade* (Wisconsin, 1967) pp. 60 ff.
2. Baikie, p. 374.
3. *The Church Missionary Intelligencer* (1853) pp. 253 ff.
4. Quoted in F. K. Ekechi, *Missionary Enterprise and Rivalry in Igboland 1857–1914* (London, 1972) p. 5.
5. The account which follows is based on Christopher Fyfe, *Africanus Horton* (London, 1972).

CHAPTER 6

1. These blunderbusses were still preserved in the 1930s. Shankland, p. 10.
2. Cf. p. 50 above.
3. Henderson, 50–2.
4. I. E. Iweka-nuno, *Akuko-Ala na onwu nke Ala-Ibo Nile*, Igbo text followed by English abridgement, (no place of pub., 1924) p. 68 of English text.
5. Hermann Köler, *Einige Notizen über Bonny* (Göttingen, 1848) pp. 110–11.
6. Ibid.
7. Nwanna Cy Nzewunwa, '*Ogu Mkpuru Oka, c.* 1888–*c.* 1890', B.A. history special project (Nsukka, 1973).
8. But cf. Basden, p. 380, for a description of 'terrible wounds' caused by iron pieces used as bullets.

9. Shelton, p. 23.
10. FO 403/200 (F.O.C.P.), Casement to MacDonald, 10 April 1894, p. 235.
11. Mrs T. J. Dennis, 'A Week's Itineration in the Ibo Country', *The Church Missionary Intelligencer* (Sep 1899) 780.
12. Rev. S. R. Smith, 'The Forward Movement in the Ibo Country', *Niger and Yoruba Notes* (1901) p. 6.
13. Nzewunwa, p. 15.
14. Afoke, MS. fieldnotes.
15. Ogali A. Ogali, *History of Item Past and Present* (Onitsha, 1960) p. 14.
16. Basden, p. 379; S. R. Smith, 'Notes from the Eastern District', *Niger and Yoruba Notes* (1904) p. 35 and my own fieldwork.
17. Jacob Ugboaja of Adazi-enu, Aguinyi, aged 90, transcribed in Ejiofor, p. 108.
18. Crowther and Taylor, p. 430.
19. Kaine, pp. 62–3.
20. Nzewunwa, p. 45.
21. Ibid., p. 34.
22. According to Igwegbe – but Aro informants question this.
23. Mazi Nkajimeje Oti of Umuekwule, Ohuhu, transcribed in Esobe, p. 160 and Mazi Oluo ha Nwosu of Ihife, Ohuhu, in ibid., p. 120.
24. Mbonu Ojike, *My Africa* (New York, 1946) p. 37.
25. Igwegbe, p. 94; Basden, pp. 373–4; NAI CSO 26/1 (File 28939), C. J. Mayne, 'Intelligence Report on the Abam Clan' (1933) p. 10.
26. Igwegbe, pp. 95–7.
27. Traditions collected by Mr Oji Kalu Oji, presented as Part II of his B. A. special project in history (Nsukka, June 1974).
28. NAI CSO 26/5 (File 29804), O. P. Gunning, 'Intelligence Report on Abboh, Uduma, Mpu and Okpanku Groups of Awgu Division' (1934) p. 4.
29. Mayne, 'Abam Report', pp. 10–11.
30. NAI CSO 26/42 (File 29881), J. Barmby, 'Intelligence Report on Akwegbe, Ohodo, Ozalla, Lejja Ede and Opir Villages of Nsukka Division' (1934) p. 5 and CSO 26/130 (File 29919), J. Barmby, 'Intelligence Report on the Igbodo Group of Nsukka Division' (1934) p. 6.
31. NAI CSO 26/224 (File 30537), J. Barmby, 'Intelligence Report on Nsukka, Ibeagwa Ani and Eror Villages' (1935) p. 4.
32. A. O. Arua, *A Short History of Ohafia* (Enugu, 1952) pp. 11, 12.
33. S. R. Smith, 'Christmas Week Itineration in the Ibo Speaking Country', *Niger and Yoruba Notes* (1898) p. 82; *Bulletin de la Congregation* (Holy Ghost Fathers) xx, 315.
34. Smith, in *Niger and Yoruba Notes* (1898) pp. 82–3.
35. Arua, pp. 11–12.
36. Ibid., p. 83.
37. Dennis, in *The Church Missionary Intelligencer* (Sep 1899) p. 780.
38. Ibid., and 'Experiences on an Itineration', *Niger and Yoruba Notes* (1904) p. 59.
39. *Bulletin de la Congregation*, XVI (Mar 1892) 358–60; XVII, 427 ff.; and XVIII, 426–7.
40. CMS CA 3/0, Buck to Crowther, 19 November 1876. (This does not state

the precise identity of the assailants, but speaks of 'War from the interior of the Ibo Country' and 'great warriors and blood thirsty people' from whom both the local inhabitants and the trader and missionary community fled. For an Onitsha comment on the Edda, cf. *Bulletin de la Congregation*, XVI, 358.)

41. NAI CSO 26/15, W. R. T. Milne, 'Intelligence Report on the Achalla Group of Onitsha Division' (1935) p. 6.
42. CSSp 192/B/IV, Shanahan to Superior General, 27 September 1910.
43. Igwegbe, pp. 83–4.
44. Esobe, p. 30.
45. Ibid, photograph, p. 31A. The trap is described on pp. 31–2.
46. Dilim Okafor-Omali, *A Nigerian Villager in Two Worlds* (London, 1965) pp. 34–6.
47. NAI CSO 26/154 (File 28583), V. Fox-Strangways, 'Intelligence Report on Isuochi, Nneato and Umucheze Clans of Okigwi Division' (1932) p. 14.
48. Jeffries, 'The Divine Umundri Kings', ch. 2. The towns he lists as members, however, cover such a large area that the present writer suspects the accuracy of his list.
49. Traditions collected by Mr Oji Kalu Oji.
50. On the Obegu raid, cf. J. C. Anene, *Southern Nigeria in Transition 1885–1906* (Cambridge, 1966) pp. 228–9 (based on fieldwork by A. E. Afigbo). Cf. also Leonard, 'A Journey to Bende', p. 201. Mr Oji Kalu Oji has collected further traditions about it.
51. CO 520/13, memo by A.B.K. on Moor to CO 16 March 1902, no. 110 and encls. CO 520/13, Moor to CO 5 March 1902, no. 91, describes how they were 'executed in the Obegu market-place in the presence of representatives of thirty-two towns . . .'
52. NAI CSO 26/147 (File 26804), G. B. C. Chapman, 'Intelligence Report on the Ikwo Clan' (1930) p. 7. The account which follows is based on this, and on the same author's report on the Ezza Clan (CSO 26/116, File 28179), on G. I. Jones, 'Ecology and Social Structure among the North Eastern Ibo', *Africa*, XXXI (1961) 117 ff. An Intelligence Report on the Izzi is listed in L. C. Gwam, A Preliminary Index to the Intelligence Reports . . . (Ibadan, 1961), but the archives officials at Ibadan could not locate it for me, nor could it be located at the Enugu archives. The most valuable source, however, was Mr James Afoke's excellent fieldnotes, which comprise Part II of his B.A. history special project (Nsukka, 1974).
53. Chapman, 'Ikwo Clan', p. 10.
54. Well described in Jones, "Ecology", *passim*.
55. What follows is based on data collected by Mr Afoke.
56. McFarlan, p. 143.
57. This paragraph is based on Afoke.
58. Robert Cudjoe, 'Some Reminiscences of a Senior Interpreter', *The Nigerian Field* (1953), p. 159.
59. Personal communication from Dr John Boston, 14 October 1970.
60. Baikie, p. 291.
61. Ankpa version, cited in full in Shelton, p. 246.
62. Elders of Ejigbo village, near Ankpa, in Ibid., p. 22.

63. Ibid., pp. 22–3.
64. NAI CSO/240 (File 29380), W. R. T. Milne, 'Intelligence Report on Ogboli Group of Nsukka Division' (1933) p. 7.
65. This point is made by Professor A. E. Afigbo, 'Igbo Historians', p. 7, and at greater length by Mr S. C. Ukpabi in a review of the book (typed copy kindly lent me by the author).
66. J. S. Boston, *The Igala Kingdom* (Ibadan, 1968 pp. 16–17, 90–1. It is difficult to know how much historical fact this legend embodies. It attributes his rise to his good looks, which won the heart of a female Atta, who married him!

CHAPTER 7

1. FO 84/1030, Hutchinson to Clarendon, 20 February 1857.
2. RH MSS Afr. 3.697, A. F. B. Bridges, 'Report on the Oil Palm Survey, Ibo, Ibibio and Cross River areas' (1938).
3. Described in Robin Horton, 'From Fishing Village to City-State, A Social History of New Calabar', in Mary Douglas and Phyllis M. Kaberry (eds), *Man in Africa* (London, 1969) pp. 37 ff.
4. For two examples, cf. James Johnson, 'An African Clergyman's Visit to Bonny', *Church Missionary Intelligencer* (Jan 1897) pp. 27–8; Hermann Köler, *Einige Notizen uber Bonny* (Göttingen, 1848) p. 2. On the general point, K. Onwuka Dike, *Trade and Politics in the Niger Delta 1830–1885*, repr. (Oxford, 1966) pp. 29–30.
5. *The Church Missionary Intelligencer* (1853) p. 258.
6. CMS G3/A3/1882/58, D. C. Crowther, 'The 3rd Visit to Okrika,' (1882).
7. FO 403/217, Kirk to Salisbury, 25 August 1895.
8. J. Pratt, 'African Town or Village Life in the Niger Delta', *Western Equatorial Africa Diocesan Magazine* (1905) p. 147.
9. CMS G3/A3/1884/129, D. C. Crowther to Lang, 30 June 1884; G3/A3/1890/142, D. C. Crowther, 'Journal of a Visit to Abonnema and Ndele', 12 August 1890; *Letters of Henry Hughes Dobinson* (London, 1899) pp. 183–4.
10. Köler, p. 154.
11. FO 84/858, Beecroft to Palmerston, no. 70, 27 October 1851.
12. Two photograph albums in the University of Ibadan library.
13. Hope Masterton Waddell, *Twenty Nine Years in the West Indies and Central Africa* (London, 1863) p. 476. For a contrasting interpretation, which I read when this book was in the press, see A. J. H. Latham, *Old Calabar 1600–1891* (Oxford, 1973) pp. 93–5.
14. Ibid., p. 477.
15. Bishop Tugwell, 'Impressions of Opobo', *Niger and Yoruba Notes* (1898) p. 13.
16. CSSp, Lejeune, in *Bulletin de la Congregation*, XXII, p. 800.
17. On Ja Ja's background and rise, cf. Dike, p. 183. For the additional detail re the reason for his enslavement, cf. Frederick Uzoma Anyiam, *Among Nigerian Celebrities* (Yaba, 1960) p. 18. The author is an Nkwerre man who cites as his source his father, Chief Anyiam Emeghara, who died in 1956 aged *c.* 105.

18. FO 84/1343, f. 322 ff., Oko Epelleh, 'Protest'.
19. On the foundation of Opobo, cf. FO 84/1308, Livingstone to Clarendon, 4 December 1869; FO 84/1326, *passim*; FO 84/1343, Hopkins to Granville, 28 January 1871.
20. FO 403/73, Ja Ja to Salisbury, 5 May 1887.
21. CMS G3/A3/1883/80, D. C. Crowther to CMS 10 May 1883; G3/A3/1886/33 (encl) Boler to Hamilton; G3/A3/1887/120, Bishop Crowther to CMS.
22. E. A. Ayandele, *The Missionary Impact on Modern Nigeria 1842–1914*, (London, 1966) p. 81.
23. Dike, p. 197, n.3 (from p. 196).
24. FO 403/74, Hewett to Ja Ja 1 July1885, encl. in CO to FO 19 March 1888.
25. FO 84/1828, Johnston to Salisbury, 24 September 1887.
26. FO 403/74, Johnston to Ja Ja, 18 September 1887 (copy), encl. in Miller Bros to Salisbury, 29 February 1888.
27. FO 403/74, Johnston to Salisbury, 2 December 1887.
28. Crowther and Taylor, p. 438.
29. Kaine, p. 41.
30. W. R. G. Horton, 'The Ohu System of Slavery in a Northern Ibo Village Group', *Africa*, XXIV (1954) 318.
31. Ejiofor, p. 69.
32. CMS CA3/02, I. Spencer, 'Araba and the Arabans'. For another estimate (400), cf. CA3/043, J. B. Wood, Report of a Visit to the Niger Mission . . . 1880.
33. Informant, F. O. Isichei of Umuaji, Asaba, aged 73.
34. Crowther and Taylor, p. 438.
35. Horton, 'Ohu System', pp. 332–3.
36. NAI CSO 26/10 (File 26769), Miller and Williams, Intelligence Report on Aboh-Benin Clans (1930–1) pp. 22–3.
37. Kaine, p. 60.
38. Ibid., pp. 94–5.
39. Crowther and Taylor, p. 435.
40. For this paragraph, cf. C. K. Meek, 'Report on Social and Political Organisation in the Owerri Division' (1933) pp. 18–19, para. 64.
41. Ogali, p. 13.
42. Igwegbe, pp. 60–1.
43. Iheagwam, traditions transcribed on pp. 78, 85 and 114.
44. G. I. Jones, 'Report on the Status of Chiefs' (Enugu, 1958) paras 74–7.
45. For these examples, cf. p. above.
46. Ikwuebisi Ejiofor of Obeledu, Aguinyi, aged *c.*75, transcribed in Ejiofor, p. 105.
47. Joseph Nwose of Etiti, Alor, aged *c.*75, in J. A. C. Onyeanuna, 'A Short History of Alor from the Earliest Times to 1917', B.A. history special project, (Nsukka, 1973) pp. 86–9.
48. Igwegbe, p. 36.
49. Elizabeth Isichei, 'Historical Change in an Ibo Polity: Asaba to 1885', *African Hist*, x, 3 (1969) 435.

50. Nweke Osine aged *c.*83 and Nwenyim Ugo aged allegedly 140, both of Idembia, Ezza – interviewed by Mr James Afoke.
51. Ogbuamazia Egbeama of Obeledu, Aguinyi, aged *c.* 90, transcribed in Ejiofor, pp. 136–7.
52. Schön and Crowther, p. 48.
53. Onuoha Duru of Nguru, aged 90, transcribed in Nwahiri, p. 59.
54. FO 2/180, Niger Coast Protectorate Annual Report, 1897–8.
55. FO 403/249, Liverpool Chamber of Commerce to Salisbury, 12 August 1897.
56. For this and the following paragraph, cf. Walter I. Ofonagoro, 'The Opening up of Southern Nigeria to British Trade and its Consequences: Economic and Social History 1881–1916', Ph.D. thesis (Columbia, 1971) pp. 190–4. I am grateful to Professor A. E. Afigbo for lending me this work, which would otherwise have escaped my attention.
57. Cecil R. Holt (ed.), *The Diary of John Holt* (privately printed, Liverpool, 1948) introduction.
58. Ofonagoro, pp. 506, 527–9.
59. Ibid., pp. 168, 483, 531; J. E. Flint, *Sir George Goldie and the Making of Nigeria*, repr. (London, 1966), Appendix I, 'The Financial History of the Niger Company'.

CHAPTER 8

1. For a study of this question on a national level, see my article, 'Images of a Wider World in Nineteenth Century Nigeria', *J. Hist. Soc. of Nigeria*, (Dec 1973).
2. For a detailed study of this process, cf. my *The Ibo People and the Europeans; The Genesis of a Relationship – to 1906* (London, 1973) ch. 6 ff.
3. CMS G3/A3/1880, Crowther, Annual Report (1880).
4. Ryder, pp. 246–8.
5. Crowther and Taylor, p. 262.
6. Ibid., p. 304.
7. For what follows, cf. A. E. Afigbo, *The Warrant Chiefs Indirect Rule in Southeastern Nigeria, 1891–1929* (London, 1972) p. 67 and footnotes; Chinua Achebe, *Things Fall Apart*, repr. (London, 1965) pp. 124–7, and details scattered through a number of Nsukka students' special projects in history, Part II (transcribed fieldnotes).
8. Afigbo, p. 67, n. 76.
9. Ibid., p. 67 and note 74.
10. Okoli, p. 101.
11. A. E. Chukwulebe, *A Book of Local History* [re Umuna, Okigwi Division] (Okigwi, 1956) p. 24.
12. C.M.S., CA/3/037/86A, J. C. Taylor, Journal entry, 23/11/1864.
13. Ibid. The list also includes 'Inan' (Anam?).
14. Okoye Imo of Obeledu, Aguinyi, aged 90 and Nwozo Onwukeme, of Adazi-Nnukwu, Aguinyi, aged 85 transcribed in Ejiofor, p. 100 and 121.
15. CMS CA3/031, Phillips to Crowther, 10 September 1879.
16. Henry Johnson, 'The Mission on the Upper Niger', *Church Missionary*

Intelligencer (Sep 1882) p. 547.

17. Afigbo, *Warrant Chiefs*, p. 57. There was apparently a similar cleavage in Nsugbe (CSSp 192/B/111, Lejeune to Superior General, 20 February 1904).
18. M. A. Onwuejeogwu, *A Brief Survey of an Anambra Civilisation* (n.d. or place of publication, but Onitsha), Section 10, n.p.

CHAPTER 9

1. For these events, cf. Isichei, *The Ibo People and the Europeans*, pp. 108–10.
2. Described in ibid., pp. 117–19.
3. Idigo, p. 28. This is the main source for what follows, supplemented by contemporary accounts in the Holy Ghost Fathers' Archives, *Bulletin de la Congregation*, XVIII, pp. 425–6; 191/A/4, Account by Fr Limbour, dated 1900, and 191/A/8, Pawlas to Director, Archconfraternity of Our Lady of Victories, 26 November 1892.
4. Idigo, p. 30.
5. Discussion following E. A. Steel, 'Exploration in Southern Nigeria', *Journal of the Royal United Services Institution* (Apr 1910) p. 446.
6. CO520/14, A. Montanaro, 'Military Report on the Aro Expedition', p. 13.
7. My knowledge of this comes from Mr James Afoke.
8. NAI CSO/26/1 (File 28939), C. J. Mayne, 'Intelligence Report on the Abam Clan', pp. 11–12.
9. *Autobiography of an Illustrious Man, Chief Eke Kalu of Elu Ohafia-Owerri Province* (Lagos, 1954), pp. 7–8 and Arua, pp. 14–17. This account is confirmed by traditions collected by Mr Oji Kalu Oji. Cf. also CO 520/10, Montanaro to Moor 4 December 1901, encl. in Moor to CO 10 December 1901, no. 416.
10. FO 84/2109, MacDonald, 'Report on the Administration of the Niger Company's Territories' (received at FO 9 January 1890).
11. CO 520/14 Montanaro, 'Military Report', p. 7 (different figures – of a comparable order of magnitude – are given on p. 14 of the same document).
12. A. E. Afigbo, 'Patterns of Igbo Resistance to British Conquest', mimeo, p. 14.
13. Chukwulebe, p. 25.
14. Cudjoe, p. 159.
15. Frank Hives and Gascoigne Lumley, *Ju Ju and Justice in the Jungle* (Harmondsworth, 1940) pp. 70–81.
16. The subject matter of this paragraph was suggested to me by Dr U. P. Isichei.
17. FO 2/101, Moor to FO, 6 May 1896 and encl. 2, Gallwey, 'Report on the Punitory Expedition to Obohia', 25 April 1896.
18. Onuoha Duru of Nguru, aged 90, transcribed in Nwahiri, p. 63.
19. Mazi Mbagwu Ogbete, aged *c.* 80, of Umuokwara, Akokwa, transcribed in Okoli, p. 64.
20. Igwegbe, p. 98.
21. Leonard, 'A Journey to Bende', pp. 203–4.
22. FO 2/101, Gallwey, 'Report on the Punitory Expedition to Obohia,' 25 April 1896.

23. FO 403/270, Gallwey to FO, 11 October, 1898.
24. FO 2/179, Gallwey to FO, 2 June 1898. Cf. also FO 2/179, March of Troops through Central Division.
25. CO 520/13, Moor to CO 14 January 1902; CO 520/14, Moor to CO, 12 April 1902.
26. CSsp 191/B/IX, Report from Lejeune, 24 November 1901.
27. This account is summarised from the numerous dispatches and enclosures in CO 520/10 and CO 520/13. There is a useful summary in CO 520/14, Monatanaro, Military Report.
28. CO 520/14, Moor, 'Political Report in Connection with the Aro Field Force Operations', f. 304.
29. Hives and Lumley, pp. 22–3.
30. CO 520/31, Extract of Report on the Owerri District.
31. CO 520/18, Moor to CO, 19 December 1902 and Heneker to Moor, 26 December 1902.
32. CO 520/15, Moor to CO, 13 August 1902.
33. CO 520/18, Heneker to Moor, 17 January 1903 (copy). Cf. also CO 250/15, Moor to CO 22 August 1902 and CO 520/18, Morrisey to Moor, 27 December 1902, encl. in Moor to CO 2 January 1903.
34. CO 520/24, 'Report on the operations in the Akwete and Owerri Districts of the Eastern Division', 1904, and CO 520/24, Egerton to Lyttelton, 30 May 1904.
35. E. A. Steel, 'Exploration in Southern Nigeria', *Journal of the Royal United Services Institution* (Apr 1910) p. 435; CO 520/15, Moor to CO, 22 August 1902; CO 520/24, Egerton to Lyttleton, 30 May 1904; CO 520/31, Officer Commanding Onitsha Hinterland Column to O.C. Southern Nigeria Regiment, 20 April 1905, encl. in Egerton to CO, conf., 13 June 1905.
36. Steel, pp. 436–8; CO 520/35, Trenchard to Deputy High Commissioner, encl. in Thorburn to CO, conf., 5 January 1905.
37. CO 520/50, Egerton to Elgin, conf., 5 December 1907.
38. CSSp 192/B/VI, Shanahan to Superior General, 10 October 1910.
39. Ibid., Léna to Superior General, 31 December 1910.
40. Ibid, Shanahan to Superior General, 27 September 1910.
41. The best-informed account of this movement is to be found in a document in the Society of African Missions Archives, Rome, based on information from a former member, SMA 14/80404/15794, Strub, 'Le Vicariat Apostolique de la Nigeria Occidentale depuis sa fondation jusqu'à nos jours' (1928). The following account is based on this, on other references in the SMA archives, on accounts in the CMS archives and periodicals, on government sources, and on an account based partly on fieldwork in the early sixties, Philip A. Igbafe, 'Western Ibo Society and its Resistance to British Rule', *J. African Hist.* XII (1971) 441 ff.
42. Igbaffe, p. 442.
43. Strub, f. 13.
44. What follows is based on ibid., ff. 13–15.
45. E. Dennis, 'The Rising of the Ekwumekwu', *Niger and Yoruba Notes* (1904) p. 84.
46. Quoted in Igbafe, p. 445.

47. CO 520/18, Fosbery to High Commissioner, 2 January 1903.
48. Ibid.
49. Strub, ff. 24–5; CO 520/24, Egerton to CO, 7 May 1904 and encls.
50. CO 520/24, Copland-Crawford, 'Report on the Rising of the Ekumeku Society . . . 1904,' 25 April 1904.
51. CSSp 191/A/II, Cutting from Depêche Coloniale, 13 June 1905, annotated, 'C'est très vrai dit le P. Lejeune.'
52. CO 520/24, Copland-Crawford, 'Report on the Rising of the Ekumeku society'.
53. This paragraph is based on Igbafe, pp. 452–3.
54. Letter from Ferrieux, dated 1 October 1910 in *Annals of the Propagation of the Faith* (1911) p. 77 (this gives another version of the whole 1909–10 war).
55. Igbafe, pp. 453–4.
56. Ibid., p. 444.
57. I am in the process of collecting material about these, for a fuller study.
58. NAI CSO 26/10 (File 26769), Williams and Miller, 'Aboh-Benin Clans' (1930–1) p. 31; J. E. N. Nwaguru, *Aba and British Rule* (Enugu, 1973) p. 85 and n. 3.
59. NAI CSO 26/147 (File 26804), Chapman, 'Ikwo Clan', p. 12.
60. Williams and Miller, pp. 30–1.
61. Nwaguru, pp. 85–9. Cf. also Talbot, *The Peoples of Southern Nigeria*, 4 vols (London, 1926) I, 273.
62. CSSp 192/B/7, Shanahan to Superior General, 3 January 1914.
63. Lugard to Flora Lugard, 15 November 1914, in Margery Perham, *Lugard: The Years of Authority 1898–1945* (London, 1960) p. 463. The Ogoni are a non-Igbo group just to the south of Igboland.
64. Chief Yaro Onaga of Agbudu, Udi, aged c.70, interview taped and transcribed by the author. I am grateful to Dr Eric Agu for his assistance in arranging my first interviews in the Udi area.
65. NAE Onprof 1/15/3, James to Governor General, 16 November 1914.
66. Ibid., conf. progress report from Capt Massey to Ag Governor, 13 November 1914, and information from Chief Onaga.
67. Informant, Chief Nnadi Donald Oji of Enugu-Ngwo, aged *c*.66.
68. This point is stressed by all informants.
69. NAE Onprof 1/15/3, James to O. C. troops, Udi, 23 November 1914.
70. Ibid., Dann to Commissioner, Onitsha Province, 12 November 1914.
71. Copy in ibid., 14 November 1914.
72. Ibid., Capt. Massey, conf. progress report to Ag Governor, 14 November 1914.
73. Chief Yaro Onaga of Agbudu, Udi.
74. Terms of surrender given in NAE Onprof 1/15/3, James to O. C. Udi, 23 November 1914.
75. CO 520/31, Egerton to Lyttelton, 16 July 1905 and encls.
76. NAI CSO 26/10 (File 26769), Chapman, 'Ikwo Clan', pp. 11–12.
77. Robert Cudjoe, 'Some Reminiscences of a Senior Interpreter', *The Nigerian Field* (1953) pp. 153–8.
78. Ibid., p. 158.

79. Ogali, p. 23.
80. Chukwulebe, p. 25.
81. CO 520/18, Fosbery to High Commissioner, 2 January 1903; also Asaba oral traditions.
82. CO 520/24, 'Report on the operations in the Akwete and Owerri Districts. . . . 1904'.
83. CO 520/31, Egerton, Journal of a cycle ride from Lagos to Calabar, entry for 14 April [1905].
84. Quoted in Ekechi, p. 214.
85. CSE 5/1/1 (File C.1576/06), Quarterly Report, Aboh, 1906. NAE.
86. CSE 5/15/14 (File C 51/1920), T. E. Rice, Director, Medical and Sanitary Services, to Secretary, Southern Provinces, 3 May 1920 (conf.) reporting a visit on 5 March. Italics in original. NAE.

CHAPTER 10

1. Quoted in A. E. Afigbo, *The Warrant Chiefs, Indirect Rule in Southeastern Nigeria 1891–1929* (London, 1972) pp. 282–3.
2. Ibid., p. 202.
3. Audrey C. Smock, *Ibo Politics, The Role of Ethnic Unions in Eastern Nigeria* (Cambridge, Mass., 1971) pp. 71–2.
4. I. F. Nicolson, *The Administration of Nigeria 1900–1960: Men, Methods and Myths* (Oxford, 1969).
5. Data from CO 520/18, Menendez, Report on Native Courts, encl. in Moor to CO, 7 January 1903.
6. Afigbo, pp. 70–3.
7. RH MSS Afr. s. 1152, A. D. N. Bain, Diary, note interleaved after entry for 25 February 1924. (This passage illustrates the illusion that there was a 'real Chief' waiting to be found.)
8. RH MSS Afr. s. 1068 (1), MS. by R. A. Stevens, f. 12.
9. *Aba Commission of Inquiry, Notes of Evidence*, p. 32, para. 500.
10. A. E. Afigbo, 'Chief Igwegbe Odum: The Omenuko of History', *Nigeria Magazine*, 90 (1966) 228.
11. Afigbo, *Warrant Chiefs*, p. 250.
12. NAE Onprof 1/8/8, conf., Onitsha Division Annual Report, 1921.
13. Igwegbe, p. 100.
14. Chukwulebe, p. 26 (the individual concerned is named in the original).
15. Afigbo, *Warrant Chiefs*, p. 309.
16. RH MSS Afr. s. 855, MacPherson, memo on Native Organisation, f. 22.
17. Afigbo, *Warrant Chiefs*, p. 285.
18. Ibid., p. 256.
19. Patrick D. Okorah, *A Short History of Uratta*, 2nd ed. (privately printed, 1963) pp. 46–7.
20. Sylvia Leith-Ross, *African Women, A Study of the Ibo of Nigeria* (London, 1939) pp. 192–5.
21. What follows is based partly on John P. Jordan, *Bishop Shanahan of Southern Nigeria*, repr. (Dublin, 1971) p. 136. Additional details (and many others I have not included) were obtained from two well-informed individuals from Agbaja, one an old man, one a younger man who remembers

the confidences of his Warrant Chief grandfather (not Onyeama). Both wish to remain anonymous.

22. Eke Kalu, p. 9. For another account of the same man, and his equally unsatisfactory predecessor, see Arua, pp. 17–20.
23. Dilim Okafor-Omali, *A Nigerian Villager in Two Worlds* (London, 1965). The contradiction between this page and earlier references to Warrant Chiefs' patronage of education is only apparent. They educated their own children and clients, but tended to see widespread education in the community as a threat.
24. NAE O.P. 391/1925, D. O. Awgu to Resident, Onitsha Province, 12 March 1926; D. O. Bende to Owerri Resident, 9 December 1925.
25. Ibid., and other documents in the same file, D. O. Onitsha to Resident, Onitsha Province, 9 March 1926; Court Clerk Achi to D. O. Awgu, 3 November 1925. For the Afikpo version, cf. D. O. Enugu to Resident, Onitsha Province, 4 December 1925.
26. NAE Onprof 1/8/8, conf., Notes on a meeting on tax held by Hunt, Resident, at Onitsha, 13 May 1927.
27. Ibid.
28. Afigbo, *Warrant Chiefs*, p. 312.
29. The account which follows is based on data in the *Report of the Aba Commission of Inquiry*, and especially the *Notes of Evidence*. There is an excellent summary of the events and their background in Afigbo, *The Warrant Chiefs*. Gailey, *The Road to Aba*, adds nothing to the official sources.
30. Notes of Evidence, page 517, para. 9769.
31. *Report*, pp. 44–6, 55.
32. Ibid., pp. 63–4, para. 187.
33. *Report*, Appendix III, 15.
34. RH MSS. Afr. s. 1068 (4), R. A. Stevens, 'Memo on the Future of Local Government in the Eastern Provinces of Nigeria' (1949) p. 2. In general, see this report *passim*, and two other documents in RH, MSS. Afr. s. 1068 (4), Stevens, and MSS. Afr. s. 546, 'Reminiscences of Sir F. Bernard Carr, Admin. Officer, Nigeria, 1919–1949'.
35. RH, MSS. Afr. s. 1068 (4) Stevens, pp. 24 ff.
36. J. S. Harris, 'Some Aspects of the Economics of Sixteen Ibo Individuals', *Africa*, XIV (1943–4) 322–4.
37. G. I. Jones, 'Chieftaincy in the former Eastern Region of Nigeria'; p. 320, in Michael Crowder and Obaro Ikine (eds), *West African Chiefs* (Ife, 1970).
38. RH MSS. Afr. s. 546, Carr, p. 30.
39. RH MSS. Afr. s. 1152, Bain, diary entry, 11 April 1930.
40. For different comments on Chadwick and Udi development see RH MSS Afr. s. 1068 (1), Stevens, p. 31; B. W. A. Onyenah, 'Community Development in Awgu Division from 1950–1971', B.Sc. in political science special project (Nsukka, 1971) iii, 5; Mrs Stanley Riggs, 'Community Development in the Eastern Region', *Nigeria Magazine*, 52, (1956) especially p. 3. These tributes are confirmed by Udi oral traditions.
41. Onyenah, p. 49.

CHAPTER 11

1. Quoted in Ekechi, p. 5.
2. Schön and Crowther, pp. 60–1 and 231.
3. CMS G3/A3/1884/66, Johnson, 'Report on the Archdeaconry of the Upper Niger'; also *Church Missionary Intelligencer* (Nov 1883) pp. 693–4.
4. CMS G3/A3/1883/129, D. C. Crowther to Lang, 30 June 1884; G3/A3/1887/87, Bishop Crowther, 'A Visit to the Markets in the Interior of Ibo', 7–21 May; G3/A3/1890/142, D. C. Crowther, 'Journal of a visit to Abonnema and Ndele', 12 August 1890; *Letters of Henry Hughes Dobinson* (London, 1899) pp. 183–4.
5. *The Church Missionary Intelligencer* (August 1876) pp. 473–4.
6. 'Autobiography of David Okparabietoa Pepple', *Niger and Yoruba Notes* (1898) pp. 13–14.
7. CSSp 191/B/II, Lejeune, Historical Account.
8. Cf. ch. 20 of Jordan, entitled 'Satan in Iboland'. For further examples see Elizabeth Isichei, 'Seven Varieties of Ambiguity: Some Patterns of Igbo Response to Christian Missions', *Journal of Religion in Africa*, (III) (1970) 210.
9. SMA 14/80403/15550, Cermenati to Superior General, 12 May 1911. Ferrieux described his own life in a letter to Poirier, dated 26 November 1906, printed in *L'Echo des Missions Africaines de Lyon* (1907) pp. 7–18.
10. CSSp 191/A/3, 'General Report on . . . the Lower Niger' (anon., n.d. but Lejeune, 1900); *Bulletin de la Congregation*, XVII, p. 430.
11. Jordan, p. 63.
12. For what follows see CSSp 191/A/1/3, Lutz, 'Les Agouleris', 3 January 1892; 191/A/4, Limbour, Short MS. history of Lower Niger Mission, 1900; see also the local history by M. C. M. Idigo, pp. 13 ff., 73 ff.
13. Lutz, 'Les Agouleris'.
14. *L'Echo des Missions Africaines de Lyon*, (1905) pp. 21–9.
15. Julius Spencer *et al.*, 'Joseph Obimgbo Egbola and his Witness for Christ', *Western Equatorial Africa Diocesan Magazine*, (1905) pp. 15 ff.
16. CMS G3/A3/1893/66, Dobinson to Baylis, 21 June 1893.
17. SMA 14/80404/15794, Strub, Le Vicariat Apostolique, p. 12.
18. CMS G3/A3/1897, Bennett to Baylis, 27 March 1897.
19. Figures in Talbot, IV, 104, 107.
20. Nigeria Census, 1931, Table 5 (2).
21. Jordan, p. 131.
22. C. K. Meek, *Law and Authority in a Nigerian Tribe* (Oxford, 1937) p. 15.
23. Eastern Region Census, 1953, Bulletin 1, Table c.
24. I. I. Ekanem, *The 1963 Census, A Critical Appraisal* (Benin, 1972) p. 65, Table 3.12.
25. Jordan, p. 100.
26. Rev. James Luke, quoted in Donald M. McFarlan, *Calabar*, rev. ed. (London, 1957) p. 109.
27. Ekechi, ch. VIII.
28. CSSp 191/A/8, A. Bindel, Historical Report on Ozubulu Mission, 1920.
29. CSSp 192/II/B, Lejeune to Superior General, 26 May 1903, gives an example.

30. Uchendu, p. 35.
31. Crowther and Taylor, p. 432.
32. Jordan, p. 88.
33. Ojike, pp. 39–41.
34. A. B. MacDonald, *In His Name* (London, 1964) pp. 108–9, 119, 120–2, 165–71.
35. Mr C. C. Onoh of Enugu-Ngwo, in a talk delivered on 29 August 1973, to the Enugu branch of the Historical Association of Nigeria.
36. Cf. note 6 above.
37. CMS G3/A3/1887/2, Annual Report, Onitsha, 1886.
38. MS. by Fr Raymond Arazu, C.S.Sp.
39. Ugwoke Ezeja of Edem Nsukka, aged 80, transcribed in A. E. Ozioko, 'Missionary Impact on Nsukka Division, 1900–1967', B. A. history special project (Nsukka, 1973) p. 54.
40. CSSp 192/B/VIII, Shanahan to Superior General, 26 January 1917. This brief account of Zappa is distilled from the voluminous records in the SMA Archives, Rome.
41. This account is based on his own autobiography, 'Story of My Life', *The African Missionary*, Nov–Dec 1919, p. 1 ff., and on traditions collected in Ezi and Asaba. Bishop Gbuji has written a short life, but it gives disappointingly little detail about his post-ordination years. (Anthony Gbuji, *The Life History of Rev. Fr. Paul Obodoechine Emecete* (Agbor, 1969).
42. *The African Missionary* (Jan–Feb 1922) p. 9.
43. CSSp 191/A/8, A. Bindel, Historical Report on Ozubulu Mission, 1920.
44. CSSp 192/B/VI, Shanahan to Neville, 20 September 1912; 191/A/3, Father Féral, Journal of a journey, Calabar-Owerri-Onitsha, 1912. 192/B/VII, Shanahan to Superior General, 3 January 1914.
45. Jordan, pp. 135–6.
46. CSSp 191/A/8, Treich, Report on Nteje, April 1920 (this gives a detailed account of the workings of the whole system).
47. CSSp 192/A/1, Reports of Lower Niger Mission to Association for the Propagation of the Faith; cf. also Jordan, p. 131.
48. CSSp 191/B/IV, Shanahan, Visite Provinciale, 1907.
49. CSSp 191/B/VI, Report by Fathers of Calabar and Anwa on schools, 26 April 1914.
50. For comments on a number of associated points, see an article by a group of seminarians in *The Voice* (1966), journal of the Major Seminary, Ibadan, and Raymond Arazu, C.S.Sp., *The Role of the Religious in the Local Church* (Ihiala, 1975), 'The Vow of Poverty', pp. 12–20.
51. From a private letter to the author.
52. Albert Omeje, aged 80, and Attah Nweleje, aged 86, transcribed in Ozioko, p. 65; cf. also pp. 90, 123, 132, 149. A rather similar point is made in P. E. H. Hair's unpublished study of Enugu (in NAE).
53. *The African Missionary* (1923) p. 81 (this example is given by a missionary in a non-Igbo area, but the attitude was widespread).
54. CSSp 191/B/III, Bishop Shanahan, circular no. 10, August 1925, laying down policy re catechumens, baptism and discipline, and pencilled memo of protest attached, and signed P.Ed.K., Treich and others to Léna, 8

March 1925, protesting re the severity of his policies.

55. Jordan, p. 74.
56. A glimpse of his early life is given in Nnamdi Azikiwe, *My Odyssey* (London, 1970) pp. 13–15. A vignette of the period in Ogoja is to be found in James Mellett, *If Any Man Dare* (Dublin, 1963). Further information from Msgr. W. Obelagu.
57. This account is based on a large number of oral histories collected by the author, who is writing a full length biography of him.
58. CMS G3/A3/1894/131, Dobinson to Baylis, 20 October 1894 (summary in Précis Book); cf. similar comments in letters from Tugwell, 11 and 17 October, nos 133 and 134.
59. E. M. T. Epelle, *The Church in the Niger Delta* (Port Harcourt, 1955) pp. 66–7.
60. Ibid., pp. 63 ff.
61. Ekechi, p. 212.
62. Ibid., p. 225.
63. Ibid., p. 198.
64. This account is based on a short biography by his daughter, Eunice C. Okediadi, *A Short Biography of the late Bishop Alphonso Chukuma Onyeabo O.B.E.* (Port Harcourt, 1956).
65. Epelle, p. 87.
66. McFarlan, p. 133.
67. There are accounts of this in McFarlan and MacDonald.
68. Dr Akanu Ibiam, 'Christian Challenge in Medical Practice', paper presented to the Fellowship of Christian Doctors Conference, 6–9 April 1972, proceedings published by the Institute of Church and Society, Ibadan, pp. 11–13.
69. This account is based on Ogbonna O. Ekeghe, *A Short History of Abiriba* (Aba, n.d.) pp. 19–21; there is another account of the same man in McFarlan, pp. 134–5.
70. Jordan, p. 103.
71. Ekeghe, pp. 36–8.
72. Blue Book (1925).
73. My knowledge of the spread of Methodism in Igboland comes from Edet A. Udo, 'The Methodist Contribution to Education in Eastern Nigeria 1893–1960', Ph.D. thesis (Boston, 1965) especially pp. 80, 85 ff., and F. W. Dodds, 'Notes on Early Days in Uzuakoli', in A. J. Fox (ed.), *Uzuakoli: A Short History* (London, 1964) pp. 93 ff.
74. Fox, p. 131; cf. also Epelle, p. 76.
75. Udo, p. 108; Fox, p. 99.
76. The account which follows is based on Ogali, pp. 16–21.
77. Blue Book (1925).
78. Epelle, pp. 51 ff; G. James Warmate, *The Niger Delta People's Hand Book* (Port Harcourt, n.d. [1963?]) pp. 23–4.
79. James Bertin Webster, *The African Churches among the Yoruba 1888–1922* (Oxford, 1964) pp. 95–6.
80. Leith-Ross, p. 251.
81. I have interviewed Rev. Martin, and a number of informants from the

area, but the best source for his life is his own autobiography (Aba, n.d., completed *c.* 1965).

82. Ajemezu Oko, aged 80, of Umunko, Nsukka, transcribed in Ozioko, pp. 144–5.
83. Okoye Imo, aged 90, of Obeledu, Aguinyi, transcribed in Ejiofor, p. 119.
84. This theme is explored more fully in Isichei, 'Seven Varieties of Ambiguity'.
85. Onitsha Christians to European missionaries, 30 August 1890, cited in Ekechi, p. 93.

CHAPTER 12

1. Figures tabulated in Otonti Nduka, *Western Education and the Nigerian Cultural Background* (Ibadan, 1964) p. 38.
2. *Report on the Review of the Educational System in Eastern Nigeria* (Official Document no. 19 of 1962, Enugu) p. 28.
3. M. O. Ijere (ed.), *Progress in Nsu* (Aba, 1963) p. 6.
4. There is a description of this school in the 1930s, in Leith-Ross, pp. 243–4.
5. M. O. Ijere (ed.), *Essays in Honour of St Charles College, Onitsha, 1928–65*, (Aba, 1965) p. 122.
6. Ibid., p. 124.
7. James Coleman, *Nigeria Background to Nationalism*, repr. (Berkeley, 1965 p. 341.
8. Nduka, p. 55.
9. Ojike, p. 85. This account of Azikiwe's experiences in America is based on the first volume of his autobiography, *My Odyssey*.
10. Editorial in *The Renaissance* (22 Jan 1974).
11. Hair, *Study of Enugu* (in NAE) p. 6.
12. Ibid., p. 9.
13. Ibid., p. 19.
14. Ikpo, p. 14.
15. Okorah, p. 14. Meek, p. 19, made a similar point re Oratta in the 1930s.
16. Isaac Nwafor, born 1885, of Orizor, Ezza, interviewed by James Afoke.
17. Quoted in Udo, p. 119.
18. Nduka, p. 39.
19. Speech reported in *Annals of the Propagation of the Faith* (1922) p. 17.
20. Okafor-Omali, pp. 129–30.
21. His life is described in ibid., *passim*.
22. Azikiwe, p. 71.
23. Ijere, *Progress in Nsu*, p. 6.
24. NAE Onprof 1/8/8, conf., Notes on a Meeting on Tax held by Hunt, Resident, at Onitsha, 13 May 1927.
25. Leo Jude Olisah, *The Facts About Ihembosi* (Nsukka, 1963) pp. 43–4.
26. Ibid., p. 49.
27. Uwa Kanu, 'The Rise of Wage Employment in Arochuku since 1900 and its Effects on the Social and Economic Life of the People', B.Sc. economics special project (Nsukka, 1966) pp. 31, 33, 36.
28. Blue Book (1935) section 23, W5, note.
29. This paragraph is based on Green, especially pp. 29–30 and ch. 4, *passim*.

30. This paragraph and the one following are based on Harris, *passim*.
31. NAE Onfprof 1/8/8, conf., Chiefs Omeli and Odo Oji of Eha town, Nsukka, letter encl. in Alakija and Alakija to Secretary of State, Southern Provinces. My knowledge of the movement now is based on an unpublished paper by Raymond Arazu, C.S.Sp.
32. Eastern Region Census, 1953, Bulletin 1, Table C.

CHAPTER 13

1. CO 520/43, Egerton to Elton, 26 February 1907, no. 84 and CO memos on it.
2. RH MSS Afr. s. 375, G. Adams, 'Five Nigerian Tales', f. 7.
3. Clement N. Anyanwu, 'Port Harcourt 1912–1955, A Study in the Rise and Development of a Nigerian Municipality', Ph.D. (Ibadan, 1971) pp. 2, 3.
4. Philip Onyeche Chinwa, born 1884 (he ran errands for the Diobu chiefs at the time), transcribed in Anyanwu, pp. 411–12.
5. RH MSS. Afr. s. 141, ff. 283–90, Firth, 'Port Harcourt: Some Notes on the Early Days' (1964). Cf. also Anyanwu, pp. 52–6 and 92–114.
6. Quoted in Anyanwu, p. 136.
7. Smock, ch. VI, *passim*, for social change and urban problems in Port Harcourt.
8. Leith-Ross, p. 247.
9. Ibid., p. 238.
10. Smock, p. 135.
11. Agwu Akpala, 'The Background of the Enugu Colliery Shooting Incident in 1949', *J. Hist. Soc. Nigeria*, III, (1965) 336.
12. Ibid., 337.
13. Hair, unpublished study of Enugu in NAE.
14. Blue Book (1935).
15. The account which follows is based on Akpala, pp. 338–40 and confirmed by local informants, not all of whom found this corruption and exploitation reprehensible 'In those days people did that . . .'
16. Quoted in Akpala, p. 340.
17. Ibid., pp. 340–1.
18. Ibid., p. 340.
19. C. C. Onoh, Talk to Historical Society of Nigeria, Enugu branch, 29 August 1973.
20. Hair, study of Enugu, pp. 4–5.
21. Ibid., p. 5, quoting a census of Enugu made by a British official in 1945.
22. For two different perspectives on twentieth century Onitsha, cf. J. C. Onyemelukwe, 'Staple Food Trade in Onitsha Market: An Example of Urban Market Distribution Function', Ph.D. thesis in economic geography (Ibadan, 1971) and Richard N. Henderson, 'Generalised Cultures and Evolutionary Adaptability: A Comparison of Urban Efik and Ibo in Nigeria', in R. Melson and H. Wolpe (eds), *Nigeria: Modernisation and the Politics of Communalism* (Michigan, 1971).
23. Meek, p. 14.
24. Henderson, 'Generalised Cultures', p. 235.

25. U. I. Ukwu, *Markets in Iboland* (published together with a study by B. W. Hodder under the title, *Markets in West Africa*, Ibadan, 1969) p. 244. Nwaguru, *Aba and British Rule* concentrates on Aba Division and says almost nothing about the growth of the city, which would make a fruitful subject for research.
26. Nwaguru, p. 78.
27. See p. 213 below.
28. Ola Balogun, 'Christmas at Aba in the early 1950s', *Nigeria Magazine*, 101 (1969) 436.
29. L. Emeka Ananti, 'Rural Migration into Aba Urban Area', B. A. geography essay, (Ibadan, 1966) p. 2. The same point is made in Hair's study of Enugu, and, by implication, in Onyemelukwe's study of apprenticeship in Onitsha Market.
30. Ibid., pp. 27–8.
31. Ibid., p. 2.
32. Ekanem, p. 63, Tables 3–11.
33. Fox, p. 29.
34. Easterfield and Uku, 'Seeds in the Palm of Your Hand', *West African Review* (Dec 1952) 1365. The present-day details are taken from Uwa Kanu, pp. 40–1, 46.
35. Quoted in C. O. E. Anozie, 'Orlu Town, A Study in Urban Land Use', B.A. geography essay (Ibadan, 1971) p. 1.
36. Kaine, pp. 102–3.
37. Azikiwe, p. 9.
38. NAE Onprof 1/8/8, conf., Annual Report Obolo Division, [Nsukka], 1921.
39. Samson O. O. Amali, *Ibos and their Fellow Nigerians*, mimeo (Ibadan, n.d. but 1967) p. 7.
40. Ibid., p. 9.
41. 1911 and 1921 census figures in Talbot, IV, 181.
42. 1952/3 census figures in Coleman, p. 77.
43. Ukwu, *Markets in Iboland*, p. 175.
44. John Oyinbo (the pseudonym of an English civil servant working in the north), *Nigeria Crisis and Beyond* (London, 1971) p. 123.
45. James O'Connell, 'Political Integration: The Nigerian Case', mimeo, p. 32.
46. Paul and Laura Bohannan, *Tiv Economy* (London 1968) pp. 182–3, 207.
47. CO 441/1, Roupell to Moor, 20 May 1899, encl. in Moor to CO, 14 June 1899.
48. Ukwu, *Markets in Iboland*, pp. 144–5; Hair, p. 6.
49. Arua, p. 22.
50. This paragraph is based on Ukwu, *Markets in Iboland*, ch. 11.
51. Eke Ucheya, *Profiles of Bende Chiefs* (Enugu, 1962), account of Azu Agwu, Okpi of Item.
52. Ananti, p. 21; cf. also Ukwu, *Markets in Iboland*, pp. 175–6.
53. Guy Hunter, *The New Societies of Tropical Africa: A Selective Study* (London, 1962) pp. 133–4.
54. Onyemelukwe, especially chs 4 and 7; also his paper presented to the

Workshop on the Peoples of Southeastern Nigeria, Nsukka, 5–8 December 1972, 'Onitsha and its Market Functions', pp. 6–7.

55. Kilby, Report on the Development of Small Industry, summarised on p. 18 of his *Industrialisation in an Open Economy: Nigeria 1945–1966* (Cambridge, 1969).

56. Ikenna Nzimiro, 'The Igbo in the Modern Setting', *The Conch*, III, 2 (1971) 166–7.

57. This account is based on two articles by Felicia Ekeijiuba, 'Omu Okwei 1872–1943, The Merchant Queen of Ossomari, A Biographical Sketch', *J. Hist. Soc. Nigeria*, III, 4 (1967) 633 ff. and 'Omu Okwei: The Merchant Queen of Ossomari', *Nigeria Magazine*, (90) (1966) 213 ff.

58. This account is based on information from Dr J. O. Ojukwu, University of Nigeria Teaching Hospital, Enugu.

59. CO 520/31, Egerton to CO, 16 July 1905.

60. Hair, *Study of Enugu*, p. 7.

61. Leith-Ross, pp. 248–9.

62. Harris, p. 326.

63. Okorah, pp. 19–20, 37–8.

64. Okafor-Omali, pp. 134–6, 138–41; the speech was quoted from memory ten years later, as 'a speech that still echoes in my mind'.

65. Ikpo, pp. 38–9.

66. This account is based on Smock, pp. 30 ff.

67. Henderson, 'Generalised Cultures', p. 240. A similar point is made by Ananti, about unions in Aba, p. 39.

68. Ananti, p. 39.

69. My knowledge of this movement comes from Elochukwu Amucheazi, 'Pressure Groups as a Factor in Eastern Nigeria Politics before 1966', paper presented to the Workshop on the Peoples of Southeastern Nigeria, at Nsukka, 5–8 December 1972, p. 7.

70. My interpretation follows Smock, pp. 17–21 and 169–72.

71. Leith-Ross, p. 109. Interesting material on these meetings can also be found in the Aba Commission of Inquiry, *Notes of Evidence*.

72. These clubs have been studied by a number of scholars, notably by Shirley Ardener and Phoebe Ottenberg.

73. *Annals of the Propagation of the Faith* (1921) p. 17.

74. Bishop Crowther in the *Church Missionary Intelligencer* (May 1874) pp. 154–5. Cf. also, for instance, CMS CA3/04, Crowther, Journal of visit to the Niger, 10 August 1868.

75. McFarlan, pp. 135–6.

76. Ibid., p. 147.

77. Jordan, p. 157.

78. Mellett, p. 23; cf. also ibid.

79. This information on dietary habits is based on evidence collected in the Nsukka area by Mr Ozioko, given on pp. 51, 55, 62, 79, 82, 87–8, 103 and 112 of his special project.

80. O. O. Akinkugbe, *High Blood Pressure in the African* (Edinburgh and London, 1972).

81. Rev. S. A. Eze, aged 60, of Nsukka, and Ugwoke Ezeja, aged 80, of Edem

Nsukka, in Ozioko, pp. 74, 55.

CHAPTER 14

1. *Awo, The Autobiography of Chief Obafemi Awolowo* (Cambridge, 1960) p. 135.
2. Ibid., p. 172.
3. Smock, p. 177.
4. Ibid., pp. 178–9.
5. *Report of the Commission Appointed to Enquire into the Fears of Minorities and the Means of Allaying Them* (London, 1958) p. 46.
6. Ibid., p. 43.
7. Quotes in John P. Mackintosh (ed.), *Nigerian Government and Politics* (London, 1965) p. 525.
8. Amali, p. 14.
9. Mackintosh, p. 525, n.3 (based on Official Document no. 20 of 1963, Enugu).
10. This and subsequent paragraphs are based on Floyd, chs 15 and 16; Kilby, pp. 73, 76, 96, 103 and 115–16; and R. Olufemi Ekundare, *An Economic History of Nigeria 1860–1960* (London, 1973) pp. 247, 304–5, 307 and 308.
11. Floyd, p. 258.
12. Kilby, pp. 149 ff.
13. Ibid., p. 100, and Walter Schwarz, *Nigeria* (London, 1968) p. 291.
14. A. Ayida, quoted in Schwarz, p. 290.
15. Floyd, p. 258.
16. Ekundare, p. 294.
17. *Report on the Review of the Educational System in Eastern Nigeria* (Official Document no. 19 of 1962, Enugu) p. 14.
18. These figures, which exclude the western Igbo, are worked out by Nzimiro, 'The Igbo in the Modern Setting', pp. 173–4. There are many inadequacies in our education statistics. Nigerian Government Education Reports (before the creation of regions) do not give detailed local breakdowns. Eastern Nigeria did not become 'an educational entity' till 1954. In the Enugu Archives, I was not able to find a consecutive run of education reports for the east (or west) since then, and those I did find usually did not break down the figures by Divisions or Provinces.
19. Mackintosh, p. 523.
20. N. C. Perkins, 'Report of the Inquiry into the Administration of the Affairs of the Enugu Municipal Council', II (1960) 393.
21. P. F. Grant, 'Report of the Inquiry into the Allocation of Market Stalls at Aba' (Enugu, 1955) p. 24.
22. R. T. Floyer and others, 'Report of the Commission of Inquiry into the Working of Port Harcourt Town Council' (Enugu, 1955) p. 33.
23. Simon Ottenberg, 'Local Government and the Law in Southern Nigeria', *Journal of Asian and African Studies*, II (1967) 27–9.
24. The account which follows is based on Richard F. Sklar, *Nigerian Political Parties' Power in an Emergent African Nation* (Princeton, 1963) pp. 143 ff.
25. Ibid., p. 183, n. 84.

26. Coleman, p. 66, Table 3.
27. Ogali, p. 29.

CHAPTER 15

1. Like my account of nationalism, my account here is based on published, and in the main secondary, sources. A brief balanced overview of the whole period (to late 1970) can be found in John Oyinbo, *Nigeria: Crisis and Beyond* (London, 1971). John P. Mackintosh, *Nigerian Government and Politics* (London, 1965) contains much detail on the early sixties. Walter Schwarz, *Nigeria* (London, 1968) is a balanced, well-informed journalist's account, to the end of 1966. John de St Jorre, *The Nigerian Civil War* (London, 1972) is the best account of the war known to me, and A. H. M. Kirk-Greene, *Crisis and Conflict in Nigeria*, 2 vols (London, 1971) is a valuable collection of documents. More partisan versions of events can be found in books written or begun during the war. Two examples are Frederick Forsyth, *The Biafra Story* (Harmondsworth, 1969) and Rex Niven, *The War of Nigerian Unity* (Ibadan, 1970).
2. Oyinbo, title of ch. 1.
3. Ibid., p. 24.
4. On this ambiguity, cf. Sklar, p. 230.
5. de St Jorre, p. 44; the Special Branch Report on the Events of 15 January 1966, as given in Kirk-Greene, I, 116, leaves three of those concerned anonymous, and names four Igbos.
6. Oyinbo, pp. 38–9.
7. Schwarz, p. 196.
8. Ibid., p. 199.
9. Oyinbo, p. 42.
10. For this paragraph cf. O'Connell, p. 32.
11. Schwarz, pp. 215–16.
12. Forsyth, p. 78.
13. Full text in Kirk-Greene, I, 451–3.
14. This account is based on de St Jorre, pp. 154 ff.
15. Ibid., pp. 394–5.
16. Ibid., p. 211.
17. Ibid., p. 376.
18. The Ahiara Declaration, 1 June 1969, in Kirk-Greene, II, p. 383.
19. Kirk-Greene's comment, II, 115.
20. de St Jorre, pp. 201 and 230.
21. Ibid., p. 377.
22. This theme is explored in detail in Arthur A. Nwankwo, *Nigeria: The Challenge of Biafra* (London, 1972).
23. Ahiara Declaration, in Kirk-Greene, II, p. 383.
24. Kirk-Greene, II, p. 468, n.2.
25. de St Jorre, p. 407.
26. Afigbo, 'Chief Igwegbe Odum', p. 222.
27. Dennis Williams, 'A Revival of Terra-cotta at Ibadan', *Nigeria Magazine*, 88 (1966) 13.

28. The first published study by an Igbo historian to take Igboland as its unit of reference was F. K. Ekechi, *Missionary Enterprise and Rivalry in Igboland 1857–1914* (London, 1971). Because of conditions prevailing in the late sixties, when it was prepared, it was based on archival sources in Europe only (and an incomplete coverage even of these), without fieldwork or research in Nigeria. The first study (if we include unpublished theses) was Dr S. N. Nwabara's unpublished doctoral thesis, 'Ibo Land: A Study in British Penetration and the Problem of Administration, 1860–1930', Ph.D. thesis (Northwestern University, 1965).
29. More, *Utopia* repr. (Oxford, 1961), Book Two, p. 140.
30. Crowther and Taylor, pp. 448–9.

List of Sources Cited

My views on bibliographies have changed considerably since I published a book with a bibliography twenty-eight pages long, in thirteen different subsections. I now think that although readers are entitled to know the evidence for specific statements – hence footnotes – they seldom require a complete list of the sources for the entire subject. To include such a bibliography would add considerably to the length, and cost, of the book, and is the less necessary because Mr J. C. Anafulu has a full bibliography of Igbo studies in the press. I also have doubts about the conventional distinction between primary and secondary sources, which I find difficult to maintain in practice, and not very helpful.

I had originally intended to omit a bibliography altogether. The difficulty here is, that, as is usual with historians, I refer to a work, after the first reference, by the name of the author only. I have very vivid memories of searching through the footnotes of a whole book in search of the first full reference, only to find on occasion, since historians are only human, that it was not given at all.

The list that follows is a compromise. It does not give any guide to archival sources, or to the voluminous mass of printed primary sources (such as Blue Books, census returns, Government Annual Reports or missionary journals) that I have used in this book, because in all these cases I give the full reference on each occasion. It seeks simply to make identification of works cited in footnotes easier. With the same aim, I have subdivided it into the least possible number of categories.

Abbreviations used to refer to archives

CMS Church Missionary Society Archives, London
CSSp Holy Ghost Fathers' Archives, Paris
FO, CO, Foreign Office/Colonial Office series, Public Record Office, London
NAE National Archives, Enugu
NAI National Archives, Ibadan
RH Rhodes House, Oxford
SMA Society of African Missions Archives, Rome

1. *Books and pamphlets (including Government publications)*

Aba Commission of Inquiry, Report (Lagos, 1930).
Aba Commission of Inquiry, Notes of the Evidence (Lagos, 1930).
Achebe, Chinua, *Things Fall Apart*, repr. (London, 1965).
Adams, John, *Remarks on the Country Extending from Cape Palmas to the River Congo* (London, 1823)
Afigbo, A. E., *The Warrant Chiefs Indirect Rule in Southeastern Nigeria 1891–1929* (London, 1972).
Allen, William and Thomson, T.R.H., *A Narrative of the Expedition . . . to the*

River Niger in 1841, 2 vols (London, 1848).
Anene, J. C., *Southern Nigeria in Transition 1885–1906* (Cambridge, 1966).
Anyiam, Frederick Uzoma, *Among Nigerian Celebrities* (Yaba, 1960).
Arua, A.O., *A Short History of Ohafia* (Enugu, n.d., [1951?]).
Awolowo, Obafemi, *Awo, The Autobiography of Chief Obafemi Awolowo* (Cambridge, 1960).
Ayandele, E. A., *The Missionary Impact on Modern Nigeria 1842–1914, A Political and Social Analysis* (London, 1966).
Azikiwe, Nnamdi, *My Odyssey* (London, 1970).
Baikie, William Balfour, *Narrative of an Exploring Voyage up the Rivers Kwora and Binue . . . in 1854* (London, 1856).
Barbot, James, *An Abstract of a Voyage to New Calabar River . . . in the Year 1699*, in Churchill's *Voyages and Travels*, vol. v (London, 1746).
Barbot, John, *A Description of the Coasts of North and South Guinea*, in Churchill's *Voyages and Travels*, vol. v (London, 1746).
Basden, G. T., *Niger Ibos* (London, 1966, first pub. 1938).
Bohannan, Paul and Laura, *Tiv Economy* (London, 1968).
Boston, J. S., *The Igala Kingdom* (Ibadan, 1968).
Chukwulebe, A. E., *A Book of Local History* (Okigwi, 1956).
Coleman, James, *Nigeria, Background to Nationalism*, repr. (Berkeley, 1965).
Crow, Hugh, *Memoirs of Captain Hugh Crow* (London, 1830).
Crowther, Samuel and Taylor, John Christopher, *The Gospel on the Banks of the Niger, Journals and Nnotices of the Native Missionaries Accompanying the Niger Expedition of 1857–1859* (London, 1859).
Curtin, Philip D., *Africa Remembered, Narratives by West Africans from the Era of the Slave Trade* (Wisconsin, 1969).
Dapper, Olfert, *Description de l'Afrique*, French trans. (Amsterdam, 1786).
de St Jorre, John, *The Nigerian Civil War* (London, 1972).
Dike, K. Onwuka, *Trade and Politics in the Niger Delta, 1830–1885* (Oxford, 1956).
Dobinson, H. H., *Letters of Henry Hughes Dobinson* (London, 1899).
Donnan, Elizabeth, *Documents Illustrative of the History of the Slave Trade to America* 4 vols (Washington, 1930–5).
Edwards, Bryan, *The History, Civil and Commercial, of the British Colonies in the West Indies*, 3 vols, 3rd ed. (London, 1801).
Egharevba, Jacob O., *A Short History of Benin*, 4th ed. (Ibadan, 1968).
Ekanem, I. I., *The 1963 Census: A Critical Appraisal* (Benin, 1972).
Ekechi, F. K., *Missionary Enterprise and Rivalry in Igboland 1857–1914* (London, 1971).
Ekeghe, Ogbonna O., *A Short History of Abiriba* (Aba, n.d.).
Epelle, E.M.T., *The Church in the Niger Delta* (Port Harcourt, 1955).
Equiano, Olaudah, *The Interesting Narrative of the Life of Olaudah Equiano*, abridged and ed. Paul Edwards (London, 1967).
Flint, J. E., *Sir George Goldie and the Making of Nigeria* (London, 1960).
Floyd, Barry, *Eastern Nigeria, A Geographical Review* (London, 1969).
Floyer, R. K. *et al.*, *Report of the Commission of Inquiry into the Working of Port Harcourt Town Council* (Enugu, 1955).
Forsyth, Frederick, *The Biafra Story* (Harmondsworth, 1969).

Fox, A. J., *Uzuakoli: A Short History* (London, 1964).
Fyfe, Christopher, *Africanus Horton* (London, 1972).
Gbuji, Anthony, *The Life History of Rev. Fr. Paul Obodechine Emecete* (Agbor, 1969).
The Gospel on the Banks of the Niger: Journals and Notices of the Native Missionaries on the River Niger, 1863 (London, 1864).
Grant, P. F., *Report of the Inquiry into the Allocation of Market Stalls at Aba* (Enugu, 1955).
Green, M. M., *Igbo Village Affairs Chiefly with Reference to the Village of Umueke Agbaja*, 2nd ed. (London, 1964).
Harcourt, H. N., *Report of the Inquiry into Oguta Chieftaincy Dispute*, Official Document no. 19 (Nigeria, 1961).
Henderson, Richard N., *The King in Every Man, Evolutionary Trends in Onitsha Society and Culture* (New Haven and London, 1972).
Hives, Frank and Lumley, Gascoigne, *Ju Ju and Justice in the Jungle* (Harmondsworth, 1940).
Hodgkin, Thomas, *Nigerian Perspectives, An Historical Anthology* (London, 1960).
Holt, Cecil R. (ed.), *The Diary of John Holt* (privately printed, Liverpool, 1948).
Hubbard, John Waddington, *The Sobo of the Niger Delta* (Zaria, 1948).
Hunter, Guy, *The New Societies of Tropical Africa, A Selective Study* (London, 1962).
Idigo, M. C. M., *The History of Aguleri* (Yaba, 1955).
Igwegbe, Richard O., *The Original History of Arondizuogu from 1635–1960* (Aba, 1962).
Ijere, M. O. (ed.), *Progress in Nsu* (Aba, 1963).
—— (ed.), *Essays in Honour of St Charles College, Onitsha, 1928–1965* (Aba, 1965).
Ikpo, W. A., *A Short History of Nkwerre Town* (Aba, 1966).
Isichei, Elizabeth, *The Ibo People and the Europeans: The Genesis of a Relationship, to 1906* (London, 1973).
Iweka-Nuno, I. E., *Akuko-Ala na onwu nke Ala-Ibo Nile* (no place of publ., 1924).
Jones, G. I., *Report on the Status of Chiefs* (Enugu, 1958).
——*The Trading States of the Oil Rivers* (London, 1963).
Jordan, John P., *Bishop Shanahan of Southern Nigeria*, repr. (Dublin, 1971).
Kaine, Esama, *Ossomari, A Historical Sketch* (privately printed in England, 1963).
Kalu, Eke, *Autobiography of an Illustrious Son, Chief Eke Kalu of Elu Ohafia, Owerri Province* (Lagos, 1954).
Kilby, Peter, *Industrialisation in an Open Economy: Nigeria 1945–1966* (Cambridge, 1969).
Kingsley, Mary, *West African Studies* (London, 1899).
Kirk-Greene, A. H. M., *Crisis and Conflict in Nigeria* 2 vols (London, 1971)
Koelle, S. W., *Polyglotta Africana* (London, 1854).
Köler, Hermann, *Einige Notizen uber Bonny* (Göttingen, 1848).
Laird, MacGregor and Oldfield, R. A. K., *Narrative of an Expedition into the Interior of Africa by the River Niger* 2 vols (London, 1837).
Leith-Ross, Sylvia, *African Women* (London, 1939).

Leonard, A. G., *The Lower Niger and its Tribes* (London, 1906).

MacDonald, A. B., *In His Name* (London, 1964).

McFarlan, Donald M., *Calabar, The Church of Scotland Mission Founded 1846* rev. ed. (London, 1957).

Mackintosh, John P. (ed.), *Nigerian Government and Politics* (London, 1965).

Meek, C. K., *Report on Social and Political Organisation in the Owerri Division* (Lagos, 1933).

——*Law and Authority in a Nigerian Tribe* (London, 1937).

Mellett, James, *If Any Man Dare* (Dublin, 1963).

Nduka, Otonti, *Western Education and the Nigerian Cultural Background* (Ibadan, 1964).

Nicolson, I. F., *The Administration of Nigeria 1900–1960: Men, Methods and Myths* (Oxford, 1969).

Niven, Rex, *The War of Nigerian Unity* (Ibadan, 1970).

Nwaguru, J. E. N., *Aba and British Rule* (Enugu, 1973).

Nwankwo, Arthur A., *Nigeria: The Challenge of Biafra* (London, 1972).

Nzimiro, Ikenna, *Studies in Ibo Political Systems: Chieftaincy and Politics in Four Niger States* (London, 1972).

Ogali, A. Ogali, *History of Item Past and Present* (Onitsha, 1960).

Ojike, Mbonu, *My Africa* (New York, 1946).

Okafor-Omali, Dilim, *A Nigerian Villager in Two Worlds* (London, 1965).

Okediadi, Eunice C., *A Short Biography of the late Bishop Alphonso Chukuma Onyeabo O. B. E.* (Port Harcourt, 1956).

Okorah, Patrick D., *A Short History of Uratta*, 2nd ed. (privately printed, 1963).

Olisah, Leo Jude, *The Facts about Ihembosi* (Nsukka, 1963).

Oyinbo, John (pseud.), *Nigeria Crisis and Beyond* (London, 1971).

Pereira, Duarte Pacheco, *Esmeraldo de Situ Orbis*, trans. and ed. George H. T. Kimble, Hakluyt Society, 2nd ser. LXXIX (1937).

Perham, Margery, *Lugard: The Years of Authority 1898–1945* (London, 1960).

Perkins, N. C., 'Report of the Inquiry into the Administration of the Affairs of the Enugh Municipal Council' (1960).

Report of the Lords of the Committee of Council Concerning the Present State of the Trade to Africa and Particularly the Trade in Slaves (1789).

Ryder, A. F. C., *Benin and the Europeans 1485–1897* (London, 1969).

Schön, James Frederick and Crowther, Samuel, *Journals of the Rev. James Frederick Schön and Mr Samuel Crowther who accompanied the Expedition up the Niger in 1841* (London, 1842).

Schwarz, Walter, *Nigeria* (London, 1968).

Shaw, Thurstan, *Igbo Ukwu, An Account of Archaeological Discoveries in Eastern Nigeria* 2 vols (London, 1970).

Shelton, Austin J., *The Igbo-Igala Borderland* (Albany, 1971).

Sklar, Richard F., *Nigerian Political Parties: Power in an Emergent African Nation* (Princeton, N. J., 1963).

Smock, Audrey, *Ibo Politics, The Role of Ethnic Unions in Eastern Nigeria* (Cambridge, Mass., 1971)

Talbot, P. Amaury, *The Peoples of Southern Nigeria* 4 vols (London 1926).

Thomas, Northcote W., *Anthropological Report on the Ibo-Speaking Peoples of Nigeria, Part I, Law and Custom of the Ibo of the Awka Neighbourhood* (London, 1913).

——Ibid., *Part IV, Law and Custom of the Asaba District* (London, 1914).
Uchendu, Victor C., *The Igbo of Southeast Nigeria* (New York, 1965).
Ucheya, Eke, *Profiles of Bende Chiefs* (Enugu, 1962).
Ukwu, U. I., *Markets in Iboland*, Part II of B. W. Hodder and U. I. Ukwu, *Markets in West Africa* (Ibadan, 1969).
Waddell, Hope Masterton, *Twenty-Nine Years in the West Indies and Central Africa* (London, 1863).
Warmate, James, *The Niger Delta People's Hand Book* (Port Harcourt, n.d. [1963?]).
Webster, James Bertin, *The African Churches among the Yoruba 1888–1922* (Oxford, 1964).
Willink Commission, *Report of the Commission Appointed to Enquire into the Fears of Minorities and the Means of Allaying Them* (London, 1958).

2. *Articles*

Akpala, Agwu, 'The Background of the Enugu Colliery Shooting Incident in 1949', *Journal of the Historical Society of Nigeria*, III (1965).
Alexander J. and Coursey, D. G., 'The Origins of Yam Cultivation', in Peter J. Ucko and G. W. Dimbleby (eds), *The Domestication and Exploitation of Plants and Animals* (London, 1969).
Azikiwe, Ben N., 'Fragments of Onitsha History', *The Journal of Negro History*, XV (1930).
Balogun, Ola, 'Christmas at Aba in the early 1950s', *Nigeria Magazine*, lol (1969).
Bradbury, R. E., 'The Historical Uses of Comparative Ethnography with Special Reference to Benin and the Yoruba', in Jan Vansina, Raymond Mauny and L. V. Thomas (eds), *The Historian in Tropical Africa* (London, 1964).
Cudjoe, Robert, 'Some Reminiscences of a Senior Interpreter', *The Nigerian Field* (1953).
Easterfield, Mary and Uku, E. K., 'Seeds in the Palm of Your Hand', *West African Review* (Dec 1952–Mar 1953).
Ekejiuba, F. I., 'Omu Okwei, The Merchant Queen of Ossomari, A Biographical Sketch', *J. Hist. Soc. Nigeria* (June 1967).
——'Preliminary Notes on Brasswork of Eastern Nigeria', *African Notes*, IV, (1967).
——'The Aro System of Trade in the Nineteenth Century', *Ikenga, Journal of African Studies*, I, 1 (1972).
Fagg, Bernard, 'The Nok Culture: Excavations at Taruga', *West African Archaeological Newsletter*, X (1968).
Harris, J. S., 'Some Aspects of the Economics of Sixteen Ibo Individuals', *Africa*, XIV (1943–4).
Hartle, D. D., 'Archaeology in Eastern Nigeria', *Nigeria Magazine* (June 1967).
Henderson, Richard N., 'Generalised Cultures and Evolutionary Adaptability, A Comparison of Urban Efik and Ibo in Nigeria', ch.8 in R. Melsom and Howard Wolpe (eds), *Nigeria: Modernisation and the Politics of Communalism* (Michigan, 1971).
Horton, Robin, 'From Fishing Village to City-State, A Social History of New

Calabar', in Mary Douglas and Phyllis M. Kaberry (eds), *Man in Africa* (London, 1969).

Horton, W. R. G., 'The Ohu System of Slavery in a Northern Ibo Village Group', *Africa* XXIV (1954).

Ibiam, Akanu, 'Christian Challenge in Medical Practice', in *Proceedings of the Conference of the Fellowship of Christian Doctors* (Ibadan, 1972).

Igbafe, Philip A., 'Western Ibo Society and its Resistance to British Rule', *Journal of African History* XII (1971).

'Inside Arochuku', *Nigeria Magazine*, 53 (1957).

Isichei, Elizabeth, 'Historical Change in an Ibo Polity: Asaba to 1885', *Journal of African Hist.*, X, 3 (1969).

——'Images of a Wider World in Nineteenth Century Nigeria' *J. Hist. Soc. Nigeria* (Dec 1973).

——'Seven Varieties of Ambiguity: Some Patterns of Igbo Response to Christian Missions', *Journal of Religion in Africa*, III, 3 (1970).

Jeffries, M. D. W., 'The Divine Umundri King', *Africa*, VIII (1935).

——'The Umundri Tradition of Origin', *African Studies*, XV (1956).

Jones, G. I., 'Who are the Aro?', *The Nigerian Field* (1939).

——'Ecology and Social Structure among the North Eastern Ibo', *Africa*, XXXI (1961).

——'Chieftaincy in the Former Eastern Region of Nigeria', in Michael Crowder and Obaro Ikime (eds), *West African Chiefs* (Ife, 1970).

Leonard, A. G., 'Notes of a Journey to Bende', *Journal of the Manchester Geographical Magazine*, XIV (1898).

Northrup, David, 'The Growth of Trade among the Igbo before 1800', *J. African Hist.* XIII (1972).

'Nri Traditions', *Nigeria Magazine*, 54 (1957).

Nzimiro, Ikenna, 'The Igbo in the Modern Setting', *The Conch*, III (1971).

O'Connell, James, 'Political Integration: The Nigerian Case', in A. Hazelwood, *African Integration and Disintegration* (London, 1967). (I read this as a mimeo and give page references accordingly.)

Onwuejeogwu, Michael, several papers in *Odinani* (Journal of Odinani Museum, Nri) I, 1 (1972) not cited separately as this issue is almost entirely his work.

Ottenberg, Simon, 'Ibo Oracles and Intergroup Relations', *Southwestern Journal of Anthropology* XIV (1958).

——'Local Government and the Law in Southern Nigeria', *Journal of Asian and African Studies*, II (1967).

Riggs, Mrs Stanley, 'Community Development in the Eastern Region', *Nigeria Magazine, 52(1956)*.

Steel, E. A., 'Exploration in Southern Nigeria', Journal of the Royal United Services Institution (Apr, 1910).

Ukwu, Ukwu I., 'The Development of Trade and Marketing in Iboland', *J. Hist. Soc. Nigeria*, III, 4 (1967).

Williams, Dennis, 'A Revival of Terra-cotta at Ibadan', *Nigeria Magazine*, 88 (1966).

3. *Unpublished Studies*

Afigbo, A. E., 'Igbo Historians and Igbo History', mimeo (Nsukka, 1972).

——'Trade and Trade Routes in Nineteenth Century Nsukka', paper presented to 18th Annual Congress of the Historical Society of Nigeria, 1972. Later published in the *Journal of the Historical Society of Nigeria*, Dec. 1973.

——'Patterns of Igbo Resistance to British Conquest', mimeo (Nsukka, 1972).

Afoke, J., Field notes on Ezza history, special project on history, Part II (Nsukka, 1974).

Amali, Samson O. O., 'Ibos and their Fellow Nigerians', mimeo (Ibadan, n.d. [1967]).

Amucheazi, Elochukwu, 'Pressure Groups as a Factor in Eastern Nigeria Politics before 1966', mimeo (Nsukka, 1972).

Ananti, L. Emeka, 'Rural Migration into Aba Urban Area', B.A. geography essay (Ibadan, 1966).

Anozie, C. O. E., 'Orlu Town, A Study in Urban Land Use', B.A. geography essay (Ibadan, 1971).

Anyanwu, Clement N., 'Port Harcourt 1912–1955, A Study in the Rise and Development of a Nigerian Municipality', Ph.D. thesis (Ibadan, 1971).

Arazu, Raymond, C. S. Sp., Interview with Ezenwadeyi of Ihembosi, taped, transcribed and translated, 1966 (in his possession).

Ejiofor, J. I., 'A Precolonial History of the Aguinyi Clan', B.A. history special project (Nsukka, 1973).

Esobe, N. E., 'A Precolonial History of Ohuhu Clan', B.A. history special project (Nsukka, 1973).

Hair, P. E. H., 'A Study of Enugu', typescript in NAE (n.d.).

Hartle, D. D., 'The Prehistory of Nigeria', mimeo (Nsukka, 1973).

Iheagwam, C. C., 'Naze Political System from Earliest Times to 1901', B.A. history special project (Nsukka, 1973).

Jeffries, M. D. W., 'The Divine Umundri Kings of Igboland', Ph.D. thesis (London 1934).

Kanu, Uwa, 'The Rise of Wage Employment in Arochuku since 1900 and its Effects on the Social and Economic Life of the People', B.Sc. economics special project (Nsukka, 1966).

Njemanze, A. U., 'The Precolonial Political and Social Organisation of Owerri Town', B.A. history special project (Nsukka, 1973).

Nwahiri, L. O., 'Nguru Mbaise before the Coming of the British', B.A. history special project (Nsukka, 1973).

Nwankwo, J. C., 'The Early Settlement of Ndikelionwu and its Neighbourhood', B.A. history special project (Nsukka, (1973).

Nzewunwa, N. C., '*Ogu Mkpuru Oka*, c. 1888–c. 1890', B.A. history special project (Nsukka, 1973).

Ofonagoro, Walter I., 'The Opening up of Southern Nigeria to British Trade and its Consequences: Economic and Social History 1881–1916', Ph.D. thesis (Columbia, 1971).

Oji, O. K., Fieldnotes on Ohafia history, special project on history, Part II (Nsukka, 1974).

Okoli, C. B. N., 'Akokwa from the Earliest Time to 1917', B.A. history special project (Nsukka, 1973).

Onyeanuna, 'A Short History of Alor from the Earliest Times to 1917', B.A.

history special project (Nsukka, 1973).

Onyemelukwe, J. C., 'Onitsha and its Market Functions', mimeo (Nsukka, 1972).

——'Staple Food Trade in Onitsha Market: An Example of Urban Market Distribution Function', Ph.D. in economic geography (Ibadan, 1971).

Onyenah, B. W. A., 'Community Development in Awgu Division from 1950–1971', B.Sc. political science special project (Nsukka, 1971).

Ozioko, A. E., 'Missionary Impact on Nsukka Division, 1900–1967', B.A. history special project (Nsukka, 1973).

Smith, S. R., 'The Ibo People', Ph.D. thesis (Cambridge 1929).

Udo, E. A., 'The Methodist Contribution to Education in Eastern Nigeria 1893–1960', Ph.D. thesis (Boston 1965).

Ugwu, M. M., 'The Agulu-Umana Village Community: Its Origin and Development to the Coming of the British', B.A. history special project (Nsukka, 1973).

Index